Mobilizing the Past

Mobilizing the Past

THE LESSONS OF HISTORY AND THE DANGER OF WAR BETWEEN CHINA AND THE UNITED STATES

Steve Chan

STANFORD UNIVERSITY PRESS
Stanford, California

Stanford University Press
Stanford, California

Library of Congress Cataloging-in-Publication Data
Names: Chan, Steve author
Title: Mobilizing the past : the lessons of history and the danger of war between China and the United States / Steve Chan.
Description: Stanford, California : Stanford University Press, [2025] | Includes bibliographical references and index.
Identifiers: LCCN 2024055982 (print) | LCCN 2024055983 (ebook) | ISBN 9781503643642 cloth | ISBN 9781503643789 paperback | ISBN 9781503643796 ebook
Subjects: LCSH: World politics—Historiography | War—Historiography | United States—Foreign relations—China | China—Foreign relations—United States | United States—Foreign relations—21st century | China—Foreign relations—21st century
Classification: LCC E183.8.C5 C3887 2025 (print) | LCC E183.8.C5 (ebook) | DDC 327.51073—dc23/eng/20250305
LC record available at https://lccn.loc.gov/2024055982
LC ebook record available at https://lccn.loc.gov/2024055983

Cover design: Jan Šabach
Cover art: Jan Šabach and Alamy

The authorized representative in the EU for product safety and compliance is: Mare Nostrum Group B.V. | Mauritskade 21D | 1091 GC Amsterdam | The Netherlands | Email address: gpsr@mare-nostrum.co.uk | KVK chamber of commerce number: 96249943

We don't see things as they are; we see them as we are.

—VARIOUSLY ATTRIBUTED TO ANAÏS NIN,
THE BABYLONIAN TALMUD, AND OTHER SOURCES

Contents

Introduction

As its title suggests, this book is about the use, misuse, and nonuse of history. It addresses how people engage history in their work. Following other scholars who have studied this topic, I discuss how policymakers have used historical analogies to frame, formulate, and choose foreign policy. More unusually, I also examine how scholars of international relations have employed history in developing their theory and offering their prognosis. In pursuing the latter inquiry, I focus specifically on how historical precedents and parallels have informed—or, in my view, sometimes misinformed—some scholars' analyses of China's rise and this country's relations with the United States. I also present and discuss historical episodes that are helpful in illuminating the dynamics that can possibly lead to an armed conflict between Beijing and Washington over Taiwan's status—episodes that are, however, usually overlooked in current discourse on Sino-American relations. These overlooked episodes may be more difficult to recall and harder for people to contemplate because of various possible political and psychological reasons or simply due to people's relative unfamiliarity with these episodes or their low salience.

International relations scholarship is replete with references to history. This is natural and understandable because history provides the material to develop our theories and validate our expectations. History is, of course, much more than just the recitation of facts, recounting one event after another. We construct and sometimes reconstruct history, giving events and sometimes also nonevents coherence and thereby enabling us to extract their meaning and comprehend their significance. The interpretation and construction of history are important parts of our self-identification. Anthony D. Smith (1986, 383) states succinctly, "No memory, no identity; no identity, no nation," and Zheng Wang (2018) argues convincingly that collective memories of the past bind people together and at the same time also set them apart from other groups.

Quite naturally, different people have different memories and understandings of the past. Moreover, we all are inevitably the product of our respective historical legacies and sociopolitical milieus and therefore cannot but be influenced by them. Thus, it is not surprising that people may have different historical interpretations and recollections—sometimes even about the same events. I believe that it was Paul W. Schroeder, a well-known historian of international relations, who said that history reminds him of the Japanese movie *Rashomon*—or something to this effect. This 1951 movie, directed by Akira Kurosawa, recounts how different witnesses have different memories of their encounters. In political science, Graham T. Allison's (1971) classic study of the Cuban Missile Crisis, *Essence of Decision*, shows how the same historical episode can be understood from different analytic perspectives. There is no "right" or "wrong" way to interpret this foreign policy episode. However, the different perspectives entail different assumptions and offer different propositions. Because they address different aspects of empirical reality, they also produce different—indeed, incompatible—conclusions and implications.

Just as with ordinary people and officials who are responsible for making foreign policy, certain historical episodes come to scholars and analysts of international relations more easily and naturally than others, and they tend to be seen through different national or cultural prisms. We may overlook, forget, and even be completely unaware of some historical episodes, while these same episodes may be indelibly etched in other people's memories even long after their occurrence. Consequently, even though we, as social scientists, strive to be objective, our views and narratives about the past are inevitably shaped by our respective backgrounds. Recognizing that the meaning of particular historical episodes is often contested, it is difficult to maintain that one's own interpretation is the only correct one.

Scholars of international relations are embedded in the social, economic, and political structures that we study, and our historical understanding reflects the influence of these structures. Michel Foucault insists that "there is no power relation without the correlative constitution of a field of knowledge," nor is there "any knowledge that does not presuppose and constitute at the same time power relations" (quoted in Pan 2012, 17). Linus Hagstrom and Bjorn Jerden (2014, 352) argue in the same vein: "Knowledge production, including scholarship, plays an important role in promoting collective understandings in which certain ideas are seen as 'legitimate' and others as 'outlandish.' Knowledge production thus becomes deeply entangled in power politics." Not to put too fine a point on it, R. B. J. Walker (1995, 6) remarks, "Theories of international relations are more interesting as aspects of contemporary world politics that need to be explained than as explanations of contemporary world politics." We should take a large grain of salt when people present their views as objective and universal truths—at least in the realm of international relations and foreign policy, which I would like to think is my field of expertise.

Stanley Hoffmann (1977) describes international relations as an American field. Americans created this field of study, US institutions train the largest number of graduate students, and the premier journals and presses for professionals in this field to publish their work are dominated by Americans and, to a lesser extent, British institutions, such as Cambridge and Oxford. In short, the field of international relations tends to be US-centric, and it thus represents predominantly US values, interests, and perspectives—which is, of course, not the same as saying there are no minority views. David Kang (2003, 2007, 2010, 2012, 2020; Ma and Kang 2024) especially calls attention to the tendency by Western scholars to impose their European or American experience and perspective on Asian realities.

Put plainly but with perhaps a small degree of exaggeration, we cannot assume neutrality or impartiality about the manner in which the profession goes about identifying international relations problems and propagating popular understandings of these problems. Of course, times are changing. For example, the International Studies Association has become more diverse in the span of my career. Still, I would argue that in the field of international relations and especially the subfield engaged in the study of war and peace, the prevailing ideas and narratives are predominantly Western and especially

American, and they tend to be self-referential, or, if you will, autobiographical. The adage "We don't see things as they are; we see them as we are" captures this book's main argument. I stress the importance of empathy and introspection—qualities that are usually in short supply.

Robert Jervis (1976, 281) observes, "International history is a powerful source of beliefs about international relations and images of other countries." His observation applies to not only officials in charge of foreign policy but also academics who study international relations. Similarly, Deborah W. Larson's (1985) remark that analogous reasoning provides scripts and schemas to assist people's understanding of foreign policy and international relations is pertinent to both government officials and academic researchers. Other scholars, such as Yuen Foong Khong (1992), study the powerful role played by historical analogies and perceived lessons of history in framing policy problems for officials, guiding their search for solutions and shaping their menu for policy choice, such as in the Lyndon Johnson administration's policymaking on the Vietnam War. As just suggested, historical precedents and parallels can be illuminating in our attempt to understand international relations and foreign policy. They can, however, also mislead by promoting mental shortcuts, top-down reasoning, premature analytic closure, and intellectual laziness and complacency. The tendency to ransack history for evidence to support one's favorite views or conclusions has been commented on by many esteemed and erudite scholars.

Although this book encompasses concerns about how leaders look to history to help them make foreign policy, I am also interested in addressing scholars' historical interpretations and constructions pertaining to China's recent rise and its implications for international peace and stability, especially the danger of a Sino-American war. What distinguishes this book from others is that I also attend to the ways in which analysts of international relations apply history in their work, or, in other words, my attention to the role of history in developing these scholars' theories about and formulating their explanations of war and peace. Instead of focusing on policymaking about one particular case, whether it be the US decision to escalate the Vietnam War, Germany's decision to launch World War I, or the decision by France and Britain to invade Egypt in the 1956 Suez Crisis, I choose an alternative approach that focuses on a specific theme. This theme refers to US scholarship on China's rise and the prospects of an armed conflict between it and the United States.

An unnamed Wall Street pundit has allegedly said, "I get nervous when people crowd to one side of the boat." Political correctness and conventional thinking always promise the safer and easier path than tilting windmills against supposedly settled lessons of history. Yet the risk of misusing history is always present (e.g., Janis 1982a; Khong 1992; MacMillan 2008; May 1975; Neustadt and May 1986b), cautioning us to be vigilant against the danger of premature consensus and intellectual closure—even for events that happened long ago. We should all be mindful of the harm that can come from sweeping generalizations ("History has taught us . . ."), categorical assertions ("Appeasement emboldens our enemy and encourages further aggression"), superficial reasoning ("Contemporary China is a replica of ancient Athens"), and facile analogies ("Saddam Hussein is a modern-day Hitler"). When people repeat popular memes, they are engaging in concurrence-seeking behavior. Academic researchers are no different. Their scholarship can contribute to creating an echo chamber that drowns out dissident or unpopular views. As children, we learned from Hans Christian Andersen's folktale of "The Emperor's New Clothes." As adults, we can all benefit from sometimes pushing the pause button, getting off the conveyor belt, and giving ourselves a moment to reflect.

International relations theories may overlook or even be mistaken about specific "minor" things, but they should get the "big picture" right—such as the end of the Cold War, the collapse of the Soviet Union, the occurrence of the two world wars, and the peaceful transition of the world's leadership position from Britain to the United States. This view, of course, goes against the grain of nomothetic generalization, which has been the dominant analytic proclivity to make statements covering as many cases or situations as possible. My view instead stresses the importance of getting "the big ones" right, even though, necessarily by their very nature, events such as those just mentioned are special and different from the "run-of-the-mill" affairs. For both reasons of good theory and sound policy, "getting China right" is important. A war between China and the United States—the world's two leading economies and most heavily armed states—would be not only a huge tragedy for the people of these countries but also an enormous catastrophe for the rest of humanity. Given the high stakes, we should also be wary that history and international relations theories can be "weaponized" by political entrepreneurs to lend legitimacy to their arguments, influence policy agenda, and mobilize political support for decisions that they have already arrived at based on other reasons.

The preceding remarks call attention to two possible uses of history in discourse pertaining to international relations and foreign policy. When I speak of the "mobilization of the past," I have in mind, first, the use of historical lessons as schemas or scripts by decision-makers to help them to process information, define problems, and make choices (or, by scholars, the use of history to develop their theories) and, second, the deployment of these lessons to justify or advocate a decision already reached on similar or other grounds—that is, to use them to steer discourse, frame agendas, and recruit support for a preferred course of action by political entrepreneurs. These two distinct ideas refer, respectively, to the "cognitive" and "instrumental" use of history in policymaking processes.

Of course, these ideas are not mutually exclusive. Scholars such as Ole R. Holsti (1962), Robert Jervis (1968, 1978), Yuen Foong Khong (1992), Deborah W. Larson (1985), and Yaacov Vertzberger (1986) persuasively show how history has shaped officials' beliefs, perceptions, and policy choices. At the same time, these officials have been known to use historical lessons and analogies to justify and advocate their decisions, such as Harry Truman's invocation of the lesson of Munich (against appeasing aggressors) to support his decision to intervene in the Korean War and Anthony Eden and George W. Bush's portrayal of Gamal Abdel Nasser and Saddam Hussein, respectively, as latter-day Hitlers. Khong (1992, 8) quotes John K. Fairbank's remark on US officials' susceptibility to exploit history as "a grabbag from which each advocate pulls out a 'lesson' to prove his point." He also points to former US secretary of state Dean Rusk in decision processes regarding the Vietnam War. His behavior illustrates "the fact that policymakers use the same analogies to *justify* their choices does not vitiate the diagnostic role of the analogies in helping the policymakers *arrive* at those choices" (16; italics in original). In the following discussion, we will encounter instances of both the "cognitive" and "instrumental" use of history, sometimes concurrently, such as when incumbent and former US officials engage in intramural policy debates in challenging or defending an existing policy of engaging China and advocating or refuting its replacement by a policy of confronting and getting tough on that country or in questioning or advocating the maintenance of a policy of strategic ambiguity toward Taiwan and arguing in favor of or against its replacement by a policy of strategic clarity that commits the United States to this island's defense.

I am troubled by prevailing US discourse on China because it tends to be consistently tilted by various errors of commission or omission in discussing that country's rise and the danger that this phenomenon has posed or is posing to international peace and stability. There are, in my view, serious distortions of history and flawed reasoning in popular narratives on Sino-American relations. In criticizing these narratives, I do not pull my punches. I may come across as being tendentious and strident. No one likes to have their ox gored and their worldviews questioned or rejected. My views can be controversial, but I do not assert that my historical interpretations are the only correct ones, having already acknowledged that it is natural and understandable that people can have different interpretations. I do, however, argue that we should not accept too easily and quickly grandiose, unqualified claims or poorly substantiated propositions about what history is supposed to have told us.

Although each of the following chapters addresses one or more discrete historical episodes, they should also be seen together as an "ensemble" whose constituent components tend to reinforce one another. Put differently, the ostensible lessons suggested by these episodes do not "float freely"—that is, they are often common components of a person's overall "historical inventory," and these components are interrelated. Thus, for example, the so-called Thucydides's Trap, referring to the ancient Peloponnesian War, and the existing conventional understanding of the origins of the two world wars invoke similar scripts and assign a common cause (namely, interstate power shifts) for these conflicts. Take another example: warnings against appeasement often refer to not only the "lesson of Munich" but also other instances of interstate aggression in the 1930s, such as those committed by the Italians and Japanese (in Ethiopia and Manchuria, respectively) and Germany's rearmament program and its violation of the Versailles Treaty. Thus, these historical recollections come often in "packages" that "thrust" policy choice in a common direction, such as when people talked about the importance of standing up against aggression *and* the danger of falling dominoes in the same context to justify the US intervention in the Vietnam War or the twin threats posed by weapons of mass destruction and international terrorism in the leadup to the US invasion of Iraq. In short, the historical narratives or references people invoke have the effect and, indeed, often the intention of reinforcing each other, and their *combined* effects on policymaking are greater than their individual impact.

The tendency for historical episodes to congregate and represent an "ensemble," or constellation, of similar, reinforcing ideas suggests that such packages lack offsetting, or countervailing, ideas. For example, when invoking the "lesson of Munich" against appeasement, people rarely remember instances in which taking a firm, uncompromising position against a prospective aggressor was equally dangerous, such as in the case of the Japanese attack on Pearl Harbor, to be discussed later. Similarly, in discussing the ongoing power shifts between China and the United States, people do not usually remember the peaceful transition of world leadership from Britain to the United States. A failure to recognize counterexamples or contrarian ideas points to the danger posed by an absence of "correctives" to moderate the tendency for all remembered historical episodes to converge on the same policy interpretation or conclusion, which has the effect of fostering unwarranted confidence on the part of decision-makers. Yet this phenomenon suggesting that people do not assign enough importance to contradictory evidence is quite natural and even inevitable given the common human tendency to seek cognitive consistency—quite aside from the usual bureaucratic or political pressure to conform to prevailing orthodoxy.

From a skeptic's view, the syndrome just described amounts to "overdetermining" the outcome of a deliberative process, or "intellectual overkill." Moreover, we are reminded of the common human tendency that once people know an event has happened (such as Richard Nixon's trip to Beijing in 1972), they tend to overestimate (retrospectively) the probability of its occurrence. This is the so-called hindsight bias, suggesting the "I knew it all along" syndrome (Fischhoff 1977; Fischhoff and Beyth 1975; Slovic and Fischhoff 1977). It gives people an unwarranted sense of certainty about their ability to predict once-future events. Relatedly, people tend to give more emphasis to events that have happened than those that could have but did not happen. They thus pay more attention to the role of shifting interstate power as a supposed cause of the Peloponnesian War and the two world wars than the nonoccurrence of war when Britain's hegemony passed on to the United States, for which reasons other than interstate power shifts are invoked as an explanation. We can also encounter a reversed situation. There is much ongoing handwringing over a possible but far-from-certain power transition in the future between China and the United States while overlooking the one and only instance in modern history when such a leadership change has occurred peacefully (i.e., the Anglo-American case).

Of course, I am also not the only dissenting voice that disagrees with mainstream thinking. My bibliographic references to other scholars' work should make this fact abundantly clear. A settled consensus on why and how an event has happened may still elude specialists even many years after an event has occurred. As just mentioned, people can also disagree about why some events did not happen. Dissidents often continue to question conventional views. Hence, I would not want to exaggerate the extent of consensus behind dominant views when I discuss below various conflict episodes pertinent to the discourse on a possible Sino-American war. My review below, however, shows that the prevailing views tend to be rather consistently distorted to dramatize the challenges to international peace and stability posed by a rising China. Moreover, there tends to be a degree of certitude on the part of those propounding these views that is, in my opinion, unwarranted and that should be at least tempered by consideration of alternative interpretations. The historical cases that some leading scholars cite do not necessarily lend support to their claims as they assert.

As I discuss in chapter 1, the outbreak of the Peloponnesian War was not preordained. It was a highly contingent outcome, just as Richard Ned Lebow (2000–2001) argues about the occurrence of World War I. Moreover, alarmist diagnoses and ominous prognoses can engender a self-fulling prophecy (Lebow and Valentino 2009). That is, if leaders believe in warnings such as Thucydides's Trap—even if these warnings are based on a dubious understanding of history—scholarship may contribute to the occurrence of hostilities that history has failed to oblige. Although most of the historical episodes I discuss below have received extensive attention from researchers in the past, this book's contribution is to bring them together and present their collective evidence to warn about biases and distortions in contemporary narratives prevailing in the United States and the West more generally about China's rise and the danger of a Sino-American war.

If this book contributes to a vigorous debate and promotes sensitivity to how other people may feel and think, it will have achieved its goal. We need more full-throated discussions to avoid the failure of the marketplace of ideas, such as when the George W. Bush administration rushed to war against Iraq under false pretenses without being checked by a skeptical Congress, critical mass media, and an informed public (Kaufman 2004). Sometimes people have to be loud and persistent, but hopefully not obnoxious, to challenge entrenched dogmas, popular myths, and the hegemony of ideas in the Gramscian sense (Gramsci 1971).

This book is a part of a large research program that I have been pursuing for the past dozen years or so. This program has produced quite a few books, journal articles, and book chapters. Although there are some inevitable overlaps among them, each publication stands on its own merit and provides a building block for my larger research agenda. Each takes on a different topic, although they have a unifying theme about the causes of war and peace with a special focus on its implications for a possible Sino-American clash. Many ideas and arguments presented below have appeared before. This is, however, the first time that I have chosen to write a book with a specific focus on the historical interpretations presented by major theories about war and peace. In my discussion below, I bring together various historical episodes to bear on these theories and popular narratives based on them. I draw on my prior research, including research conducted for pending publications, for this purpose. Of course, I also introduce many new materials to bolster my arguments and expand my study.

In the following analysis, I introduce six armed conflicts from the past. Four of them have been featured prominently in international relations theories on war. They are the Peloponnesian War, the two world wars, and Japan's attack on Pearl Harbor. I also include the Falklands/Malvinas War and the ongoing Russo-Ukrainian War, even though they have not received nearly as much attention from international relations analysts in developing their theories on war. Nevertheless, these conflicts have received extensive media coverage, and the latter conflict is still ongoing as of the time of this writing. Even though these wars are perhaps less consequential, say, compared to the two world wars, I will show that they offer important insights about the nature and possibility of a Sino-American collision. In addition to the six cases of interstate wars just mentioned, I will discuss two episodes that ended without war. They are the peaceful transition of world leadership from Britain to the United States and the peaceful resolution of the Cuban Missile Crisis, both representing cases where "the dog did not bark." Except for the two world wars, each of these cases will be the subject of attention for a separate chapter (chapters 1–7). I tend to see the two world wars as one large conflict with an interlude of peace (Carr 2001 [1939]). Thus, I present my discussion of them in a single chapter (chapter 2).

Besides those episodes mentioned above, I also introduce briefly other poignant cases, such as the *Mayaguez* affair, the Suez Crisis, US involvement in the Bay of Pigs invasion of Cuba, its invasion of Iraq and interventions in Lebanon and Somalia, and NATO's (North Atlantic Treaty Organization) attacks on Libya and Serbia. These and other cases are the subject matter for chapter 8. This chapter discusses how historical analogies have influenced policymakers, including non-Americans. It is not specifically focused on Sino-American relations and the role of history in scholarship, although it is clearly relevant to both. Washington's decisions to fight in Korea and Vietnam and the legacy of China's intervention in the Korean conflict have obviously been salient historical reminders in the minds of both US policymakers and academic researchers. They have been the subject of much analysis. I have not dedicated individual chapters to discuss them, although references to these historical episodes are sprinkled throughout the text.

The so-called lessons of the 1930s, especially that of the Munich Conference in 1938, have loomed large for Western officials in the 1950s, 1960s, and 1970s not only for Americans but also for British and French policymakers. They continue to be important and relevant for many officials and scholars who advocate a hard-line policy to rebuff and contain perceived Chinese aggression and an emergent threat from Beijing. I have referred often to these putative lessons throughout the text and especially at the start of chapter 3 in the context of the crisis about the Suez Canal in 1956 and in my comparison of the historical experiences of Habsburg Spain and imperial Britain. I have not dedicated a separate chapter to the Munich Conference and the so-called lessons of the 1930s.

This decision certainly does not mean that I dismiss their influence on policymakers, scholars, and political pundits. In fact, chapter 3 tries specifically to juxtapose popular understanding about what happened in Munich in 1938 and its historical consequences with the Japanese decision to attack Pearl Harbor in order to show the danger of simplistic warnings against appeasement. My discussion of Britain's accommodation of a rising United States (in chapter 4) also challenges this conventional wisdom. Ironically, one can also almost hear Vladmir Putin complaining about Mikhail Gorbachev's unilateral concessions to the West for being responsible for Russia's subsequent troubles (Kupchan 2010, 397), including the ongoing war in Ukraine (chapter 7). Of course, the word "appeasement" is never used to describe Britain's "accommodation" of the United States and Russia's "concessions" to the West. No one (at least those who publish in leading US academic venues on international relations) to my knowledge has referred to these episodes as evidence to warn about the dangerous consequences of appeasement. Evidently, what is bad for the goose is not necessarily also bad for the gander. "We don't see things as they are; we see them as we are." This is one example of my complaint about how history has been deployed in political discourse and even scholarship. Those who experienced the events of the 1930s have passed from the scene, although the so-called lesson of Munich is still alive and around. It figures prominently, if not always explicitly, in the statements and writings of those Americans who are now advocating a get-tough policy on Beijing.

These people are highly critical of Beijing's alleged expansionist policies, even though no Chinese leader has advocated purchasing Borneo, controlling the Strait of Malacca, or annexing Mongolia, whereas Donald Trump has publicly declared his intention to purchase Greenland, take over the Panama Canal, and incorporate Canada as the fifty-first state of the United States while at the same time refusing to rule out the use of military force to achieve these goals (Smith and Lee 2025). How would Americans react to any such Chinese declaration? This reaction tells us about the extent of hypocrisy and double standard in the conduct of and discourse on foreign policy. In chapter 9, I turn my attention specifically to the question of which historical precedent provides an appropriate analogue for contemporary China. The answer to this question may not be as easy or straightforward as one may think. Of course, Graham Allison's (2015, 2017) recent formulation of Thucydides's Trap points to ancient Athens as a parallel for modern China. How appropriate is this analogue? On the occasion of the hundredth anniversary of World War I, there were also essays written about whether Wilhelmine Germany offers useful lessons for contemporary China so that Beijing would not repeat the same mistakes that had resulted in Berlin's self-encirclement and an even worse outcome for it in the ensuing devastating war that resulted in its demise (e.g., Wolf 2014; see also Shirk 2023). Of course, there are also thoughtful writings suggesting that contemporary China is far from being a replica of ancient Athens. It is also different from the *Kaiserreich* in some important respects. Therefore, Germany in the early twentieth century, not to mention Athens some 2,500 years ago, is a misleading example to inform us about today's China (e.g., Chong and Hall 2014; Solingen 2014).

It is, of course, an interesting and important phenomenon that when Americans speak about rising powers as revisionist states, including officials and scholars, they seldom include the United States in the ranks of these countries, even though it clearly belonged to this category from roughly the mid-1800s to the early 1900s (highlighted by the Mexican-American War of 1846–1848 at one end and the Spanish-American War of 1898 and the US participation in World War I in 1917 at the other end), then again after World War II (after the European states were exhausted and laid in ruins), and for a third time after the USSR's (Union of Soviet Socialist Republics) collapse, catapulting it to the status of a unipolar power without any peers in sight. To his credit, Allison warns Americans to be more careful when they demand the Chinese to be "more like us." Allison reminds his readers that the United States had applied a sharp elbow and practiced "muscular" policy when Theodore Roosevelt was its president.

Should we consider the United States then as an analogue for China now? This question has probably never occurred to many Americans, scholars and officials included. Another awkward question asks, What could account for the discrepant experience between the ascending United States from roughly the mid-1800s to the early 1900s, on the one hand, and imperial Japan after the Meiji Restoration during roughly the same period, on the other hand? Specifically, Washington succeeded in establishing a regional hegemony in the Western Hemisphere, while Tokyo encountered serious resistance in a similar quest, even though the former appeared to have acted more like a revisionist state, and the latter, as a conformist state. It seems that for all of us, some historical occurrences are recalled more easily than others—even when it comes to remembering our own history.

We also often settle on different historical parallels when studying a current situation depending on whether it applies to us or others. Few US officials acknowledge publicly how Americans had settled their civil war when they say the United States opposes any "nonpeaceful" means by Beijing to take over Taiwan. More Americans were killed by fellow Americans in our civil war than in any war against foreigners. In warning about Xi Jinping's designs for Taiwan, few Americans pause to ponder why Abraham Lincoln enjoys such an exalted place in US history (although he was not very popular when he was alive).

In the book's conclusion, I summarize my major arguments. I discuss especially the danger of misappropriating history, presenting simplistic, one-sided, and hence misleading conclusions that impair sound policy and scholarship. These errors can be due to motivated bias, the natural human tendency to resort to mental shortcuts, or lazy and sloppy thinking. These causes are not mutually exclusive. I discuss lessons to be drawn from those historical episodes studied in the preceding discussion, specifically steps that we can take to mitigate various threats to making valid inference—precautions to guard against or at least ameliorate mistakes in our rush to recruit history to confirm our theories and support our arguments. I also ask whether the shoe fits the other foot, emphasizing the importance of empathy and introspection.

If a reader has made it thus far, it would be obvious that I contest many popular ideas and mainstream accounts intended to explain why wars have happened or peace has endured in the past. My discussion shows how history may be distorted and misappropriated. I argue that alternative and more persuasive explanations are possible for some historical episodes compared to those being currently presented in popular narratives and circulating in prevailing discourse. Moreover, some important lessons are being overlooked—lessons that are highly pertinent to Sino-American relations and the prospects and consequences of a possible war between them. Thus, some historical episodes, such as the Peloponnesian War in ancient Greece and the two world wars, often mentioned in connection with China's recent rise and the associated danger of a Sino-American war, are, in my view, not suitable historical analogues for contemporary international relations—at least not in the way that they are usually presented. At the same time, other episodes, such as Japan's attack of Pearl Harbor, the Falklands/Malvinas War, and the Cuban Missile Crisis, do not usually come up in popular and even scholarly discourse on Sino-American relations and yet appear to offer some valuable lessons or insights that have been heretofore overlooked.

These proclivities call attention to my remark that people have different recollections and interpretations of history. They usually remember those episodes that tend to be consistent with their expectations or support their preexisting beliefs even when the specific past event they invoke does not match well with a current situation. Conversely, they often fail to apply an analogy or precedent from the past when it can actually offer some useful parallels to and instructive caveats for the present. Thus, what people see from history depends in part on where they stand on an issue. In other words, people sometimes overlook or ignore uncomfortable but pertinent episodes from the past. History can be mobilized selectively to advocate, justify, and legitimate a policy that has already been decided on for other reasons, as in the instrumental view of history's role in policymaking. In the garbage can model of decision-making (Cohen, March, and Olsen 1972), to be discussed later, solutions can be looking for problems to which they can be plausibly applied just as a recognition of problems can motivate efforts to search for solutions. The former tendency describes how people who have a preferred policy are constantly on the lookout for issues or occasions to apply it. In the concluding chapter, I associate this tendency to the law of the instrument. If given a hammer, a young child may use it for purposes other than its original intended use—for example, as a toy, a weapon, or a utensil for eating food. In international relations and foreign policy, history can be used to define a problem and formulate a response to it (history's cognitive role as distinct from its instrumental role). It can therefore be used to explain a policy. But just as easily or commonly, it can be mobilized and deployed to justify or hide the real reasons behind a policy.

ONE

The Origin of the Peloponnesian War

Thucydides, who lived in ancient Greece some 2,500 years ago, has recently gained name recognition among Americans who are not typically interested in or knowledgeable about the classic world. This phenomenon owes its development to the influential writing of Graham T. Allison (2015, 2017), a Harvard professor, who has popularized the idea of Thucydides's Trap.

In a nutshell, Allison warns his readers that China and the United States may be headed for war. The reason? He cites Thucydides's explanation of the origin of the Peloponnesian War. In his masterpiece, *The History of the Peloponnesian War* (see discussions by Balot, Forsdyke, and Foster 2017; Jaffe 2017; Kagan 1969; Mynott 2013; Strassler 1998), Thucydides writes that the rise of Athens and the consequent fear felt by Sparta were the root causes of this conflict, which devastated ancient Greece. This observation has been turned into a maxim taken by Allison to mean that when a rising latecomer catches up to an established, leading state, the danger of war between them becomes elevated. According to him, when this development occurred in the past, war ensued in twelve of sixteen cases—or, if you will, the odds of a war happening was about 75 percent. Allison claims that his compilation represents the universe of such historical cases. On this basis, he warns that we are entering another period of heightened danger for war to break out as China is catching up to the United States.

Allison's work has been remarkably influential. It has reached the highest level of policymakers. He was reportedly invited to Zhongnanhai, the compound where top Chinese leaders have their offices and residences. China's President Xi Jinping has been quoted saying, "We must all strive to avoid falling into Thucydides Trap" (Yicai Global 2017) and that this trap "can be avoided . . . as long as we maintain communication and treat each other with sincerity" (Shi 2020). Allison's work has also "caught fire" among academics and the informed public.

One indication of this influence is attested by the fact that Allison's proposition has apparently won many converts, even though it goes against the central tenet of realism, which has long claimed that a balance of power promotes international peace and stability. From this traditional realist perspective, one should welcome the development whereby the balance between Chinese and US power has become more equalized (even though the United States continues to be predominant). In fact, however, this development has become a source of anxiety and even alarm because, in Allison's account of Thucydides's Trap, it augurs war. That this perspective has so easily and thoroughly displaced the traditional realist tenet urging states to undertake policies to balance power is quite remarkable. It represents a paradigmatic shift for international relations analysts, and yet there has been scant evidence of a serious debate among these scholars on this paradigmatic change transforming their discipline (Chan 2024; Chan and Hu, forthcoming-a).

To be sure, Allison was not the first one to have written about the putative effects of interstate power shifts on the increased danger of war. Other works, such as those of A. F. K. Organski (1958), Organski and Jacek Kugler (1980), Robert Gilpin (1981), Charles F. Doran (1991), and Doran and Wes Parsons (1980), have also discussed this topic prior to Allison's more recent introduction of Thucydides's Trap. Reacting to Allison's work, other scholars warn of the danger of misinterpreting Thucydides, whose writing is, in their view, much richer, nuanced, and sophisticated than the simple aphorism attributed to him—namely, Sparta's fear of Athens's rise was the basic cause of the Peloponnesian War (e.g., Bagby 1994; Kirshner 2019; Lebow 2007). These critics point to many analytic problems with Allison's study in what has now become known as Thucydides's Trap (e.g., Chan 2019, 2020a, 2020b, 2020c, 2021b;

Chan et al. 2021; Lee 2019; Lebow and Tompkins 2016; Platias and Trigkas 2021; Welch 2015). Yet it appears that these objections have been swamped by a much larger number of academics, the lay public, and even officials embracing Allison's rendition of Thucydides's Trap. I will not go into details to discuss all the objections that have been raised about Allison's thesis. I will instead point out a few of the more salient ones pertinent to this study's topic.

Allison's study recalls the Peloponnesian War between Athens and Sparta in the ancient Greek world. Thus, unlike power-transition theory (to be discussed in chapter 2), whose scope limits it to the industrial age, his formulation of Thucydides's Trap is presumably not bounded by time. Yet the earliest war included in his case files is the struggle between Spain and Portugal in the late fifteenth century. Was there any transitional warfare in the intervening one thousand years (that is, roughly between 2,500 BCE and 1,500 CE) that should be included? Recall that Allison claims that the sixteen historical cases included in his compilation represent the entire *universe* of episodes that correspond to the phenomenon being described as Thucydides's Trap—that is, all historical cases that fall within the scope of this formulation's claim. It is not clear, however, what criteria Allison applies in deciding which states, how much power shifts, and what kind of wars warrant inclusion in his compilation. Which ones should be included and which ones excluded from this inventory?

One presumes that Allison's formulation pertains only to wars among major states, but the precise definition of such states is missing from his analysis. He includes the Sino-Japanese War of 1894–1895 in his case files but not the subsequent Japanese invasion of China dating conventionally from 1937 to 1945. Both the First Opium War fought between China and Britain (1839–1832) and the Second Opium War waged by Britain, France, and the United States against China (or the so-called Arrow War, 1856–1860) are missing from his case inventory. The Spanish-American War (1898) is also absent. Perhaps this omission is because Allison did not consider Spain to be a "ruling power" in the late 1800s. Perhaps the two opium wars are omitted for the same reason: that China was no longer a "ruling power" when these wars were fought. But then why is the Sino-Japanese War (1894–1895) included in the case files? Or is it possible that Allison does not consider the two opium wars to have met his criterion of war, such as according to the number of their combat fatalities? In the absence of a clear and explicit definition of what it means to be a "ruling" or "rising" power and what constitutes "war," one cannot be sure.

Allison also does not provide instruction on how to measure national power or to determine the precise time period during which power shifts are supposed to be occurring for the pertinent pairs of countries to raise the danger of war between them. Should a conflict happen before, during, or only after the period of power shifts, and how much should power be shifted between two countries to raise the danger of war between them? In short, the criteria for admissible evidence to confirm or reject his proposition are unclear. For instance, China has overtaken Russia, Germany, and Japan in recent decades in terms of the size of their respective economies. Should the fact that there has not been a war among China and these other states count against the proposition of Thucydides's Trap?

Does Athens (a "rising" power) provide a fitting analogue for contemporary China? Is the United States a suitable replica of Sparta (an established, or "ruling," power)? Even someone with only a casual acquaintance of ancient Athens knows that it is usually considered the cradle of Western democracy, a naval power, and a commercial powerhouse in its day. In contrast, the hallmarks of Sparta were its people's martial spirit and their austere lifestyle. It was an oligarchy living in constant fear of rebellion by its slaves. It was also famous for its infantry fighting in phalanx formation. Do these traits of ancient Athens and Sparta correspond with our knowledge about contemporary China and the United States, respectively? That is, is ancient Athens a suitable facsimile of contemporary China, and is ancient Spartan an appropriate parallel for the contemporary United States? For us to accept the thesis of Thucydides's Trap, we would have to overlook the obvious incongruities between the pertinent pairs (that is, contemporary China is equivalent to ancient Athens, and the contemporary United States is equivalent to ancient Sparta) and to put all our analytic eggs in one basket—namely, that the power shifts ostensibly happening between the two ancient Greek city states and currently between China and the United States are historically accurate and have comparable effects. In fact, we do not have any direct evidence to indicate that power distribution was shifting between these two Greek polities. The closest we could come to arguing that changes in their relative power were occurring to present a possible cause of their ensuing war is to point to their leaders' perceptions. Yet Allison did not offer any systematic evidence pertaining to this possibility.

The preceding remarks in turn call our attention to the fact that Thucydides's Trap presents a monocausal explanation of war—that power shifts between states trump all other possible factors that can cause war, such as states' differences in ideology or political orientation, their disputes over territory, their leaders' personalities and ambitions, and the nature of their economic system, as Marxists would allege. In my view, monocausal accounts are inherently dubious for explaining complex sociopolitical phenomena, including war. Wars can result from multiple and not necessarily mutually exclusive causes or pathways. For instance, they can happen due to the push of domestic politics, the pull of alliance entanglement, and/or mistakes in officials' judgments (Welch 2015, 2020).

Moreover, wars do not suddenly happen out of the blue. There is typically a long history involving multiple steps that eventually lead to the outbreak of armed hostilities (Senese and Vasquez 2008). This observation in turn suggests that there are usually several exit ramps on the way to war, or, in other words, opportunities for leaders to deescalate crises and avoid war. From this perspective, war need not be an inevitable outcome, which, of course, Allison acknowledges even though he invokes only one cause or independent variable—namely, power shifts between the pertinent pair of countries. There is typically a dangerous constellation of factors—often featuring recurrent crises, armament races, tight and interlocking alliances, and diplomatic brinksmanship in addition to power shifts—that creates a combustible environment—one that can be more easily ignited by a precipitant, such as Sarajevo in 1914, to become a large conflagration (Lebow 2000–2001; Thompson 2003). In other words, wars tend to stem from a combination of variables and not a single one, such as power shifts.

For readers to accept Allison's monocausal explanation of the Peloponnesian War and apply it to the contemporary world, they would have to suspend their disbelief that nothing has happened since ancient Greece that would have changed the effect of power shifts on war occurrence. To make such a large transhistorical leap from the Greek world some 2,500 years ago to modern international relations, we would have to dismiss the relevance or importance of changes that have happened in the intervening years, such as the advent of modern states, nationalism, and nuclear weapons, to mention just a few obvious ones.

To illustrate this point, there was, of course, a huge power shift between the United States and the USSR before and after the latter country's collapse and disintegration. Leaders in the Kremlin accepted retrenchment and Russia's greatly diminished international stature. Yet even in view of these disastrous (from their perspective) developments, they were evidently not overly concerned about being attacked by the Americans. Their possession of nuclear weapons made all the difference in reassuring them that this attack was unlikely. Fear of an ascendant United States did not produce war in this instance, even though the huge power shift in this case should have presented an "easy" case for confirming the warning of Thucydides's Trap.

If war did not happen in this case, why should we expect its occurrence in other contemporary situations? This example points seemingly to an obvious and important omission in Allison's case inventory. This omission may be due to the fact that the USSR was never a "ruling" power. If anything, the United States came closer to being a "ruling" state, whose power rose even further after the USSR's demise, conferring upon it the status of a unipolar hegemon. Setting aside the designation of "ruling" and "rising" states, however, a large shift in relative power did occur between these two leading countries, and it did not produce a war. In light of this discussion, Thucydides's Trap appears to be a formulation constructed to lend an aura of authoritativeness and timelessness to Allison's analysis. In other words, Thucydides's name is invoked as "a legitimating strategy for our presentist arguments" (Zarakol 2020).

> While Thucydides thought he was observing something deep and likely to be repeated about the human condition in the war between Athens and Sparta (as many historians do about the episodes they are writing on), he was not at all thinking with our post-nineteenth century IR [international relations] concepts.
>
> This point is simultaneously banal and important. We tend to read IR concepts back into classical texts and periods not because they are brilliantly trans-historical, but because presenting them as such is a legitimation strategy for our presentist arguments. . . . [I]t is much easier to take our beliefs about dynamics from the present and read them into various historical episodes, historical texts and the thinking of historical figures, such as Thucydides. Confirmation bias, if you will, passing as *argumentum ad verecundiam* [argument from authority or appealing to an authority to support one's argument]. Allison has not learned what he thinks from Thucydides, nor do we have any reason to believe that Thucydides would have agreed with Allison; Allison is simply calling his own

> argument "Thucydides's Trap" and thus giving it the appearance of being timeless (when it is not). There is no reason to concede Thucydides to Allison. (Zarakol 2020)

As already stated, we do not have any direct evidence that the power relationship between Athens and Sparta had in fact shifted to Sparta's detriment before they started fighting. Did Spartan leaders perceive a threat emanating from such a possible shift? Indeed, would Thucydides have agreed with Thucydides's Trap in its contemporary version? Athanassios Platias and Vasilis Trigkas (2021, 18; italics in original) suggest that "it was not *solely the increase* of the Athenian power but the *character of Athenian power* that exacerbated Spartan fear." Specifically, Athens's aggrandizement and its efforts to undermine Sparta's alliance were, in their view, the cause of the latter's perception of threat.

In a similar vein, James Lee (2019) questions whether Thucydides would agree with the view that Allison attributes to him. According to Lee, Athens's imperial expansion, rather than its growth of power, was the source of alarm for Sparta. This is an important distinction. It separates what a state *has* from what it *does*. The distinction being drawn here also describes the main difference between Kenneth N. Waltz's (1979) balance of power theory and Stephen Walt's (1987) balance of threat theory. In this regard, power-transition theory offers a more satisfactory explanation of war because it incorporates not only power shifts but also the revisionist intentions and conduct of a rising upstart to explain the outbreak of war. The difference between Waltz and Walt is that whereas the former argues threat inheres in power alone, the latter contends that intention also matters.

My reference to what a state *does* reflects Walt's theory because a state's behavior indicates its intention. As just mentioned, proponents of power-transition theory introduce the variable "revisionism" to suggest a rising state's (aggressive) intention. It is important to note, however, in actual practice, nearly all quantitative analyses of power-transition theory omit "revisionism" as an explanatory variable, and they are therefore similar to Thucydides's Trap in that both focus exclusively on interstate power shifts to explain war.

Why is this distinction between power and threat important and relevant in the current context? US scholars tend to focus on China's rising power, as in Allison's rendition of Thucydides's Trap, thus suggesting that other countries should be concerned about the threat posed by this development regardless of Beijing's intentions. They tend to instead underscore the benign nature of US hegemony, or, in other words, its nonthreatening behavior and its benevolent intention rather than its unrivaled power. This tendency is especially pronounced in liberal accounts of international order (Ikenberry 2001, 2008, 2011, 2012) and hegemonic-stability theory (Kindleberger 1974, 1981, 1986). Of course, I am referring here to relative emphasis as many scholars also point to China's revisionist tendencies and the United States' unprecedented power in their analyses. My point is that these relative differences often reflect shuttling logic depending on which country is being analyzed. An emphasis on China's increased power also deflects the view, albeit a minority one, that given their historical ties, China's neighbors do not see its growing power to be threatening (Kang 2003, 2007, 2010, 2012, 2020).

Indeed, Xinru Ma and David Kang (2024) show that power-transition theory—derived from European experience—cannot account for infrequent war and protracted peace in premodern East Asia. Dynastic changes in East Asia tend to be the result of internal challenges rather than foreign conquest, and neither interstate power shifts nor dissatisfaction with the prevailing order—the two key variables in power-transition theory—is able to explain this history. Instead, Ma and Kang point to the relevant governing elites' "common conjecture," or shared understanding, about their states' respective roles and statuses in a legitimate hierarchical order as the principal reason for this enduring reality. Mutual accommodation, rather than appeasement, aggression, balance of power, and systemic anarchy (featured so prominently in Western Realpolitik reasoning), provides a more accurate description and explanation of East Asian history over 1,500 years. While agreeing with their analysis, my argument in this book is that formulations such as Thucydides's Trap and power transition do not *even* explain Western or European experience satisfactorily.

Significantly, Thucydides's discussion can just as easily be interpreted to say that rather than Athens's increasing power, it was its aggression that caused the Peloponnesian War. After all, the Corinthians, who pleaded for help from Sparta to resist Athens, had complained that the Spartans had been too slow and even oblivious to the danger posed by Athens and too lethargic in responding to Athens's aggressive actions that had expanded its empire and imposed punitive tributes on its subordinates. If we must transport ancient

Greece to contemporary international relations, this interpretation could as well be applied to the United States' hyperactivity and its global reach, which are the causes behind resistance to Washington's modern-day empire. Such an interpretation may not be correct, but this example suggests that Thucydides's writing can be used to reach quite different analytic and policy conclusions.

As just noted, although Allison and others emphasize Thucydides's aphorism that it was Athens's rise and the fear that this development had aroused in Sparta that had caused the Peloponnesian War, one could just as easily construct different narratives about this conflict. In his account, Thucydides does not assign any moral superiority to his home polity, Athens, with its version of democracy by the standards of its time. He instead describes Athens as a "tyrannical empire" and reminds his fellow Athenians of the danger of this situation. He reminds his readers of Athenian leader Pericles's warning to his compatriots: "Nor can you now give [the empire] over for already your government is in the nature of a tyranny, which is both unjust for you to take up and unsafe to lay down" (quoted in Platias and Trigkas 2021, 229). Moreover, Pericles cautions Athenians "not to extend your empire at the same time as you are fighting the war [in Sicily] and not to add self-imposed dangers, for I am more afraid of our own mistakes than the strategy of our opponents" (quoted in Kagan 1969, 192).

To contemporary ears, these statements can sound very much like a warning against imperial overstretch, involving self-injurious policies, which Paul Kennedy (1987) warns the United States about. By imperial overstretch, Kennedy has in mind the tendency for a dominant imperial power to extend its foreign commitments beyond its available resources. Allison could very well have written an alternative account of Thucydides's Trap, referring to unforced errors committed by a country in its pursuit of an overseas empire. As Thucydides's account makes abundantly clear, hubris, ambition, and vanity—and not necessarily interstate power shifts—can present an intoxicating brew causing self-destructive behavior, such as that of overreach. Allison's historical rendition appears to be motivated by his recognition of a contemporary development—namely, China's rise—which in turn inspired him to refer to Thucydides to warn about the danger that this development poses to international peace and stability—and, of course, also to the United States' dominant position in international relations.

Allison's rendition of Thucydides's Trap and, as we shall see in the next chapter, power-transition theory as formulated by A. F. K. Organski and Jacek Kugler (1980) both emphasize structural factors characterizing the interstate system as the decisive determinant of war and peace. More specifically, they both assign analytic priority to the shifting balance of power among major states as the principal cause of armed conflict. Yet even a casual reading of *The History of the Peloponnesian War* would tell us that Thucydides's account is far richer, nuanced, and complex than the monocausal explanation represented by the contemporary summation of his thesis.

Moreover, Thucydides's own account suggests that war between Sparta and Athens was far from preordained or inevitable. It happened due to a combination of factors, each being highly contingent in itself. For example, Sparta's assembly was closely divided on whether to respond positively to Corinth's plea for assistance. King Archidamus urged caution and moderation, and he warned against any rash decision to rush to war. He pointed out the hardships and risks of a war and thus tried to restrain his countrymen from a direct confrontation with Athens. His views were opposed by Sthenelaidas, who appealed to his audience's sense of pride and indignation, exhorting them to seek revenge against perceived insults from Athens. Sparta's assembly was thus split between a war party and a peace party, and its support for Corinth was far from a foregone conclusion. In the end, it agreed to lend support to Corinth based on a split decision. Even after this decision was reached, Sparta continued to send peace envoys to Athens, asking Pericles to rescind the Megarian Decree aimed at crippling a Spartan ally. In other words, there was still an option to exit from war and confrontation, and even after Pericles rejected Sparta's demand, actual combat did not commence for another year. Fighting only started after Thebes, one of Sparta's allies, launched an invasion of Plataea, thus precipitating war and forcing Sparta's hand.

On the Athenian side, its decision to assist Corcyra in a conflict with Corinth was also a close call. Its assembly met twice, with the second meeting reversing the original decision favorable to the Corinthians. Even then, Athens only extended defensive assistance to Corcyra, refraining from any offensive commitment that would have made a war more likely with Sparta (which, as noted just now, decided to support Corinth also in a close call). Moreover, had Pericles decided to rescind the Megarian Decree, this decision could have avoided a war with Sparta. His refusal to do so made Athens appear overly aggressive and harsh in Spartan eyes.

In short, history could have easily taken a different turn at several pivotal points. Had the relevant decision-makers made a different choice at any of these points, war could have been avoided. We will encounter this theme again later, such as in the timing of the dual assassinations in Sarajevo that triggered World War I and the accidental convergence of several events that precipitated the Falklands/Malvinas War. A major problem with the way in which supposed lessons of history are frequently invoked is that they often strongly imply a certainty or inevitability on how things eventually turn out that is not warranted by the fact that these are highly contingent affairs. Robert Jervis (1976, 321) writes, "Accidents, chance, and lack of coordination are rarely given their due by contemporary observers. Instead, they suspect that well-laid plans give events a coherence that they would otherwise lack."

Before concluding this chapter, three additional observations are pertinent in evaluating propositions such as Thucydides's Trap. First, the way in which Allison frames this aphorism—which is not based on the rich and nuanced account given by Thucydides himself—points to a single factor—namely, power shifts among countries—to be the root cause of war. As already pointed out, Thucydides's Trap as formulated by Allison offers a monocausal explanation of war. Its focus on the changing distribution of power among states suggests an emphasis on the structural properties of the interstate system. This emphasis in turn means that human agency is not accorded nearly as much importance. The very premise of structural explanations of war, such as the one offered by Allison's rendition of Thucydides's Trap, contends that structural forces will overwhelm human agency and, moreover, when presented with similar circumstances, such as the phenomenon of interstate power shifts, decision-makers—regardless of their personality, background, or beliefs—will likely respond similarly. This quality gives Thucydides's adage a seeming quality of being ageless. Indeed, the danger of war warned by Thucydides's Trap assumes that officials never learn. That is, they will repeat the same mistake again and again in almost a robotic fashion so that war recurs whenever and wherever the distribution of power makes states more equal in their capabilities.

Second, Thucydides's Trap as formulated by Allison presents a bivariate proposition stipulating a causal connection between interstate power shifts and the outbreak of war. Yet we all know that power shifts in themselves do not cause war. That is, whether war results from power shifts depends on decision-makers' perceptions of and reactions to these changes. Stated differently, the simple bivariate relationship posited by Thucydides's Trap omits critical intermediate steps that connect power shifts to the outbreak of war. As currently formulated, the linkages connecting these two phenomena are missing. We are not told what are the causal mechanisms that would incline leaders to choose war when presented with information on power shifts. At least in the customary translation of Thucydides's aphorism, fear was supposed to be the source motivating Sparta's reaction to Athens's rise. Contemporary discourse on Thucydides's Trap, however, fails to specify or test any cognitive, affective, or any other factors (possibly including organizational momentum, bureaucratic politics, domestic partisanship, and economic rent seeking) that mediate between the putative cause (power shifts) and the ostensible effect (war), or, in other words, that provide the causal connection from power shifts to the outbreak of war.

Third, the idea of equifinality suggests that there can be multiple pathways to war (Chan, forthcoming-a). As mentioned earlier, war can result from the push of domestic politics, the pull of foreign alliances, and a variety of reasons that cause misperception or misjudgment. These explanations or pathways need not be mutually exclusive. Indeed, one way to assess the danger of war is to emphasize and focus on the *interactions* of factors that are conducive to the occurrence of armed hostilities. Armament races, entangling alliances, diplomatic brinksmanship, recurrent crises, and states that are ensnared in enduring rivalries can all contribute to the danger of war. Moreover, the combined influence of these factors is greater than the sum of each factor's separate effect. Naturally, the more tightly coupled are the different parts of an interstate system and the more mutually sensitive are those factors conducive to war, the greater is the probability of a possible positive feedback loop producing amplification. The risk of contagion and the domino effect (one thing leading to another) would then become more elevated.

TWO
The Causes of the Two World Wars

Graham T. Allison's introduction of Thucydides's Trap was predated by power-transition theory (Kugler and Lemke 1996; Organski and Kugler 1980; Tammen et al. 2000), which, as its name suggests, is also concerned with changes in states' relative power as a cause of war. Rather than being specifically inspired by China's rise, A. F. K. Organski (1958) wrote long before this more recent development about how an approaching power parity between the world's two leading states presages war. Although both Thucydides's Trap and power-transition theory emphasize the effect of power shifts on war occurrence, the latter formulation also introduces a second variable, the rising state's revisionist agenda, as an additional factor in determining the prospect of war. Unlike Thucydides's Trap, Organski's power-transition theory is specifically concerned with interstate dynamics during the industrial age and with the struggle between the two states at the very pinnacle of interstate hierarchy for world domination. Thus, the Peloponnesian War would not meet the scope conditions of power-transition theory and thus would not fall within its purview. In contrast, Allison's cases include preindustrial states and states other than the world's two leading powers. Unlike Thucydides's Trap, we have a much clearer idea about power-transition theory's scope conditions and its operational definitions of national power and transitional period (which is supposed to start when a latecomer's gross national product reaches 80 percent of the established leader's economy).

Both Thucydides's Trap and power-transition theory are characterized by important missing links. That is, they do not tell us the intermediate steps that connect changes in states' relative power at the systemic or interstate level of analysis to officials' decisions to initiate or accept war at the group or individual level of analysis. Of course, the former formulation refers to Sparta's fear as a motivation for war, and the latter points to the *interaction* between power shifts and revisionist impulses as a cause of war. In practice, however, research to date hardly incorporates explicitly and systematically "fear" or "revisionism" as intervening variables to explain the outbreak of major war. To the extent that empirical research on power-transition theory examines *only* power shifts as their explanatory variable for war occurrence (thus excluding "revisionism" as a second variable, whose interaction with power shifts is supposed to precipitate war), it does *not* really offer a valid test of this theory (for an exception, see Sample 2018). As with Thucydides's Trap, by focusing on *just* power shifts, power-transition theory presents us with a bivariate analysis, thus offering a monocausal explanation of war when analysts either simply bypass the "revisionism" variable or proclaim it as a matter of assertion without providing any systematic evidence.

Although power-transition theory has been understandably applied by international relations scholars to study the implications of China's rise (e.g., Chan 2008, 2017; Levy 2008b; Rapkin and Thompson 2003, 2013), it has also been a topic of study for those who are interested in understanding how power shifts affect international peace and stability more generally. Indeed, this latter interest has predated more recent studies in the wake of China's rise. The two world wars were the primary exhibits in the earlier studies. Some studies in the pertinent literature address theoretical issues (e.g., DiCicco and Levy 1999; Thompson 1996; Vasquez 1996), while others take up empirical work, whether engaging in large-*N* statistical analyses or in-depth case studies (e.g., de Soysa, Oneal, and Park 1997; Greve and Levy 2018; Houweling and Siccama 1988; Kim 1991, 1992; Lebow and Valentino 2009; Lemke and Reed 1996; Lobell 2016).

As just remarked, power-transition theory originally looked to the two world wars to provide its empirical foundation and its main source of historical support (for discussions on the two world wars, see Berghahn 1973; Fischer

1967, 1975; Hilgruber 1981; Robertson 1963; Taylor 1961; Tuchman 1962). Put simply, proponents of this theory claim that in both of these cases, war was instigated by a rising Germany in a failed bid to displace Britain as the leading global power. In this respect, too, power-transition theory is more specific than Thucydides's Trap in arguing that the responsibility for instigating war laid with a revisionist upstart seeking to supplant an incumbent hegemon and to upend the existing international order. In contrast, Allison's formulation only suggests that wars frequently happen when there are power shifts among states without, however, stipulating how analysts should measure power shifts or identify those states that are inclined to start war. Although Organski and Kugler (1980) include the Franco-Prussian War and the Russo-Japanese War in their original analysis, these two conflicts do not actually meet their own stipulation limiting their theory to wars between *just* the world's two most powerful states fighting over which one of them should be the global hegemon. This stipulation naturally leads Organski and Kugler and other scholars to look for pertinent evidence from the two world wars as their primary source of evidence. Of course, this same stipulation also limits—and should limit—the number of historical cases that meet their criterion for admissible evidence.

Parenthetically, that Organski and Kugler chose to focus on the four wars just mentioned raises the question of selecting on the dependent variable (war). They essentially ask whether there is evidence of power transition in these cases of war. But they overlook cases when peace endured even in the presence of power transition, such as the Anglo-American case to be discussed in chapter 4. There is, of course, also the possibility of war happening in the absence of power transition. In making causal attribution, analysts face challenges posed by "idiosyncrasy" and "irrelevance." These threats to making valid inference refer, respectively, to the phenomena that similar "treatments" (in this case, power transition) have produced different results (in this case, war and nonwar) and that dissimilar "treatments" (the presence and absence of power transitions) have produced the same results (such as when wars have happened whether there was or was not a power transition between the belligerent states).

As Michael D. Swaine and Ashley L. Tellis (2000, 227) point out,

> The fact remains that direct attacks on a hegemon by rising challengers are rare and infrequent in modern times. The best examples of such a

> war . . . remains the French attack on the Dutch United Provinces under Louis XIV. Most systemic wars in fact occur because (a) some rising states attack other rising states to consolidate their power but nonetheless manage to precipitate systemic war because the existing hegemon enters the fray on behalf of the weaker side to preempt a future challenge that may be mounted by the stronger rising power (the Italian wars); or, (b) some rising states attack key allies of the existing hegemon or important neutrals in a search for regional gains, which nonetheless precipitates systemic war because the existing hegemon enters the fray on behalf of the ally or the neutral to prevent a shift in the future balance of power (the Spanish wars, the Napoleonic wars, and the First and Second World Wars).

Significantly, the above passage points to the possibility of reciprocal causality. Not only can interstate power shifts cause war, but also wars may be initiated or fought to pursue power gains or to prevent others from making these gains. The latter possibility is as likely as—perhaps even more likely than—the former possibility.

Just as I have indicated in my discussion of Thucydides's Trap, the historical basis for power-transition theory's claims is problematic in several ways (e.g., Chan 2004b, 2008, 2017; Lebow and Valentino 2009). Here, I focus on Organski and Kugler's (1980) interpretation of the two world wars as an Anglo-German contest, which is a controversial proposition used to support power-transition theory for two main reasons. First, the United States had already overtaken Britain prior to World War I, not to mention World War II, and Germany never came even close to matching US capabilities. There was therefore never a power transition between Germany and the United States—a nonevent that cannot possibly be used to explain the two world wars. In order to finesse this problem, Organski and Kugler exclude the United States from their analysis of the origins of the two world wars, thus avoiding a direct test of their own theory. They argue that the United States was outside international relations' central system, which was located in Europe then. This argument is contentious because the United States played a decisive role in determining the outcome of World War I, and the central system for international relations had arguably moved westward to include it prior to World War II, if not already having occurred earlier, before World War I. As already mentioned,

Organski and Kugler instead pitch these two conflicts as a struggle between Britain and Germany, even though Britain had already lost its primacy to the United States before the start of World War I in 1914. Moreover, in the one and only occasion in modern history when the baton of world leadership was passed from one country to another—namely, the Anglo-American case—this power transition happened peacefully, thus contradicting their theory. In this case, we have the phenomenon of "the dog that did not bark," or the occurrence of the unexpected, from power-transition theory's perspective; peace was preserved, even though there had been a power transition between the world's two most powerful states.

Second, the characterization of the two world wars as a German challenge to Britain's preeminent global position is also questionable. As Reinhard Wolf (2014, 193) indicates, "World War I hardly fits the notion of a conflict chiefly motivated by the rising power's desire to defeat the reigning hegemon." On the contrary, a strong case can be made that Germany found itself at war with Britain on both occasions *not* because Berlin had wanted to fight London but rather because its diplomacy had been unable to persuade London to stay on the sidelines (e.g., Chan 2008, 2020a; Chong and Hall 2014, 18). It is true that Berlin had started these wars deliberately, but the real target of Germany's aggression was Russia / the USSR (Chong and Hall 2014; Copeland 2000; Lieber 2007; Van Evera 1999). Specifically, Berlin had a preventive motivation, seeking to destroy an emergent powerhouse to its east while it still had a brief window during which it had an advantage in waging this campaign.

Seen in this light, it was a sense of insecurity and a fear that their country was poised to experience relative decline that motivated German leaders to start war. From the perspective of prospect theory (Kahneman, Slovic, and Tversky 1982; Kahneman and Tversky 1979, 2000), Berlin's behavior can be interpreted to suggest "gambling for recovery," or, more accurately, "gambling to forestall decline," due to its aversion to prospective loss. In this view, the threat to international peace and stability originated from a declining state rather than a rising state. The policy implication of viewing interstate power shifts in this light is enormous. Instead of pointing their fingers at a rising state, such as China, as the instigator of war, as the participants in the current discourse on power transition in the West and the United States suggest, it is the established but declining state that is the more likely source of this danger.

Michael Beckley (2023) argues that "peaking powers"—those countries that have previously experienced high growth rates but have entered or are expected to enter a period of economic slowdown—are likely to become more aggressive and expansionist. In response to their actual or expected loss compared to their own past or compared to their international counterparts, these are the states most likely to seek exclusive foreign economic zones, engage in protectionist policies, and spend heavily on their armament programs. Coming from a different angle, Thomas Christensen (2001) writes that even if China fails to catch up to the United States, it can pose a problem. Indeed, a China facing economic stagnation, even decline—one that is beset by domestic instability and motivated by extreme nationalism—can be more threatening to international peace and stability than a growing or rising China.

The logic of Beckley's and Christensen's analyses receives greater support from what we know about human psychology, such as those tendencies suggested by prospect theory, as just mentioned, and the idea of relative deprivation (Gurr 1970). The latter idea suggests that the disappointment stemming from reality failing to meet a person's or country's expectations is a powerful source of social turmoil or political instability and a strong motivation to challenge the status quo. A vigorous debate between proponents of power-transition theory and others who take the opposite view that peaking or declining states are the more likely source of threat to international peace and stability would be quite beneficial. But the current dominant discourse hardly even acknowledges the existence of arguments and evidence that are contrary to its standard script—one that asserts ritualistically that "history teaches us that rising powers are likely to provoke war" (Shirk 2007, 4). It is unclear whether the generalization just cited about what history teaches us includes the United States when it was a rising power or, for that matter, others such as Britain and France during their years of ascendance in international relations.

History in fact does not support the proposition that rising powers provoke war—or at least war against the established, dominant power. When subjected to critical scrutiny, empirical support for power-transition theory turns out to be quite limited and even dubious. As the remark by Swaine and Tellis introduced earlier suggests, rising powers rarely challenge an established, dominant state directly. Naturally, whether rising powers provoke war depends also on how one identifies these states and defines war. A quick illustration suggests that, for example, although China has overtaken Germany, Japan, and Russia in recent years, war has not broken out. Nor has war occurred when Germany and Japan surpassed—at least in terms of their relative economic sizes—Russia / the USSR after World War II.

There are, moreover, important questions about how to measure national power and determine the timing of a power transition (e.g., Beckley 2018; Rauch 2017). Depending on how these issues are settled, an analyst's research results can be seriously affected. Even though one need not agree with these decisions made by Richard Ned Lebow and Benjamin Valentino (2009, 40), the conclusion they reach from their historical analysis is persuasive: "Should war come between the United States and China in the future it will not be a result of a power transition. The greater risk is that conflict will result from the misperception that such a transition is imminent, and the miscalculation by decision-makers in the United States (or China) that China will soon be in a position to do what no state has done before—unilaterally dictate the rules of the international system. Power transition theory would be made self-fulfilling—generating its own corroboration where history has failed to oblige."

Significantly, although rationalist theory disagrees with prospect theory on the basic nature of human judgment and decision-making, these otherwise opposing perspectives agree that a rising state is unlikely to initiate war because it can expect a continuation of the ongoing trend to produce further gains for it. Only when its growth is stalled or reversed would it make sense for this upstart to insist on immediate status recognition commensurate with its capabilities or achievements. Or, in other words, a rising state is likely to postpone its demand for full status recognition because it anticipates making further gains. Robert Powell (1999, 199) explains, "If the distribution of benefits mirrors the distribution of power, no state can credibly threaten to use force to change the status quo and the risk of war is smallest. If, however, there is a sufficiently large disparity between the distribution of power and benefits, the status quo may be threatened regardless of what the underlying distribution of power is."

This view does not point to the distribution of interstate power per se but rather to the discrepancy between a country's power and the rewards (or recognition) that it receives from the international community as the source of discontent and grievance motivating it to resort to war as a way to redress its sense of relative deprivation. When a state feels that its share of benefits (or recognition) is less than that which its power (or accomplishments) should entitle it to, this sense of being undercompensated or underrecognized causes it to demand "its place in the sun," sometimes even if it means going to war to rectify this injustice. In this view, power is a means to acquire benefits (or recognition) from the international system and not necessarily an end in itself. Examples of the rewards, benefits, or recognition being sought can include permanent representation on the United Nations (UN) Security Council, the acceptance of a country's currency as the medium for international transactions, the adoption of its language as the lingua franca, the privilege of hosting international events and headquarters of international organizations, a seat at summitries or at the negotiation table for important issues, and, in a previous era, the spoils of colonial conquest.

Of course, states can fight over their relative power. But Powell's statement quoted above suggests that power can also be a means to gain tangible (e.g., territory, resources) and intangible (e.g., prestige, status, influence) rewards. A state's motivation to go to war or stay in peace is due to the difference between its belief about how many rewards (or how much recognition) that it is entitled to due to its power, on the one hand, and the actual amount that it receives from the international community, on the other hand. Grievances occur when a state perceives that the amount of benefits it receives falls seriously short of the amount that it feels it deserves; or, in other words, it has received fewer rewards and less recognition than it feels that its capabilities should entitle it to. Conversely, those states that are overcompensated are satiated and would prefer to maintain the status quo that works to their relative advantage.

This perspective in turn prompts us to ask why those satiated established states fail to accommodate the rising but undercompensated states. After all, it takes two to fight. Wars are then not just a matter of pushy latecomers insisting on their place in the sun. They are also due to the resistance by the established but declining states to make room for rising states and their reluctance to trim their sense of entitlement even in the face of their relative decline. Various political, bureaucratic, and psychological reasons come to mind as possible explanations of the established but declining states' insufficient or tardy responses to the rising states' demands for accommodation. Recognition of this phenomenon would then redress power-transition theory's biased view assigning the responsibility for starting war solely to rising states.

Earlier writers on power transition (e.g., Gilpin 1981; Organski and Kugler 1980) recognize that some states are undercompensated in terms of benefits or status recognition compared to their achievements or capabilities, and other states are overcompensated. They acknowledge forthrightly that the rules of international order are rigged to favor the established states to the detriment of the later arrivals—an observation that has usually been overlooked in more recent and politically motivated discourse on the ostensible dissatisfaction and revisionist tendencies of rising states.

In response to US calls for China to abide by a "'rules-based' international order," Beijing retorts that it will only respect the UN Charter and not some "house rules" determined by the United States and a select group of its allies (denisli34 2021). While accusing China of being a revisionist state, Western commentators give scant attention to how other rising powers in the past, including Britain and the United States, conducted themselves in their quest for international influence and global preeminence. How did they reach the pinnacle of international power? Did they violate the then-prevailing rules and norms of international order when they were rising powers? I will discuss later the case of the United States.

Both Wilhelmine Germany and Nazi Germany were aggressive and ambitious, and they both appeared to be insecure powers fearful that their best days would soon be behind them. There is, however, one significant difference between them. It is, even in retrospect, difficult to imagine how the basic rules and norms of international order would have been altered if Wilhelmine Germany had prevailed in World War I. Put differently, in what ways had Wilhelmine Germany acted as a revisionist power, distinguishing its conduct from that of other imperial powers during its time, such as Britain, France, Russia, and the United States? In contrast, it is easier to imagine how Nazi Germany would have introduced major changes to the international order if it had won World War II. Its dogma on the superiority of the Aryan race would have arguably introduced a new doctrine to international order, although other countries were also espousing racist views and policies during the time when Nazi Germany was a rising power. In the years prior to and immediately following World War I, there was also much talk of the superiority of the Anglo-Saxon race, the "white man's burden," *mission civilisatrice*, and eugenics. Indeed, as I will point out again later, when the victorious Allies met at the Versailles Conference after World War I, they rebuffed Japan's demand that they recognize the principles of racial equality and sovereign equality among all states. I will return to this issue later when discussing revisionist foreign policy and revisionist history.

As indicated earlier, power-transition theory presents the two world wars as a failed German bid to challenge and displace Britain as the then-reigning global hegemon. This contention or characterization is the linchpin for this theory. Therefore, it is important to emphasize that although Berlin did start both world wars, it did not fit—especially in 1914—the description of a cocky, overconfident upstart itching for a fight to claim the mantle of world domination from London. Prior to World War I, German leaders saw their country isolated and their only major ally, Austria-Hungary, besieged by many severe internal and external problems, appearing to be well on its way to further decline and possibly even disintegration (Schroeder 2004). They feared that their strategic position would deteriorate further with the passage of time—especially in view of Russia's emergence as a new great power. "They saw themselves encircled, blocked, threatened with demotion or even disappearance. German chancellor Bethmann Hollweg wondered 'if there is any purpose in planting new trees' on his estate near Berlin, as 'in a few years the Russians would be here anyway'" ("*Guardian* View" 2014).

German leaders felt a sense of urgency to act before their strategic position became even more precarious. They started a preventive war against Russia in 1914 and again against the USSR in 1941 in order to seize a closing window of opportunity before they lost their fleeting military advantage (Copeland 2000; Lebow 1984; Levy 2008c; Van Evera 1999). Stephen Van Evera (1984, 84) explains, "The First World War was in part a 'preventive' war, launched by the Central powers in the belief that they were saving themselves from a worse fate in later years." In 1918, former German chancellor Hollweg acknowledged, "Lord yes, in a certain sense it was a preventive war . . . [motivated by] the constant threat of attack, the greater likelihood of its inevitability in the future, and by the military's claim: today war is still possible without defeat, but not in two years!" (quoted in Mearsheimer and Rosato 2023, 143). He reportedly said, "Our military men were fully convinced that now [July 1914] they could *still* come out of a war victorious; but in a few years, i.e., 1916, after the completion of the Russian railroads, [this] would no longer be so" (quoted in Lebow 1981, 229; italics in original). Just prior to the war, Germany's foreign secretary Gottlieb von Jagow observed, "Russia will be ready to fight in a few years. Then she will crush us by the number of her soldiers; then she will have built her Baltic fleet and her strategic railways. Our group in the meantime will have become steadily weaker. . . . I do not desire preventive war, but if the conflict should offer itself, we ought not to shirk it" (quoted in Mearsheimer and Rosato 2023, 143–44). Fritz Fischer (1975, 402) notes how Helmuth von Moltke, chief of the German General Staff, expressed his serious concern in May 1914, just three months before the outbreak of the war: "In two to three years Russia would have finished arming. Our enemies' military power would then be so great that he [Moltke] did not know how he could deal with it. Now we were still more or less of a match for it. In his view there was no alternative but to fight a preventive war so as to beat the enemy while we could still emerge fairly well from the struggle. The Chief of Staff therefore put it to me that our policy should be geared to bringing about an early war."

Moltke warned that time was running out: "For a number of years, the [power balance] has shifted substantially to the detriment of the allied Monarchies" (quoted in Herrmann 1995, 169). At the kaiser's war-council meeting in December 2012, Moltke said, "I believe a war is unavoidable and the sooner the better" (quoted in Röhl 1994, 162). "By June 1914 . . . with relative military power now at its height, German leaders switched policy: in the face of the latest Balkans incident, they pushed Austria to invade Serbia. This was designed to force Russia to act, allowing Germany to blame Russia for the major war only Berlin wanted" (Copeland 2000, 57). German leaders sought war in the summer of 1914 because, in their opinion, their country had reached the peak of its power, and, moreover, they "believed that their state was inevitably and profoundly declining versus Russia," and they made sure to "cut off all possible last-minute negotiations, making war truly inevitable" (60).

Adolf Hitler had also expressed a sense of urgency before World War II, warning that "favorable circumstances will no longer prevail in two or three years' time" and that Germany would face "certain annihilation sooner or later" if it did not launch a preventive war at a moment most propitious to it (quoted in Van Evera 1999, 77–78, 96–97). Hitler was disappointed and even infuriated rather than pleased when the Munich Conference in 1938 defused the immediate crisis and denied him an excuse to attack Czechoslovakia. He "believed Chamberlain had cheated him out of [a military victory over Czechoslovakia] at Munich" (Claar and Ripsman 2016, 169).

In both world wars, Berlin's intent was *not* to pick a fight with London, although its brusque and clumsy diplomacy had antagonized and alienated Britain. Germany would have much rather had Britain stay neutral in the impending war. That, in the end, Britain nevertheless joined the fray indicated that Berlin's diplomacy had failed rather than its eagerness to fight London. Adolf Hitler blamed London for failing to see that "an Anglo-German combination [made] the most natural of alliances" (quoted in Schweller 1998, 114) and for not realizing that the USSR was "now the greatest power factor in the whole of Europe" (quoted in Robertson 1963, 54). He declared, "Everything I undertake is directed against the Russians; if the West is too stupid and blind to grasp this, then I shall be compelled to come to an agreement with the Russians, beat the West, and then after their defeat turn against the Soviet Union with all my forces" (quoted in Copeland 2000, 135). On another occasion, he declared, "Originally I wanted to work together with Britain. But Britain has rejected me again and again. It is true, there is nothing worse than a family quarrel, and racially the English are in a way our relatives. . . . It's a pity that we have to be locked in this death struggle, while our real enemies in the East can sit back and wait until Europe is exhausted. That is why I do not wish to destroy Britain and never shall" (quoted in Higgins 1966, 55).

These words make it clear that Hitler saw the USSR as Germany's real and principal enemy. Rather than wanting to fight Britain, Germany had "sought to keep [it] out of the war" in 1914 (Vasquez 1996, 42). "Britain for him was clearly an undesirable sideshow" (Copeland 2000, 139). Hitler had "explained . . . that the eastern campaign was inevitable, and that we [Germans] therefore must conduct it in a preventive and offensive manner to avoid [the possibility] that the Russians could overrun us at a later time after longer appropriate preparations," according to Germany's lieutenant general Franz Halder's diary (quoted on 142). Reflecting the same preventive logic, General Alfred Jodl stated that war with the USSR was inevitable, and "it was better . . . to have this campaign now, when we were at the height of our military power" (quoted in Warlimont 1962, 111–12).

The Nazis looked to their east for expansion to create Lebensraum (living space) for their Reich. In their study of World War I, Nazli Choucri and Robert C. North (1975) use the term "lateral pressure" to describe the demand of a growing population and economy for additional land and resources. Chief of the German Army's General Staff Lieutenant General Franz Halder viewed Operation Barbarossa—the code name for Germany's invasion of the USSR—to be imperative to eliminate a "long but steadily rising political danger" (quoted in Leach 1973, 132).

Moreover, and contrary to power-transition theory's depiction, World War II was not a bilateral struggle between Britain and Germany for global domination. It was more about two concurrent regional contests, with Germany and Japan fighting almost entirely separately in two regions (Europe and Asia) without military coordination (Levy 2008b, 28–30). Neither Berlin nor Tokyo aspired to global domination as power-transition theory would suggest. Both were more interested in establishing a regional sphere of influence.

The characterization of World War I as originating from a German desire to displace Britain as the global hegemon is also mistaken. For one thing, Britain was certainly no longer the world's dominant power by 1914. And for another, this conflict was more about mastery over Europe rather than an attempt by Berlin to seize global domination. Moreover, rather than a burning desire for acquisitive accumulations, German leaders were motivated more by their sense of insecurity and aversion to losses. These words also apply to German policies prior to World War II—albeit to a much less extent. Stephen Van Evera (1999, 79) observes that "preventive motives were evident in most wars." The historian A. J. P. Taylor (1954) goes even so far as to argue that every war fought among great powers between 1848 and 1918 started as a preventive war and not as a war of conquest.

The implications of this discussion are straightforward. In current Western discourse, a rising China is usually portrayed as an arrogant, assertive power, and it is cast in the role of instigating a potential war and bent on upending the existing international order. Instead of power-transition theory's depiction of an aggressive, impatient upstart itching for a fight, wars can be caused by the preventive motivation of an insecure established power poised to suffer imminent or inexorable decline. This view contradicts power-transition theory's contention that the incumbent hegemon is by definition satisfied with the status quo and committed to its defense even while suffering declines. Such reasoning is captured by Ronald L. Tammen et al. (2000, 9) when they assert, "By definition, the dominant power is satisfied . . . [and therefore] is the defender of the status quo. After all, it creates and maintains the global or regional hierarchy from which it accrues substantial benefits."

Yet why should a dominant but declining power be committed to the existing international order, even if it had a leading role in creating its rules and institutions? Why should we not expect it to revise these rules and institutions to halt and reverse its decline? Recent actions by Washington, especially during Donald Trump's first administration, present plenty of evidence of the United States rejecting or withdrawing from international accords and organizations, such as the World Health Organization (WHO), the Paris Climate Agreement, the Trans-Pacific Partnership, and the Iran nuclear deal (Joe Biden has since reversed Trump's decision to withdraw from the WHO and abandon the Paris Climate Agreement but Trump withdrew the US from them again for a second time in the early days of his second presidency). Barry Buzan (2004, 184) observes, even before the Trump first administration, that recent US actions suggested "nothing less than an assault on the international social structure built mainly by the US over the previous half-century, and therefore a seismic shift in US grand strategy." This shift in US policy could even be discerned before the George W. Bush administration. For instance, voting patterns in the United Nations showed that the United States became increasingly isolated in this world body during the Clinton administration.

The same logic presented above would incline one to ask, Why would a rising state want to precipitate a war and overthrow the international order that has enabled its ascendance? Why not let the ongoing trend be its friend so that, to paraphrase Paul Kennedy (1980), with the passage of time, mastery of Europe would fall into Germany's lap peacefully? A parallel with China's current predicament is also obvious. Should there be an armed conflict between Beijing and Washington over Taiwan, it would not be because China wants to fight the United States and claim global hegemony. China is still a regional power whose capabilities do not extend very far from its borders. Fighting the United States would be its last resort and not its first preference. Should this conflict occur, it would indicate that Beijing's diplomacy to persuade Washington to stay out of its civil war had failed.

The last sentence is, of course, a reference to the possibility that the United States would intervene militarily on Taiwan's behalf in a crisis over this island's status. Taiwan is seen by Beijing as a breakaway province—a legacy of China's unfinished civil war. Ever since Harry Truman's order in 1950 for the Seventh Fleet to intervene in the Taiwan Strait to prevent a Chinese invasion of Taiwan, it has enjoyed de facto independence due to US support (Chan, forthcoming-c). Beijing has declared that Taiwan's status is its core interest, representing its highest national priority. It is determined to achieve its goal of national reunification with Taiwan.

There are obvious similarities and also differences between Germany in 1914 and China today. Geographic reality places both countries in a crowded neighborhood, hemmed in by other great and middle powers. Therefore, these countries' increased capabilities cannot but concern, even alarm, their respective neighbors. In contrast to Germany and China, the United States resides in a neighborhood that places it in a league by itself, and it has only two weak states and fish as its neighbors. Although the preceding discussion challenges power-transition theorists' characterization of an arrogant and overconfident Germany seeking a showdown with Britain to claim the former country's mantle as the world's leading state, I do not deny that other factors were also present. German chancellor Bernhard von Bülow told the Reichstag in 1897, "We wish to throw no one into the shade, but we also demand our own place in the sun" (Wikipedia 2024c).

Why do I bring up this idea that rising states demand "a seat at the table"? It is because contrary to power-transition theory and certainly Allison's rendition of Thucydides's Trap, "war and violence occur because of *grievances* and not just power" (Vasquez 2009, 133; italics in original). Wilhelmine Germany—one may also include imperial Japan until its defeat in World War II in this depiction—harbored resentment about not being accorded the respect and recognition that it believed it deserved. Contemporary China can be characterized in the same way. They share, if you will, a "chip-on-the-shoulder" syndrome, feeling that the established powers had tried to block or thwart their countries' ascent and had inflicted gratuitous insults on them (such as US racial discrimination against Asians—more specifically, against the Chinese—in its immigration laws of 1875, 1913, and 1917 and the refusal by Western countries at the Versailles Conference to acknowledge the equality of states and races). Status denial was and is a strong motivation for these countries as well as contemporary Russia (Buzas 2013; Larson and Shevchenko 2010, 2019; Lebow 2010; Murray 2010, 2019; Pu 2019; Renshon 2016, 2017; Ward 2017). Power-transition theorists emphasize rising states' insistent demand to be admitted to the select club of great powers as part of the cause for war (namely, the attribution of revisionist motivations to these states). These scholars, however, do not ask the other part of the story—namely, Why do the established but declining states refuse to accommodate the latecomers? Why do they not trim their international profile, downsize their foreign commitments, and, most importantly, accept a demotion in their status and entitlements commensurate with their diminished capabilities?

To summarize, contrary to power-transition theory's characterizations, the world wars were *not* a struggle for global domination waged by the two most powerful states in the world. These conflicts were more cases of coalitional warfare fought mostly over whether Germany should be the master of Europe and, in World War II, also over whether Japan should rule over East Asia. While Britain and Germany did fight and the United States (an extraregional power as far as the European and, in World War II, Asian countries were concerned) did join the fracas (one might add, belatedly), this fight was more about regional hegemony, and it happened not because Berlin had wanted to initiate a war with London but rather because it was unable to persuade London to stay on the sidelines. Instead of a cocky, arrogant, and overconfident upstart, Germany in 1914 and, as we shall see shortly, Japan in 1941 were insecure, anxious, and, in Japan's case, even desperate, gambling (almost quite literally) their nations' respective fates in a bid to forestall decline and, in Japan's case, defeat. The story told by power-transition theory is a caricature and indeed a distorted and misleading representation of history.

Finally, the preventive motivation loomed large in Germany's calculations in the leadup to both world wars. Berlin was motivated to launch a *preventive* war to forestall a more precarious future (for preventive war, see Bell and Johnson 2015; Copeland 2000; Levy 1987, 2008c; Mueller et al. 2006; Schweller 1992; Silverstone 2007; Trachtenberg 2007; Van Evera 1999). This rationale was explicitly used by the Bush administration to invade Iraq in 2003 (Ricks 2006), claiming that Saddam Hussein already had or was developing weapons of mass destruction—claims that turned out to be false. This was an instance of preventive war, even though US officials have misnamed their attack on Iraq as a preemptive strike (for this distinction, see Reiter 1995).

It is perhaps not too surprising that most American scholars do not stress Germany's preventive motivation when discussing the origins of the two world wars. Had they done so, the obvious parallel would be that instead of seeking to challenge the United States for world domination, China today would be anxious about the possibility that it might become the victim of a preventive war launched by Washington. The two world wars would then imply that the next two decades would be the most dangerous time for China because it would have grown enough to concern Washington but still perhaps not strong enough to deter the United States. Of course, such a conjecture does not usually come up in US narratives on China's rise—narratives that tend to instead emphasize the danger of a rising, dissatisfied China starting a war.

In a rare departure from the dominant narrative, Christopher Layne (2004, 116; italics in original) writes, "Given that the Iraq War has demonstrated U.S. willingness to use preventive war or preemptive strategies to counter *future* threats, rising great powers will have good reason to view the transitional interval as one during which they will be vulnerable." Similarly, Robert Gilpin (1981, 191–93) points to the fears of a declining power rather than the ambitions of a rising latecomer as a cause for war. Still, the very idea that the United States would consider launching a preventive war would appear to be ludicrous and unimaginable to most Americans, even though Washington did at one time consider initiating an unprovoked attack against China's nuclear facilities at Lop Nor (Burr and Richelson 2000–2001). That this very idea is likely to be seen as outlandish is itself an interesting reflection of how people view history. Randall L. Schweller (1992) argues that democracies do not initiate preventive wars, although this proposition has been challenged by Jack S. Levy (1987, 2008c), who shows that democracies have done so and come close to doing so on several occasions.

Not to put too fine a point on it, consider the following episode. Bob Woodward and Robert Costa (2021) report that in final days of Donald Trump's first presidential term, General Mark Milley, head of the US Joint Chief of Staff, made secret phone calls to his Chinese counterpart, General Li Zuocheng, on October 30, 2020, and again on January 8, 2021. Milley felt that he had to make these calls to reassure Li that the United States was not planning to attack China. He was ostensibly worried that Donald Trump might "go rogue" by starting a nuclear war in the waning days of his administration. He reportedly said, "General Li, I want to assure you that the American government is stable and everything is going to be OK. We are not going to attack or conduct any kinetic operations against you. . . . Gen. Li, you and I have known each other now for five years. If we're going to attack, I'm going to call you ahead of time. It's not going to be a surprise" (quoted in Morris 2021). When Trump learned about these phone calls, he accused Milley of committing a "treasonous act" that was "so egregious that, in times gone by, the punishment would have been death!" (de Vries 2023).

To summarize my arguments, prevailing discourse on and theory about the two world wars are misleading in several respects. Although Wilhelmine and Nazi Germany were aggressive states responsible for initiating these conflicts, the former was motivated more by fear than greed. The *Kaiserreich* went to war in 1914 because it was worried, even obsessed, about the prospects of its impending (relative) decline and wanted to forestall a more dangerous future when it would have to confront an emergent Russian colossus in addition to its immediate neighbor France. It dreaded the prospect of having to fight a two-front war after Russia became a more formidable opponent. It was also fearful of losing its only significant ally, Austria-Hungary, which was already on a steady course of decline. This multiethnic empire even faced the danger of disintegration. Berlin felt isolated and encircled, and as a latecomer in its quest for an overseas empire, it felt that its just demands for recognition had been rebuffed by France and Britain. Its diplomacy could be brusque and overbearing, much of it fueled by its felt grievance over status denial. It would be a stretch, however, to claim that it had wanted to challenge and displace Britain as the existing global hegemon, and it would be much more accurate to say that it was primarily interested in establishing a predominant position in Europe—a feat that the United States had accomplished in its home region, the Western Hemisphere. Although Wilhelmine Germany has often been described as a revisionist state, it is not clear how its conduct was different from that of its predecessors or contemporaries. What had it done that Britain, France, Russia, and the United States had not done? It is also unclear how the then-prevailing rules and norms of international order would have been altered and what would have been the nature of new ones introduced by Berlin had Germany won the war.

Nazi Germany would appear much more interested in aggrandizement and conquest, although it was also driven by fear of encirclement and the prospect of a more ominous future in which the USSR could match and perhaps even overtake its power. Greed and fear—to acquire gains and forestall future losses—were both present in its policy agenda. It is also easier to imagine that Hitler's vision of a postwar world would entail more fundamental revisions of the rules and norms of the existing international order. Thus, Hitlerian Germany would fit the description of a revisionist state better than Wilhelmine Germany. Still, it would be a mischaracterization to describe his ambitious gambit as a bid for world leadership. As with its predecessor, Nazi Germany was more interested in securing a preponderant position in its home region, Europe. It sought to consolidate its gains, establishing Festung Europa, a fortified European bastion against an inevitable assault led by Britain and the United States. As discussed earlier, on both occasions (1914 and 1941), German leaders were strongly motivated by a preventive motivation. Rather than deliberately picking a fight with Britain, it would be more accurate to say that Germany was unable to persuade London to stay neutral in both world wars.

Of course, the struggles initiated by Berlin in 1914 and again in 1938–1941 had obvious implications for which country would be the world's next dominant power, but this goal of claiming a global hegemonic position was not what Berlin had set out to achieve. The outcomes of both world wars had the effect of further securing the position of leading global power for the United States—a status that it had already acquired before World War I and that was further consolidated and confirmed at the end of this conflict and certainly after World War II. Britain was exhausted by both world wars, but it was already eclipsed by the United States before 1914.

The implications for contemporary China's rise should be obvious. China is still a regional power, and it can hardly be described to be competing to take over the preponderant global position occupied by the United States as the world's sole superpower. Rather than deliberately picking a fight with the United States, China would much rather prefer to avoid such a fight. And, as discussed earlier, rather than challenging and undermining the existing international order, China would be more motivated to preserve it as the existing rules and norms have assisted its remarkable ascent since 1978. The question that is typically overlooked in the current discourse about power transition is why the dominant global power, the United States, should have an unwavering commitment to defend the rules and norms of international order as they have increasingly worked against its interests. Why should it not alter, or, in other words, revise, these rules and norms to arrest and reverse its relative decline? Of course, having the capabilities to alter or revise these rules and norms is also important in addition to having the incentive to do so. As the world's most powerful country, the United States has the greatest wherewithal to introduce and implement these changes in order to forestall or prevent a further erosion of its dominant global position.

Researchers of international relations often do not indicate clearly what they mean by revisionism or revisionist behavior. They also usually eschew applying explicit indicators and systematic data to assess a country's revisionist tendencies. Plausible indicators could be which country has been more often outvoted in the UN General Assembly or its Security Council—the world's most authoritative bodies for determining the rules and norms of international order. Which country has fought more wars and undertaken more armed interventions abroad in recent history? Which country continues to outspend the *combined total* of military outlays made by the world's next ten or twelve countries with the highest defense expenditures? Which country among the world's major states has recently withdrawn from international organizations and international accords—as Nazi Germany, Fascist Italy, and imperial Japan had done in withdrawing from the League of Nations before World War II (the United States never joined the League of Nations)? Finally, which country has been the target of most complaints about unfair trade practices filed with the World Trade Organization (WTO)?

Data to answer these questions are readily available, but few international relations analysts have bothered to consult them when they attribute revisionist tendencies to China, for example. If they had, they would have, for example, reached the following conclusion about alleged unfair trade practices. "The United States has made more frequent use of WTO exceptions to protect domestic industries from foreign competition than any other country," and foreign countries "have initiated more complaints at the WTO against the US for violating trade-exception rules than against any other nation or region, including the European Union" (Broz, Zhang, and Wang 2020, 432). As another example, compared to China and other major states, the United States has been far more likely to find itself among a small minority of countries objecting to roll call votes passed by an overwhelming majority in the UN General Assembly—even if we consider just motions relating to human rights (Chan, Hu, and He 2019; Ferdinand 2014; Primiano and Xiang 2016). None of the indicators mentioned in the above examples are perfect, but they will all contribute to improving the current state of affairs by giving empirical content to and engaging in explicit comparisons about different countries' revisionist tendencies.

As just implied, revisionism is not a binary category in juxtaposition to its opposite idea of being committed to the status quo. Rather, it is more useful to treat it as a matter of gradation and also to be systematic and clear about the benchmarks being applied (that is, how a country's ostensible revisionist tendencies compare with its own past and with that of other countries' past or current conduct). I will return to this concept of revisionism in the book's conclusion. For now, it bears repeating that although power-transition theory has been much talked about, actual empirical attempts to confirm its claims have been deficient because, among other things, one of its two principal independent variables that are purported to explain the onset of systemic wars—namely, states' revisionist tendencies—has rarely been incorporated in these studies.

In conclusion, history did not comport in the way power-transition theory expected it to. The two world wars constitute the main—indeed the *only plausible*—source of historical support for this theory. Yet they do not correspond to its characterization of these conflicts as epic struggles started by Germany, an overconfident and impatient upstart, to challenge Britain as the incumbent global hegemon so that Berlin could take London's place as the world's next dominant power. These wars did not follow this theory's script, and they did not substantiate its proposition as it claims. This is a devastating blow, especially considering that the only historical case involving a change in the identity of global hegemon in the modern era, the one occurring between the two states at the very top of international pinnacle—the one involving Britain and the United States (a topic for chapter 4)—was peaceful.

THREE

The Lesson of Munich, US Intervention in Korea, and Japan's Attack on Pearl Harbor

The Munich Conference held in 1938 presents perhaps the most emblematic example of history providing an important policy-relevant warning. This event, held among the leaders of Germany, Italy, Britain, and France, is typically remembered today as a symbol of appeasement because these countries were seen to pressure Czechoslovakia to yield to the German demand to annex the Sudetenland, a part of Czechoslovakia populated by German-speaking residents. This episode is supposed to demonstrate the folly and naivete of democratic leaders—specifically, France's Edouard Daladier and Britain's Neville Chamberlain, who had supposedly believed Adolf Hitler's promise that once satisfied with the Sudetenland, Germany would not have any further territorial claims in Europe. Chamberlain was ridiculed for believing that concessions made to Hitler at the Munich Conference had "secured peace for our time," and his umbrella became a symbol of appeasement. The orthodox view of the lesson of Munich held sway until it began to be challenged by scholars, such as A. J. P. Taylor (1961), Donald C. Watt (1965), and Paul Schroeder (1976), although, in most people's mind, this episode continues to be associated to this day with the stigma of ineptitude and cowardice.

The concessions made by France and Britain at Munich were not thought to be intended to buy time for them to better arm themselves in a forthcoming fight against Germany as Hitler had suspected (Beck 1989; Ripsman and Levy 2008). Chamberlain professed, "I hope . . . that my colleagues will not think that I am making any attempts to disguise the fact that, if we now [at the time of the Munich Conference in 1938] possessed a superior force to Germany, we should probably be considering these proposals in a very different spirit. But we must look facts in the face" (quoted in Mearsheimer and Rosato 2023, 194–95). There is also a human tendency to see a historical outcome to be more certain and inevitable than is warranted—what psychologists have called "hindsight bias" (e.g., Fischhoff and Beyth 1975). At the time of the Munich Conference, Hitler's behavior could be compatible with two competing hypotheses—that he had limited demands and was only interested in reuniting German-speaking people in one nation, or he had an insatiable appetite to expand territory under Germany's control. It was not until later when he started to seize ethnically non-German areas that he disclosed his true character as a serial aggressor (Jervis 1968, 479).

Moreover, the lesson of Munich is supposed to mean that appeasement would only embolden an aggressor, making a future war more likely and devastating. However, proponents of this view do not actually engage in a counterfactual analysis to demonstrate that had Hitler been opposed earlier and more resolutely, he would have been deterred from further aggression. As Richard E. Neustadt and Ernest R. May (1986b, 43) observe, "The point of each analogy from the 1930s was that something had not been done which, if done, might have staved off World War II." This proposition is implicit in the argument against appeasement but almost never taken up explicitly by those invoking the lesson of Munich, insinuating that a firmer policy to rebuff or deter a would-be aggressor would have avoided war. The possibility that Hitler was a megalomaniac who could not be deterred is not usually given serious consideration.

The notoriety of the Munich Conference is often associated with other supposed "lessons of the 1930s," referring to the unchecked aggressions committed by Italy against Ethiopia and by Japan against China. These lessons exercised a powerful influence in policymaking, such as on US officials when they decided on military intervention in Korea and Vietnam (e.g., Janis 1982b; Khong 1992). Following up on their own observation, Neustadt and May

(1986b, 43) ask, "What was it that Truman thought those earlier decision-makers [of the 1930s] should have done?" They surmise that his answer, at the time when he was deciding what the United States should do upon hearing the news that North Korea had attacked South Korea, would have been as follows: "In Manchuria and Ethiopia the League powers should have threatened or used force to compel Japan, then Italy, to cease aggression, and restore preexisting conditions. In the Rhineland and Austrian crises the signatories to the Versailles Treaty should have done likewise, compelling Hitler to withdraw his troops from the Rhineland and Austria. In the Czech crisis the Western powers should have declared their willingness to fight instead of pressing the Czechs to concede" (43).

Yet, as already remarked, these are suppositions that have never been submitted to a thorough examination. Moreover, rival hypotheses—such as the proposition that Hitler was a megalomaniac who could not have been stopped regardless of the nature of policies undertaken against him, that appeasement made sense to buy precious time in order to make military preparations to resist him more effectively at a later time, or a that a firmer policy to oppose him in 1938 was infeasible or at least politically costly in view of the nature of British domestic opinion and opposition within the Commonwealth—are rarely given due consideration. Alas, history is seldom unambiguous enough to provide definitive proof supporting a claim. John J. Mearsheimer and Sebastian Rosato (2023, 47) quote Nobel laureate in economics Paul Krugman remarking that "in the social sciences, it is much harder to [distinguish] . . . between serious ideas and pseudoscience. . . . Partly this is because one cannot perform controlled experiments: evidence in social science is always historical evidence, and history is complicated enough that its lessons are seldom unambiguous."

Perhaps Truman was a bit too critical of the leaders of Britain and France at Munich in 1938 as the United States had refused to even join the League of Nations. His invocation of the lesson of Munich also reflected post hoc reasoning. It was easier to argue in retrospective that Britain and France should not have conceded to Hitler's demand to annex the Sudetenland. Upon hearing news that North Korea had attacked South Korea, his and his advisors' first instinct was to perceive it as a deliberate aggression planned and orchestrated by Moscow and as a probe designed to test the West's resolve. They assumed that Pyongyang had acted at the behest of Moscow and that it was a surrogate of the Soviet Union. Moreover, the threat facing the West came, in their view, not just from North Korea but more ominously from a monolithic Communist bloc that included China (e.g., Janis 1982b). They were concerned that the loss of any country to Communism would cause a chain reaction, leading other countries to also succumb to it in the fashion of a series of falling dominoes.

Given these views, it was natural that Truman and his advisors thought that much more was at stake than just the fate of Korea. They applied their understanding of past events in Europe to analyze Asia and never bothered to ask whether it was appropriate to frame and interpret the Korean conflict from this perspective. Moreover, they saw their opponents in Korea as Communists rather than nationalists. Finally, they jumped to the conclusion that this conflict was tantamount to an instance of international aggression with one country's armed forces crossing an international border to invade another rather than the resumption of a civil war in which both sides belonged to the same nation. In short, their decision to intervene in this conflict was based on multiple and potentially dubious assumptions. Neither Truman nor his advisors questioned the validity of these assumptions. Had anyone among these officials challenged these suppositions, they would perhaps have taken more time to consider the US response to the outbreak of armed hostilities in Korea—especially in view of the fact that just five months earlier, in January 1950, US secretary of state Dean G. Acheson (1950) had given a speech at the National Press Club, placing Korea outside the US defense perimeter in Asia. If any of the assumptions just mentioned were taken away, they would have seen events in Korea in a different light, and their decision to fight there could have been different. In combination, these assumptions amounted to analytic overkill, or, in the parlance of social scientists, their decision to intervene in the Korean War was overdetermined. Significantly, many of these same assumptions were repeated later in motivating US intervention in the Vietnam War.

Decision-making by US officials in the case of the Korean War is instructive in that the lesson of Munich had a powerful influence in framing the policy problem for them. Moreover, this historical analogy worked in a top-down fashion to determine the nature of US response to the outbreak of armed hostilities. In other words, the decision premise established by the Munich lesson would have ruled out "softer" options, such as to broker a ceasefire or negotiate a political settlement with the help of the United Nations and even, outlandish as it may sound, to engage in diplomatic cooperation with the USSR and China to contain the war—not to mention the option of doing nothing. Framing the policy problem in terms of their perceived lesson of Munich, a decision by US officials to intervene militarily in that conflict became highly likely, if not inevitable.

Parenthetically, collaborating with Moscow to arrange a truce is actually not as much of an outlandish idea as it may appear because this was how several subsequent wars between India and Pakistan and among Israel and its Arab neighbors were brought to an end. Of course, Washington has also worked with Moscow and Beijing in efforts to contain Iran's and North Korea's nuclear programs. My point here is simply that once the attack by North Korea on South Korea was seen through the prism of the Munich lesson, some obvious policy options (such as armed intervention) could be deduced or at least became highly probable, while others were excluded from consideration. Naturally, the more limited and ambiguous the information available to decision-makers—such as immediately after the outbreak of armed hostilities in Korea when Truman and his advisors met at the Blair House to deliberate the US response to it—the greater their reliance on historical analogies. In their rush to reach a decision, Truman and his advisors took for granted the supposed lesson of Munich. They did not examine critically its applicability to the situation in Korea nor the other assumptions influencing and shaping their policymaking.

Interestingly, although they were both part of the history of World War II, people have not juxtaposed the lesson of Munich with Japan's decision to attack Pearl Harbor. The latter attack in December 1941 has, of course, been the subject of extensive research, but its implications for effective deterrence against aggression have not resonated with those who are opposed to appeasement. Asked plainly, what does the Pearl Harbor attack tell us about the results of resolute opposition to aggression, a firm refusal to appease?

My conclusion from Japan's attack on Pearl Harbor is that the United States succeeded in convincing Tokyo that it would definitely intervene to fight Japan should Tokyo commit aggression against the European colonial powers in Southeast Asia. In other words, war happened because Washington stood its ground—the opposite of appeasement. Another conclusion from this case is that leaders could knowingly precipitate a war even when they realized that their country was eight or nine times weaker than its enemy. These conclusions appear paradoxical, and yet, as I will try to show below, they are pertinent to the Sino-American standoff today over Taiwan.

Japanese officials were keen observers of World War I, and one of the lessons they drew from this conflict was that Germany had lost because of its vulnerable dependency on foreign sources to supply its strategic resources. They saw their country in a similar predicament and were determined to rectify this vulnerability (Barnhart 1987). Japan's territorial expansion abroad—in Korea, Taiwan, and China—was intended to secure its supply of vital minerals and foodstuff as well as overseas markets for its manufactures. Japan's aggression against China, however, caused opposition from the Western countries, especially the United States, which had insisted on an "open door" policy toward China—that is, other countries should have equal access to the Chinese market. To force Japan to give up the gains it had made from its invasion of China, Washington joined the British and Dutch in imposing an economic embargo on Japan, denying it strategic material, such as brass, oil, and iron ore.

This embargo placed Japan in a stranglehold as its economy and military were heavily dependent on the import of such resources from abroad. In the face of this embargo, Japanese planners estimated that their petroleum stockpile would be depleted in two years and that they would have only eighteen months of fuel supply left should there be a war (Barnhart 1987, 141; Butow 1961, 234; Ike 1967, 188; Prange 1982, 234–35). After this interval, their fleet and air force would not be able to wage war, and, according to head of Japan's Planning Board General Suzuki Teiichi, Japan's economy would collapse within two years if the United States continued with its oil embargo (Feis 1962, 252).

Japanese leaders faced three options, none of them palatable to them. They could yield to US pressure and give up their gains in China, which, in their eyes, would be tantamount to giving up their country's aspiration to be recognized as a great power—something that they were dead set against. They could do nothing, in which case, with the passage of time, they would have lost the war without having fired a shot. In other words, doing nothing was also not an acceptable option because the United States would then be in a position to dictate terms to Japan after starving it of essential raw resources. The third and remaining choice was to attack the United States at a time and place of Japan's choosing to maximize strategic surprise and to buy time for Japan in the hope that after administering a devastating blow to the US Pacific Fleet, Japanese forces might be able to seize the European colonies in Southeast Asia to satisfy their resource shortages and build a strong defense in preparation for an inevitable US counterattack.

On July 25, 1941, Washington froze all Japanese assets in the United States and brought all of Japan's financial and trade deals with the United States under government control. This action imposed a stark choice on Tokyo, forcing "Japan to choose between making terms with [the United States] or making war against [the United States]" (Feis 1962, 239). In order to finesse this predicament, Tokyo made a final offer to Washington to settle their dispute before deciding to attack Pearl Harbor. The so-called Plan B proposed that Japan withdraw its troops from southern French Indochina and reassign them to the northern part in exchange for the United States agreeing to supply Japan with sufficient fuel and refraining from interfering with Japan's invasion of China. This proposal was rejected by Washington, which demanded complete and unconditional Japanese withdrawal from Indochina and China before the United States would resume its oil exports to Japan (Ike 1967, 95–99, 169–70, 263). Japanese leaders refused to accept the US terms, which they saw to be tantamount to forfeiting their country's demand to be recognized as a great power and to accepting the status of a "third rate power" (196–98, 238).

Why attack the United States rather than go after the European colonies in Southeast Asia (e.g., British Malaya, Dutch Indonesia, and French Indochina)? Because Tokyo was convinced of Washington's deterrence threat—that is, that the United States would wage war on Japan if it were to attack these European colonies. The United States was standing in their way to seize Southeast Asia. Rather than having Washington declare war on Japan, Tokyo decided to seize the strategic initiative by attacking the United States first. As just described, none of the options available to Japanese leaders were palatable. They decided to take the bull by its horns, and they opted for what appeared to them the least objectionable course of action. They chose war against a formidable adversary, which, in their own judgment, was eight to nine times stronger than Japan (Russett 1969; Wohlstetter 1962).

In short, as in the case of Germany fighting Britain in the two world wars discussed in chapter 2, Japanese leaders would have rather preferred not to have to fight the United States if they could find a way to mitigate their dire circumstance caused by a critical shortfall of vital strategic materiel without doing so. The idea that as a cocky, impatient rising power, Japan was itching to challenge the United States does not fit historical reality. The proposition that Tokyo's behavior represented a bid for world domination would be even more of a stretch. Japan was aggressive and ambitious, but its leaders' aspirations were more focused on East Asia. They sought hegemony in their home region—just like the United States sought to do by propagating and enforcing the Monroe Doctrine. The Japanese had their own version, the so-called Greater East Asian Coprosperity Sphere. Obviously, some historical analogies are easier to recall or imagine than others.

There is plenty of documentary evidence to support the two conclusions that I have mentioned earlier: that Japanese officials were sure that the US deterrence threat against Tokyo was credible (that is, Washington would definitely fight Japan if it were to seize the European colonies in Southeast Asia) and that their country was much weaker than the United States and could not hope to prevail militarily, especially if their war against the United States became a protracted struggle allowing Washington to bring the full weight of US military might to bear on Japan.

The proposition that Japanese officials were convinced by Washington's deterrence threat—that they could not attack the European colonial powers without having to also fight the United States—is critical to understanding their decision to attack Pearl Harbor. Robert J. C. Butow (1961, 317) summarizes the collective judgment of Japanese officials in these words: "On the key issue of whether Japan could attack the Netherlands alone, or Great Britain and the Netherlands, without having to take on the United States as well, the answer was a definite 'No.'" Japan's top naval officer responsible for the Pearl Harbor attack, Admiral Yamamoto Isoroku, indicated that "our operations against the Netherlands Indies are almost certain to develop into a war with America" (quoted in Prange 1982, 11). The Japanese military, especially the navy, judged that "it was absolutely impossible to think of Britain and the United States as separate entities; consequently an attack on the Philippines would be the prerequisite for a successful advance to the South [that is, Southeast Asia]" (Butow 1961, 204). In Japanese thinking, any operation to seize the Dutch East Indies (today's Indonesia) to address Japan's dire need to make up for its oil shortfall caused by the US embargo would be the equivalent of "undertaking war against the United States" (204). In short, Tokyo saw a united front of Western powers plus China arrayed against Japan. Attacking one of them meant fighting the others as well. Japan could not seize the European colonies in Southeast Asia and at the same time bypass US opposition.

This Japanese assessment was correct. Even though the United States was not technically at war, it had agreed secretly to coordinate its actions with Britain (Feis 1962, 165–70). Top US leaders had agreed that should Japan get into a fight with Britain in Southeast Asia (specifically in assaulting Singapore and Malaya), "we [the United States] would have to fight" (Wohlstetter 1962, 266). The counselor at the US embassy in Tokyo, Eugene Doorman, had warned Japanese officials that "the American people were determined to support Britain, even at the risk of war; that if Japan or any other country menaced that effort it would have to expect to come to conflict with the United States" (quoted in Feis 1962, 160). Britain's prime minister Winston Churchill conveyed the same message publicly: "The British declaration [of war against Japan] will follow within the hour" should there be a conflict between Japan and the United States (quoted in Jones 1954, 302). Thus, Japan was boxed in—it could not fight any Western power without bringing in the others, and yet to concede to Washington's demands on giving up the fruits of Japan's conquest in China was unacceptable, and with each passing day, Japan was getting weaker due to the Western economic blockade.

On the proposition that Japanese leaders were fully aware of their country's lopsided weakness relative to the United States, there was also little doubt. The United States commanded a much larger domestic resource and industrial base compared to Japan, which was heavily dependent on foreign raw material to sustain its economy and war machine. For instance, Japan's capacity to produce steel was only one-seventeenth of that of the United States, and it had to import 80 percent of its oil needs, 75 percent of its scrap iron, and 95 percent of its copper from the United States (Barnhart 1987, 144–46). Such overwhelming dependency gave Washington a huge amount of leverage to cripple Japan's economy and its capacity to wage war, and both Tokyo and Washington were aware of this fact. Top US leaders also understood its implications. US ambassador to Japan Joseph C. Grew wrote to President Franklin D. Roosevelt that instead of having a deterrent effect on further Japanese aggression, Washington's action "would tend to push the Japanese people onward in a forlorn hope of making themselves economically sufficient" (Feis

1962, 137). Both President Roosevelt and his Secretary of State, Cordell Hull, were convinced that "an oil embargo against Japan would provoke Tokyo to attack Dutch East Indies" (Barnhart 1987, 196).

Japanese leaders were aware that time was not on their side. As summer and fall came and went in 1941, they increasingly believed that a war with the United States was a "now-or-never proposition" (Butow 1961, 320; see also Ike 1967, 200). "Japan's military leaders agreed that if they waited another six months, they might as well forget about [fighting a war] and admit defeat by default" (Prange 1982, 235). Thus, Japanese leaders realized that delay and inaction would have meant the fate of a slow but inevitable economic strangulation by the Americans. Once their stockpile of oil was exhausted, the Americans would have won the war without having fired a shot. Time was working against Japan. Navy chief of staff Admiral Nagano Osami remarked, "In various respects the Empire is losing materials; that is, we are getting weaker. By contrast, the enemy is getting stronger. By the passage of time we will get increasingly weaker and we won't be able to survive" (quoted in Ike 1967, 130–31). At the Laison Conference on July 21, 1941, he repeated this assessment:

> As for the war with the United States, although there is now a chance of achieving victory, the chances will diminish as time goes on. By the later part of next year, it will already be difficult for us to cope with the United States; after that the situation will become increasingly worse. The United States will probably prolong the matter until her defenses have been built up, and then try to settle it. Accordingly, as time goes by, the [Japanese] Empire will be put at a disadvantage. If we could settle things without war, there would be nothing better. But if we conclude that conflict cannot ultimately be avoided, then I would like you to understand that as time goes by we will be in a disadvantageous position. (Quoted on 106)

Prime Minister Konoe Fumimaro made a similar argument, pointing out that "if we allow this situation to continue, it is inevitable that our Empire will gradually lose the ability to maintain its national power, and that our national power will lag behind that of the United States"; and in his view, Japan should "try to prevent the disaster of war by resorting to all possible diplomatic measures. If the diplomatic measures should fail to bring about favorable results within a certain period, I believe we cannot help but take the ultimate step in order to defend ourselves" (quoted in Mearsheimer and Rosato 2023, 149).

At the imperial conference in November 1941, Japan's new prime minister, Tojo Hideki, asserted that Japan could not

> let the United States continue to do as she pleases, even though there is some uneasiness. . . . Two years from now we will have no petroleum for military use. Ships will stop moving. When I think about the strengthening of American defenses in the Southwest Pacific, the expansion of the American fleet, the unfinished China Incident, and so on, I see no end to difficulties. We can talk about austerity and suffering, but can our people endure such a life for a long time? . . . I fear that we would become a third-class nation after two or three years if we just sat tight. (Quoted in Mearsheimer and Rosato 2023, 150)

Again, as for Germany's leaders, top Japanese officials felt a sense of urgency—even desperation. The passage of time pressed on them to make a final decision. The United States was getting stronger by the day, while Japan was becoming weaker. As the US embargo took its toll, Japan faced economic strangulation—losing its contest with the United States without putting up a fight. Hara Yoshimichi, the president of the Privy Council, expressed this view when he said, "We cannot let the present situation continue. If we miss the present opportunity to go to war, we will have to submit to American dictation" (150). One might add that Japan would have to submit to American dictation *by default*.

In short, the Pearl Harbor attack represented for the Japanese more a desperate gamble than a cocky, overconfident upstart eager for a fight against the world's premier power. As we have seen, this sense of foreboding and even dread about an increasingly unfavorable future also characterized German leaders' thinking prior to the two world wars. Japanese leaders did not have any illusions about defeating the United States. Admiral Yamamoto stated, "In the first six months of war against the U.S. and England I will run wild, and I will show you an uninterrupted succession of victories; I must also tell us that, should the war be prolonged for two or three years, I have no confidence in our ultimate victory" (Ray, n.d.). Concurring with this view, Admiral Nagano indicated at the imperial conference on September 16, 1941, "Our Empire does not have the means to take the offensive, overcome the enemy, and make them give up their will to fight. Moreover, we are short on resources at home, so we would very much like to avert a prolonged war" (quoted in

Ike 1967, 139). Japanese officials pinned their hopes on seizing the European colonies to replenish their resource stockpile and establishing a strong defense to inflict heavy casualties on the Americans when Washington launched its expected counteroffensive.

Bruce M. Russett (1969, 135; italics in original) explains the Japanese decision calculus best in these words: "Japanese leaders realized that given the overwhelming strength enjoyed by the United States, Washington *could* win any war, [but] they decided that it might not *choose* to win a *long* war." Russett (135) continues on to observe that "Japan's sole strategy involved dealing maximum losses to the U.S. at the outset, making the prospects of a prolonged war as grim as possible, and counting, in an extremely vague and ill-defined way, on American people's 'softness' to end the war." Of course, there was a paradox, or, if you will, a glaring inconsistency, in this Japanese thinking—or, rather, wishful thinking. As already reported, they realized that they could not win a long war against the United States. Yet they pinned their hopes on such a protracted struggle that would somehow, in their mind, persuade the Americans to negotiate a political settlement with them.

Japanese leaders decided on war against the United States as "the only escape from [their] dilemma . . . by blunting one of its horns—to accept war with the U.S., but to attempt it under circumstances where the chances for victory were higher" (Russett 1969, 134). They went to war with their eyes wide open, realizing that they were gambling on a very risky course of action—one that turned out to be disastrous for their country. In this case, Washington's policy of firmness and a refusal to appease turned out to have backfired. Paradoxically, the Japanese leaders realized that it would be difficult—indeed, impossible—for them to reach a permanent settlement with the United States without compromising their vision for their country, and absent this settlement, they would be perpetually vulnerable to US economic coercion (Barnhart 1987, 263). Again, time was working against Japan—whose economy was put on a starvation diet by the United States while the balance of power increasingly tilted in favor of Washington. Japanese leaders chose war rather than succumbing to US pressure and giving up their ambition for their country, even though they understood that the odds were stacked heavily against them in such a fight and even though "knowing to a person that Japan could not win a prolonged conflict and that any US-Japanese war would likely last several years" (Taliaferro 2016, 193). War happened in this case not because of appeasement; rather, its occurrence could be traced to something closer to the opposite of appeasement.

Finally, Japan's decision to attack Pearl Harbor obviously ended badly for it. Just as with Germany's leaders in 1914 and 1938, we have here an example of leaders deliberately choosing war but more out of a sense of desperation and an aversion to loss than greed for gain. War happened not because they were asleep at the wheel or because they were guilty of blundering or sleepwalking into war. They took a huge gamble, which they realized could have disastrous consequences—but they were still willing to roll the dice.

What does Pearl Harbor have to do with China's rise and the possibility of a war between it and the United States? The key takeaway from Japanese decision-making in the Pearl Harbor case is that one should not back an adversary into a corner, leaving it with only a choice between surrender and lashing out. Another moral of this case is that defeat in war may not be the most dreadful thing for some leaders. Renouncing their country's status and aspiration or giving up other cherished goals (such as national reunification with Taiwan in China's case) may be even more distasteful and unthinkable than the specter of military defeat. Still, another strong implication of the Pearl Harbor case is that the balance of power between two prospective belligerent states is *not* the only consideration—and perhaps not even the most important one when leaders decide on war or peace. Japanese leaders went to war against the United States in full realization that it might very well end very badly for their country.

Hence, the emphasis given by Thucydides's Trap and power-transition theory to the relative power of states can be misplaced. That is, a country with weaker capabilities—much weaker capabilities—can still decide to go to war against a stronger foe. Relative commitment to a national cause or dedication to religious faith also matter, and they can sometimes trump considerations of relative power, as the United States should have learned from its misadventures in Vietnam and Afghanistan. Having the biggest guns is not everything, and a willingness to endure hardship and tolerate casualties is also relevant. After all, China had fought the United States in Korea when it was much weaker than today. If the lesson of Korea means anything, it warns that Washington should not underestimate Beijing's resolve to fight when it sees its important national interests threatened. That underestimation was responsible for the strategic surprise that caught General Douglas MacArthur off guard and sent his troops on the longest retreat in US history.

The above remarks should not be construed to suggest that power considerations are unimportant in or irrelevant to international relations—only that they are not the only or sometimes even the most important factor in these relations. As I will show in chapter 4, shifting balance of power certainly made a difference in the history of evolving Anglo-American relations in the 1800s and early 1900s. Growing US strength and relative British weakness, in part caused by London's overcommitments abroad, meant that effective resistance to US demands became increasingly difficult for Britain, and these considerations forced it to increasingly accommodate US interests and eventually accept Washington's dominance in the Western Hemisphere.

There has recently been a public debate among US academics and former US officials about whether to change Washington's policy toward Taiwan (e.g., Benson 2022; Blanchette et al. 2022; Christensen et al. 2022; Initiative for US-China Dialogue on Global Issues 2020; Glaser et al. 2020; Haass and Sacks 2020; Zelleke 2020). Since the United States and China established diplomatic relations in 1979, this policy has been described as strategic ambiguity. It is designed to present a dual deterrence by Washington, preventing Beijing from using force against Taipei and, at the same time, discouraging Taipei from declaring independence. In carrying out this policy, Washington refuses to precommit itself as to how it would act in a future contingency involving Taiwan. In the recent policy debate, some former officials and media commentators have argued that Washington should abandon this policy and replace it with a new policy of strategic clarity—meaning to publicly commit itself to defend Taiwan in a possible war against China. Such a change could create a moral hazard if it emboldens Taipei to declare formal independence and thus provokes a Chinese attack on the island—precisely what the US deterrence policy is supposed to prevent in the first place (Benson 2012).

The important point from the above discussion on Pearl Harbor, however, is that such a policy of strategic clarity would lock in both Washington and Beijing, leaving less policy space for their officials to maneuver in attempting to avoid a confrontation. This change would commit US prestige and reputation to the defense of Taiwan. However, Beijing also has its prestige and reputation to consider. As Thomas C. Schelling (1966, 125) indicates, it is "equally important . . . to help to decouple an adversary's prestige and reputation from a dispute; if we cannot afford to back down we must hope that he can, and if necessary, help him [to do so]." At the height of the Cuban Missile Crisis in 1962, Soviet leader Nikita Khrushchev communicated to John F. Kennedy that the first thing to do in resolving a dispute is for both sides to stop pulling at the opposite ends of a rope, making a knot tighter.

An effective demonstration of one's resolve and firmness does not necessarily prevent war's occurrence. As explained above, Japanese leaders were convinced that Washington was determined to fight on behalf of the European colonial powers should Japan try to seize their colonies in Southeast Asia. Therefore, bypassing US resistance was impossible if Japan had to acquire these territories to alleviate its acute resource shortfall. The same logic argues that if Beijing places a higher priority on its goal of national reunification with Taiwan than avoidance of conflict with Washington, a US policy of strategic clarity does not decrease the danger of war and in fact tends to increase this danger. It is tantamount to throwing away the steering wheel in the game of chicken in an effort to convince one's counterpart that it must swerve if a collision is to be avoided.

Obviously, proponents of a US policy of strategic clarity—committing the United States to defend Taiwan against a Chinese assault—believe that Washington still enjoys a military edge in an armed clash across the Taiwan Strait. However, whether it will continue to maintain this edge and for how long may not have been considered adequately by these advocates of policy change. Even more to the point, facing a lopsided disadvantage—as in the case of Japan vis-à-vis the United States on the eve of Pearl Harbor—does not mean that the target of a deterrence policy will be dissuaded. Relative stake in a dispute, relative dedication to one's cause, and relative willingness to suffer privation in a conflict are also relevant and may be more decisive in influencing the occurrence and outcome of a conflict than relative capabilities. What had transpired in the Vietnam and Afghan Wars should have made this point self-evident.

Even though they had some premonitions, US leaders in the Pearl Harbor case did not realize more clearly that their Japanese counterparts would dread the renunciation of Tokyo's imperialist ambitions more than the prospect of defeat in a war. Evidently, those who are urging Washington today to adopt a policy of strategic clarity with respect to Taiwan—to publicly commit the United States to defend this island against a Chinese attack—believe that Beijing can be deterred from attacking Taiwan because it would rather renounce or at least delay its goal of national reunification than suffer defeat in an armed conflict with the United States. They obviously believe that a declaration of Washington's commitment to defend Taiwan would demonstrate US resolve, showing that the United States is at least as much committed to defend Taiwan as China might be committed to its goal of national reunification. What might have been overlooked, however, is that the credibility of an actor's resolve has to be assessed in proportion to its stake in a dispute. Just as US leaders would ask their Chinese counterparts to consider whether seizing Taiwan would be worth the risk and cost of fighting the United States, Chinese leaders would ask themselves what stake Washington has in Taiwan's future to warrant the United States taking on the risks and costs of fighting China.

In the Pearl Harbor case, Japanese leaders were convinced that Washington saw itself as having a sufficiently large stake in Southeast Asia's future so that they did not doubt the US determination to fight their country if it should try to seize the European colonies there. Ironically, Washington's threat to intervene against Japan caused it to attack the country issuing the deterrence threat before invading its protégés. In this case, Washington's policy of extended deterrence worked, but it directed Japanese aggression to itself because it was blocking Japan's access to Southeast Asia (Iriye 1981; Russett 1969). One can hardly argue that war happened because the United States made the mistake of appeasement. Quite the contrary.

It is more difficult for extended deterrence to succeed than direct deterrence (e.g., Fearon 1994, 2002; Huth 1988a, 1988b; Huth and Russett 1988). Extended deterrence refers to a country committing itself to the defense of a protégé if another country attacks this protégé, whereas direct deterrence refers to a country's effort to deter an attack on itself. In Schelling's (1966, 36) words, "The difference between the national homeland and everything 'abroad' is the difference between threats that are inherently credible, even if unspoken, and threats that have to be made credible." In practicing extended deterrence, the country issuing the deterrence threat faces difficulty not only with respect to the target (the country that it wishes to deter) but also with respect to its protégé. French president Charles de Gaulle insisted that his country must have its own independent nuclear force de frappe. To paraphrase him, if the USSR were to attack Paris, would the United States retaliate against Moscow and St. Petersburg, thereby risking the destruction of New York and Los Angeles in a possible Soviet retaliatory strike? De Gaulle was, of course, questioning the reliability of the US nuclear umbrella to protect France to the same extent that it would protect the US homeland.

For reasons given by de Gaulle, Washington's promise to defend Taiwan would appear as "hot air" unless it was made credible by backing its words with deeds. The more costly US actions in its preparation to defend Taiwan and the greater the risks Washington accepts in undertaking this deterrence threat, the more credible is its threat to come to Taiwan's defense. By taking on these costs and risks, the United States would distinguish itself from a country that is just bluffing. These remarks in turn call attention to Washington's actions that have the effect of boosting its credibility to defend South Korea, Japan, and the Philippines, such as stationing US troops on their soil, establishing a joint command with their military, undertaking joint military exercises, and signing a defense treaty with them (Fearon 1997). If Washington fails to carry out similar actions in its relations with Taiwan, this failure communicates that its commitment to defend Taiwan is weaker than that to its other allies. Indeed, in contrast to South Korea, Japan, and the Philippines, Taiwan is not, strictly speaking, an ally because it does not have a formal security treaty with the United States. This treaty was abrogated unilaterally by Washington when it switched its diplomatic recognition from Taipei to Beijing in 1979.

This chapter's discussion warns us to be skeptical about sweeping generalizations and dogmatic assertions along the lines of "history has taught us this or that." Of course, history can be illuminating and informative. However, history does not usually lend itself to supporting overconfident, simplistic, and one-sided arguments that overlook its nuances, complexities, and ambiguities. Just as those who ignore history are likely to repeat mistakes of the past, others who are certain about their understanding of history are prone to make the opposite mistakes. The problem with those who are convinced that they have understood history correctly, such as the more outspoken and adamant proponents of the lesson of Munich, is that they have often not considered seriously alternative explanations for the conduct of those officials being criticized by them. Moreover, they usually do not bother to ask whether there are counterexamples that contradict their favored explanation and emphatic admonition. As my discussion of the Japanese decision to attack Pearl Harbor suggests, resolve and credibility in deterrence attempts can actually backfire—that is, contrary to the supposed lesson of Munich, determination to stand one's ground and refusal to compromise (or appease) can also have deleterious consequences. History is too complex to warrant oversimplified assertions and dogmatic injunctions to do this or to avoid that.

The law of the instrument, commonly attributed to Abraham Kaplan or Abraham Maslow (and is thus otherwise known as Kaplan's hammer or Maslow's hammer; Wikipedia 2024b), reminds us that if you give a hammer to a small child, she will use it for any and all purposes. In other words, there is a temptation to apply lessons of the 1930s or that of Munich to any or all situations pertaining to foreign policy. Such practice can foster mental rigidity and intellectual complacency if these supposed lessons are followed blindly without a careful analysis of their appropriateness for and relevance to the problem at hand.

This chapter presents another argument. There is often a tendency for scholars of international relations and officials in charge of foreign policy to emphasize the relative capabilities or power of the respective parties involved in a dispute. It is easier to tally the number of troops, tanks, and missiles for each side but much more difficult to grasp and evaluate intangible qualities, such as the contestants' relative resolve, stamina, and morale. US analysts tend to focus their attention on the military capabilities of China and the United States in their studies of a possible clash over Taiwan's status. They are far less likely to assess these countries' less quantifiable and more elusive qualities, such as those just mentioned. During the Vietnam War, the United States relied heavily on body counts (that is, combat fatalities) of the Viet Cong to assess its progress in this conflict without probing more deeply to grasp Hanoi's dedication to its cause and its willingness to suffer casualties. In their air campaign to bomb North Vietnam, US officials searched vainly for Hanoi's breaking point—that is, its threshold for enduring pain beyond which it would presumably cry uncle. Washington consistently underestimated Japan's and North Vietnam's willingness to fight despite their lopsided military disadvantages.

An additional takeaway from this chapter is that time is not neutral. Officials are and should be forward-looking, anticipating what the future will hold for them and other countries. My discussion of Germany's decision to start a preventive war and Japan's decision to attack Pearl Harbor points to the importance of time and timing. With the passage of time, Japan's strategic position became progressively weaker compared to the United States. Japan's opponent could outwait it, but Tokyo could not delay its decision forever because soon it would have lost the war by default if it would have exhausted its strategic reserve of important resources.

There is also the issue of path dependency, meaning that once officials start a particular policy course, it may be difficult or even impossible for them to reverse it. Path dependency therefore argues that actions undertaken today may open some options tomorrow but also foreclose others. Myopia is an enemy of good policy. Although they might have had some vague premonitions, it is not clear whether US officials had given enough thought to how their decision to embargo strategic materiel destined for Japan could have serious consequences down the road. The parallel with a possible conflict between the United States and China over Taiwan's status should be clear. Although US advocates for a harder line against China and a stronger and more explicit guarantee to defend Taiwan evidently believe that the United States holds a military edge over Beijing now, it is not clear whether they have thought through the long-term implications of their advocacy. As time passes, will this balance of power evolve? Having committed the United States to Taiwan's defense, can this commitment be easily undone? Would their recommendation for Washington to adopt a policy of strategic clarity lock the United States and China in a situation that they could only extricate themselves from with great difficulty?

Among other considerations, the tragedy of the Vietnam War was that having staked US reputation to the defense of Saigon, this commitment made the reversal of a failed policy more difficult politically and psychologically, thereby causing additional unnecessary human, financial, and reputational costs to the United States and suffering by the Vietnamese people before this conflict was finally ended. Those who now advocate a public US commitment to defend Taiwan argue that this commitment is important to communicate US reliability as an ally (they obviously forget that Washington had once before abandoned Taiwan when it switched its diplomatic recognition to China and unilaterally canceled its defense treaty with Taiwan) without, however, asking whether the damage done to the US reputation would be even greater if Washington were to change its mind later.

Reversing the clock on these comments urging greater attention to thinking forward and considering contingencies resulting from one's own actions, I conclude this chapter with a look back to history. Many people have commented that although Europeans have generally put their animosities stemming from World War II behind them, historical reconciliation has been much more difficult in Asia, shown especially by the persistent bitter division between the Japanese, whose leaders continue to visit the Yasukuni Shrine (a memorial site for Japan's war dead, including those convicted of war crimes), on the one hand, and the Chinese and Korean victims of Japan's aggression, who complain about its lack of remorse and attempts to whitewash history, on the other hand (Markovits and Reich 1997; Z. Wang 2012, 2018). Many readers may recall the vivid photo showing West German chancellor Willy Brandt kneeling at the memorial to commemorate the Warsaw Ghetto Uprising when he visited this site in 1970. One main—though hardly the only—reason is the Japanese people's recollection and understanding of the war in the Pacific reflect in part their belief that their country was not entirely or solely culpable for this conflict, which, in their view, had stemmed from Japan's defensive response to the dire circumstances that had been imposed on it. Moreover, they perceive that the United States and the West had applied double standards to Japan's quest for an empire compared to these countries' own overseas expansion and foreign aggression. Here, then, is another example of how history may be remembered and interpreted differently by people in different countries. Memories of how that conflict ended should also caution Americans to be more sensitive when they preach to the rest of the world about the danger of nuclear weapons falling into the wrong hands. So far only one country has ever used these awesome weapons of destruction—and twice against civilian targets of an enemy that had, for all practical purposes, been defeated already.

Finally, China and Japan share important similarities in the history of their political economies, and yet they decline to bury their grievances stemming from the past, or what Barry Buzan and Evelyn Goh (2020, 20–21, 35, 50–51) describe as a "narcissism of small differences." Their continued alienation enables and sustains the role of the United States as the ring holder, or the adjudicator, in East Asia. Of course, China, Japan, and the United States have all aspired to be the hegemon of their respective regions, and all three have claimed their uniqueness or exceptionalism in their construction of history and their promotion of their self-image. Importantly, however, Beijing has self-consciously indicated that its economic development and political governance do not provide a universal model for others to emulate, evident when it emphasizes that they reflect "Chinese characteristics." In contrast, even though Americans believe in their country's exceptionalism, Washington seeks to export its economic and political models, such as in promoting various color revolutions abroad to engineer regime change and in urging others to adopt capitalism and market reform (the so-called Washington Consensus). One compelling reason to avoid calling the current Sino-American tension a new cold war is that China is not waging an ideological campaign against the United States in an effort to promote the adoption of its economic and political systems abroad as the USSR did during the Cold War. There are other reasons to avoid calling today's world a return to the days of the Cold War, when Washington and Moscow were engaged in an ideological competition. China is not leading a military alliance against the United States and the West, and it is far more embedded in the global economy than the USSR ever was (Christensen 2021). Characterizing today's Sino-American tension as a new cold war is too facile and misleading, presenting us with another example of misapplication of historical analogy.

FOUR

The Reasons for the Peaceful Anglo-American Power Transition

I turn now to a discussion of Anglo-American relations. Unlike the other cases discussed in this study, peace was maintained, even though there was a power transition between these two countries. A common belief points to these countries' democratic institutions and cultural affinity as the reasons for their peaceful relationship (e.g., Schake 2017). Some people (e.g., Friedberg 2011) contend that if China were a democracy, a power transition between it and the United States would not be so concerning for Americans.

This proposition immediately raises the question of whether, during those years when the United States was catching up to Britain and eventually overtaking the latter country—say, the last five decades of the nineteenth century and the first decade of the twentieth century—these countries were indeed democracies. If by "democracy" we mean regular elections with universal adult suffrage, then both countries would not qualify because women and racial minorities were denied the right to vote until much later. The description of these countries as democracies would then be a distortion, representing an example of "conceptual stretching" (G. Sartori 1970, 1033–53 passim).

Perhaps one can consider both countries to be liberal but undemocratic during the period of their power transition, and it was their liberal rather than democratic institutions that had played a role in contributing to their eventual peaceful power transition (Owen 1994, 1997). Another possible way to approach the question is to ask how the United States had reacted to the ascendance of Japan—a treaty ally and fellow democracy—during the 1970s, 1980s, and even in the 1990s. It may be difficult for Americans to recall that many of them, including prominent scholars, saw Japan as not only an economic challenger but also a prospective security threat (Ma and Kang 2024, 160–64). Ma and Kang (163) cite a *Newsweek*/Gallup survey from September 1989 reporting that "52 percent of Americans thought the economic power of Japan was a greater threat to the United States than the military power of the Soviet Union" and refer to the portrayal of this threat from Japan in Michael Crichton's 1992 novel and subsequent movie *Rising Sun* and Tom Clancy's 1994 novel *Debt of Honor*. Judged by the titles of scholarly books published during that era, the fact that Japan was a democracy and ally did not incline Americans to take that country's rise with equanimity. These books had sensational titles, such as *Japan as Number One* (Vogel 1979), *Trading Places: How We Are Giving Our Future to Japan and How to Reclaim It* (Prestowitz 1990), *Agents of Influence: How Japan's Lobbyists in the United States Are Manipulating Western Political and Economic Systems* (Choate 1990), *Blindside: Why Japan Is Still on Track to Overtake the U.S. by the Year 2000* (Fingleton 1995), and even *The Second Pearl Harbor: Say No to Japan* (Pickens, Choate, and Burke 1992) and *The Coming War with Japan* (Friedman and LeBard 1991)! These books were alarmist and wrong, and contemporary Americans' narratives about China are in many respects eerily reminiscent of their earlier reactions to Japan's rise.

Contrary to the belief of those who attribute democratic institutions and cultural affinity to be the main reasons for the peaceful transition between Britain and the United States, John Mearsheimer (2001, 2006) argues that any country that is catching up to, not to mention overtaking, the United States will face strong opposition from Washington. The nature of their political institutions or regime ideology is irrelevant. Realists like him and Christopher Layne (see later discussion) are intellectually more consistent. Even though interstate power shifts are featured prominently as *the* overriding variable determining the prospects of war and peace in formulations such as Thucydides's Trap and power-transition theory, when it comes to explaining the peaceful leadership transition between Britain and the United States, this variable disappears inexplicably in the dominant discourse. This discourse instead points to variables traditionally championed by liberals—namely, democratic institutions and cultural affinity—to explain an obvious and important anomaly from the perspective of those who advocate Thucydides's Trap and power-transition theory.

In other words, there is a tendency to shuttle logic (a "shell game" of heads I win, tails you lose) to explain away historical phenomena inconsistent with one's favored theory. Ironically, as explained below, the suggestion that the Anglo-American transition turned out to be peaceful because of Realpolitik reasons—specifically, the shifting balance of power between London and Washington—tends to get short shrift in accounts that would otherwise emphasize this variable. Moreover, as explained later, the prevailing explanation of this Anglo-American case does not give nearly enough weight to the role of accidental timing and the serendipitous role of geography. And finally, it evades the uncomfortable discrepancy in the experience of a revisionist United States and a conformist Japan in seeking admittance to the select club of great powers. Prevailing Western narratives, of course, disregard the weight of historical evidence and reverse these labels, describing the United States as a status quo power and Japan as a revisionist one.

As for the argument that cultural affinity would ease the turbulence of a power transition, history is replete with countries with such affinity going to war against each other, including those of the Prussians and Austrians, the ongoing war between Ukraine and Russia, and civil wars that had been fought by the Vietnamese, Koreans, Chinese, and, indeed, Americans. The Jews and Arabs have cultural affinity, and obviously their relationships have not been entirely peaceful in recent times. Buzan and Goh (2020) write about Sino-Japanese alienation and estrangement despite considerable similarities between their cultures and historical experiences. These observations do not deny that cultural affinity may play a role in the peaceful relations among states, only that there must be some other variable(s) that in combination or interaction with cultural affinity creates this peaceful effect.

Parenthetically, Charles A. Kupchan (2001, 6) presents yet another view, stating, "Unlike reigning hegemons in the past, the United States will not fight to the finish to maintain its primacy and prevent its eclipse by a rising challenger." This view appears to be largely based on his sense that domestic opinion is unlikely to support such a policy by Washington. Kupchan's emphasis on domestic politics (*Innenpolitik*) is obviously in contrast to Mearsheimer's (2011) thesis, mentioned just now, that gives primacy to external politics (*Außenpolitik*). There was, of course, popular resistance to US participation in World War I, and isolationism has had a long and influential tradition in American politics (Kupchan 2020). Circumstances may change in the future, but in the past, US public opinion could occasionally be quite belligerent, even though it could also be "pretty prudent," as suggested by the titles of articles written by Bruce W. Jentleson (1992) and Jentleson and Rebecca Britton (1998). John R. Oneal, Brad Lian, and James H. Joyner Jr. (1996) also support this assessment.

If democratic institutions and cultural affinity were the principal reasons for the peaceful Anglo-American power transition, how can one reconcile this claim with the fact that these countries had in fact fought in the American War of Independence and again in the War of 1812? Moreover, there were several instances when these countries came close to exchanging blows. While the relationship between London and Washington did become amicable after the first decade of the twentieth century, it was competitive and turbulent before this transformation. Recent claims that these countries have always had a friendly relationship have a distinct post hoc flavor. Like the other episodes addressed in this study, it presents revisionist history, as their relationship had been quite stormy in much of the nineteenth century (Bourne 1967; Layne 1994; Rock 1989, 2000). International relations analysts, who ought to know better, often appear to have historical amnesia.

Kenneth Bourne (1967, 408) tells his readers that "the United States remained an enemy of Britain's calculations . . . until 1895–96. Until after the Venezuelan affair [the boundary dispute between Venezuela and British Guiana in 1895–1896] any increase in the territory and strength of the United States was regarded as a direct threat to the British possessions and British power and influence in the western hemisphere." This feeling was reciprocated, such as when Theodore Roosevelt wrote in 1918, "For the first ninety years the British Navy, when, as was ordinarily the case, the British Government was more or less hostile to us, was our greatest threat" (quoted in Zakaria 1998, 177). In view of these countries' contentious relationship, William R. Thompson (1999, 213) remarks, "The most difficult position to defend is the extreme argument that democratization was primarily responsible for the decline of Anglo-American conflict." He goes on to note, "In the late eighteenth century and early nineteenth century, the British ruling elite had seen the United States as a revolutionary challenger to the status quo, both internationally and potentially within the British domestic politics. The Americans, for their part, did not consider the British political system of the same period to be particularly democratic" (213).

The idea that the Anglo-American power transition was peaceful because of their common democratic institutions and shared cultural affinity tends to be revisionist history. After all, these same factors did not prevent their fighting in the American Revolutionary War and the War of 1812. These countries also came close to blows in 1845–1846 over their dispute over Oregon. As Christopher Layne (1994) observes, the evolution of Anglo-American relations from being turbulent to amicable has more to do with the changing balance of power between these two countries, leading to increasing British accommodation of American power and concessions to American demands over time. Their political institutions and culture have been relatively constant factors over the years and, as such, cannot account for the *changing* nature of their relationship. Note also that British concessions to the Americans are usually described as accommodation rather than appeasement. The latter term would, of course, raise eyebrows given its association with the so-called lesson of Munich. Such verbal contortions attest to the view that scholarship on international relations can be seriously biased and distorted.

The contention that the United States would welcome and accept China's rise if only it were a democracy is not persuasive. This proposition reminds one of the quintessential American sayings "It does not have a Chinaman's chance." Since the establishment of diplomatic relations between these two countries in 1979, Beijing has renounced its support for armed insurgency abroad, its objection to arms control agreements, and its opposition to international organizations, such as the United Nations. It has, moreover, opened its economy to international trade and investment, and it has become deeply embedded in the global economy since then. Its society has become more open compared to the Maoist years, and its people's living standards have improved vastly. None of these developments have prevented the sharp recent deterioration in Sino-American relations (Chan 2023).

Proponents of the argument that democratic institutions and shared cultural heritage were responsible for the peaceful Anglo-American power transition would expect these countries to refrain from making coercive threats against each other or planning war against each other. As Christopher Layne (1994) points out, scholars holding this view would also have to show that their proposition offers a better explanation than competing hypotheses, such as the contention that the transformation of Anglo-American relations was due to an inexorable change in the balance of power between these two countries, forcing London to succumb to Washington's pressure and agreeing to accommodate US interests. In the border dispute between the British colony of New Brunswick and the US state of Maine (the so-called Aroostook War in 1838–1839), both sides mobilized their troops. Although this conflict ended without fighting, their actions indicate that a resort to arms was not ruled out from the outset.

The *Trent* affair (1861) and the boundary dispute between Venezuela and British Guiana (1895–1896) are equally revealing. They show that war was on the minds of British and American leaders. USS *Jacinto* under Union command had intercepted Britain's RMS *Trent*, and two Confederate envoys traveling on this vessel were captured and imprisoned by Union soldiers. Many in Britain saw this action as casus belli. US secretary of state William H. Seward was informed by a US citizen residing in Britain that "the people [in Britain] are frantic with rage, and were the country polled I fear 999 men out of 1000 would declare for war" (quoted in Layne 1994, 16). Prime Minister Lord Palmerstone delivered an ultimatum, giving the Americans seven days to apologize and release the two prisoners, or else he would resort to force. He told his cabinet, "I don't know whether you are going to stand for this, but I'll be damned if I do" (17). He ordered military preparations, including reinforcing Britain's forces in Canada and its navy in North America. He told Queen Victoria, "Great Britain is in a better state than at any former time to inflict a severe blow upon, and to read a lesson to the United States which will not soon be forgotten" (19). Even though President Abraham Lincoln had wanted to take a hard line, Washington yielded to British pressure in the end, mainly out of a concern that Britain might join the Confederacy in opposing the Union in the then-ongoing US Civil War.

However, by 1895–1896, the balance of power had shifted decisively in favor of the United States, which interjected itself in a boundary dispute between Venezuela and British Guiana. US secretary of state Richad Olney told London that American "honor and interests" were at stake in this dispute, "the continuance of which it cannot regard with indifference" (quoted in Layne 1994, 22). He demanded international arbitration to settle this dispute. The United States was now in a stronger position, and Britain buckled under

Washington's pressure and acceded to US terms. Both Olney and President Grover Cleveland thought that applying the "Monroe Doctrine as a lever, the United States could ram a diplomatic settlement down Britain's throat" (Eggert, quoted on 23). "The United States was willing to fight Britain if necessary in order to establish America's primacy in the Western Hemisphere" (24).

British prime minister Lord Salisbury realized that the Americans were not bluffing, and he said that war "in the not distant future has become something more than a possibility" (quoted in Bourne 1967, 337). In the end, London yielded to Washington's pressure despite Salisbury's own preference to take a harder line. He lamented, "It is very sad, but I am afraid America is bound to forge ahead and nothing can restore the equality between us. If we had interfered in the Confederate Wars, it was then possible for us to reduce the power of the United States to manageable proportions. But two such chances are not given to a nation in the course of its career" (quoted in MacMillan 2013, 38).

After the settlement of the boundary dispute between Venezuela and British Guiana, Washington continued to consolidate its regional hegemony and to pressure London for additional concessions. Theodore Roosevelt insisted on "[driving] the Spaniards out of Cuba" and openly wished for "an immediate war with Great Britain for the conquest of Canada" (Morris quoted in G. Allison 2017, 95). Prior to the settlement of their dispute in 1903, British Canada and the United States had quarreled over the drawing of the boundary between them in the Northwest—a dispute during which Theodore Roosevelt had threatened that, should diplomacy end in an impasse, "I shall take the position which will prevent any possibility of arbitration hereafter" and that the United States would "act in a way which will necessarily wound British pride" (quoted in Tilchin 1997, 44). He declared that "in the event of specious and captious objections on the part of the English, I am going to send a brigade of American regulars up to Skagway and take possession of the disputed territory and hold it by the power and the force of the United States" (quoted in Wood 1927, 115). The Alaskan-boundary dispute dissipated only after London yielded to US pressure and agreed to set up a commission, later accepting its decision to settle the matter practically in favor of all US claims with only minor concessions to Canada.

London also gave up its objection to the construction of the Panama Canal, thus in effect conceding US naval control of the Western Hemisphere and its dominant influence in the Pacific. Thus, as Washington's power grew and concomitantly London's power declined, Britain made successive concessions to accommodate US demands (Zeren and Hall 2016). This view was shared by Stephen R. Rock (1989, 32), who observes, "Between 1895 and 1905, Britain gradually retreated from the Western Hemisphere and removed herself as an effective obstacle to the exercise of American authority in that region of the world." Similarly, Graham T. Allison (2017, 197) explains that Britain's concessions to US demands reflected "cold realism," which it was simply not in a position to resist. Ali Zeren and John A. Hall (2016, 113) conclude, "There is little sense in talking about 'passing the baton' of liberal hegemony. It is very important not to accept such language. For one thing, Great Britain never exercised hegemonic power, being but one of a small number of great powers; the situation of the United States, both at the end of World War II . . . and still more from 1989, has been entirely different. For another, the manner in which the United States took powers from Great Britain was altogether more brutal."

The *Trent* affair, the Anglo-Venezuelan boundary dispute, and other episodes such as those involving relations with Canada suggest strongly that neither democratic institutions (if we can consider countries without universal adult suffrage to be democratic) nor cultural affinity can explain the peaceful nature of the Anglo-American power transition. Both countries' behavior and their statements show that London and Washington had not given up the thought of applying coercion and resorting to violence as a way to resolve their disputes. War was always an option for one or both of them. This is an important point. Karl Deutsch and his coauthors (1957) write about the emergence of a "security community" in the North Atlantic region. By "security community," they mean a group of people or states for whom the idea of going to war against one another has become "unthinkable." In other words, members of a security community have renounced force as a way to settle their disagreements. Although a security community did eventually develop for Britain and the United States, this does not mean that they had always ruled out the use of force against each other prior to this development.

Although Britain and the United States managed to avoid war after 1812, there were several "close calls" that could have easily ended in armed hostilities between them. As just indicated, it should not be overlooked that these countries did come to blows on two occasions—in the War of American Independence and the War of 1812. Political institutions and cultural affinity change slowly. Those who point to these variables as the decisive determinants in the peaceful transition of global leadership from Britain to the United States would have to explain how these relatively constant factors could have accounted for the evolution of their relations from being turbulent to being cordial. They would have to also show that these variables rather than some other changes—such as the shifting power balance between London and Washington—were responsible for this evolution. Rather than being always peaceful and amicable, the Anglo-American relationship only evolved to become so over time. "For London, the 'special relationship' was a myth devised 'to enable Britain to withdraw gracefully" from those areas where British and American interests clashed (Hyam, quoted in Layne 1994, 27–28). As C. J. Lowe and M. L. Dockrill put it, this made "the 'pill'" of appeasing the United States "more palatable to swallow" (quoted on 28).

Analyses of the peaceful power transition between Britain and the United States sometimes reflect the practice of "selecting on the dependent variable"—that is, the decision by analysts to select a case that they know to have ended in peace and reason backward to search for factors that could have accounted for this outcome without, however, asking whether these same factors had also been present in cases that had ended in war, such as the Austro-Prussian War mentioned earlier, involving states with close cultural affinity. This type of analysis also often overlooks cases where peace persisted even in the absence of shared democratic institutions or common cultural affinity, such as China's peaceful overtaking of Germany, Japan, and Russia in recent decades.

My earlier comments questioning the role of cultural affinity should not be mistaken to mean that it was irrelevant to this peaceful process. As with most things in life, its role is contingent upon other factors. Among these other factors are strategic necessity and one or both countries' desire to reduce overcommitments in their security policies (Kupchan 2001). Thus, London's willingness to accommodate Washington reflects in part the fact that it was facing multiple competitors and challenges. In the period between the mid-1800s and early 1900s, there were several rising states: Japan, Russia, and Germany, in addition to the United States. British leaders decided to retrench and focus their attention and resources on Germany, which is located closest to their home islands.

Two other points made by Kupchan (2010) are pertinent. First, cultural affinity does not in itself foster peace and stability among countries. As already mentioned, many wars have been fought by groups or states sharing similar cultural heritage. The peaceful transformation of Anglo-American relations was also the product of political entrepreneurship. The process of creating amity and a "we feeling" usually starts with a unilateral concession by one party, which is subsequently reciprocated by the other. This is a top-down process initiated by the elites who, as political entrepreneurs and for their own political agenda, start to construct and propagate a friendly view of their counterparts in the other country. It requires a considerable amount of time before benign images of the other country start to permeate to the mass level with the further construction and propagation of narratives of mutual friendship—narratives that gradually gain increasing popular acceptance over time.

The process just described can also operate in reverse to construct and spread an enemy image, although it appears that this transformation can occur more rapidly than the process required to turn former enemies into friends (Rousseau 2006). There was a time when the American elite, including the then-future US president Woodrow Wilson, held kaiser's Germany in high esteem, perceiving it as a model constitutional monarchy, a paradigm of the rule of law, and an example par excellence of an efficient bureaucratic state (Oren 2003). But as World War I approached, their opinions changed rather abruptly so that German leaders were then portrayed as Teutonic marauders bent on aggression and destruction.

There were also several changes in popular US views of China from images of yellow peril and a land of coolies to a heroic nation resisting Japanese aggression. Of course, there was a reversal of this view after Beijing intervened in the Korean War, thus putting China and the United States in a direct armed conflict. Americans' views of China changed swiftly so that the Chinese were now seen as godless, Red hordes doing the Kremlin's bidding in Asia, whereas Americans' views of the Japanese were transformed from being conniving aggressors to loyal allies contributing to building an anti-Communist bulwark in Asia. After Richard Nixon's visit to Beijing in 1972, there was yet another burst of fascination with China, as represented by the so-called panda mania. Americans' views of China improved markedly as these two countries became practically allies in their joint opposition to the USSR.

This sense of friendship and cooperation took another downturn as official relations between China and the United States deteriorated in more recent years. Both elite and mass opinions in the United States have become highly critical of China, even though many of the characteristics that are usually mentioned nowadays by Americans to be objectionable about China—such as its Communist ideology, its single-party rule, its authoritarian government, and its suppression of people's political rights—have not changed since Richard Nixon's trip to Beijing and Jimmy Carter's diplomatic recognition of China. If anything, there have been changes since then that should make China appear more acceptable to the United States, such as improvements in the Chinese people's living conditions, their greater social freedoms, and the opening of China's economy since Nixon's and Carter's decisions and since the time of Sino-American strategic partnership to oppose the USSR. Changes in China's foreign policy—such as its renunciation of support for violent insurgencies abroad, its acceptance of and support for arms control agreements, and its active participation in multilateral diplomacy and international organizations, like the United Nations—should also be congenial to American interests and values. Notwithstanding these changes, however, these countries' bilateral ties have suffered serious deterioration in recent years. In short, public opinion about another country can be quite malleable, and it usually follows the ups and downs in the official relations between two countries and reflects governmental actions and pronouncements.

Second, cultural affinity is not a necessary condition for states to get along and enter into collaborative relationships. As just pointed out, there was a time when China and the United States were practically allies in their joint opposition to the USSR, when China's government was more repressive, and its society and economy were more closed than now. Even though they had a subsequent fallout, Beijing and Moscow were allies in a close strategic partnership in the 1950s, and their relationship has shown another rapprochement more recently despite the fact that they do not share any cultural affinity. Similarly, the Concert of Europe after the Napoleonic Wars—consisting of countries with different cultures and political affinities—managed to enhance cooperation among those great power that had vanquished Napoleon, enabling them to keep peace and stability in Europe until 1848.

As Charles W. Kegley Jr. and Gregory A. Raymond (1994) show, when states agree on the basic norms and rules of international relations, peace and stability are likely to prevail—regardless of their cultural affinity or regime characteristics. The basic norms and rules representing a restrictive international order enhancing peace and stability pertain to leaders' agreement to recognize the legitimacy of other ruling elites, respect other countries' traditional spheres of influence, accept the sanctity and binding nature of international agreements, and adhere to the rules governing the use of force. Other scholars, such as Robert Gilpin (1981) and Yuen Foong Khong (2001), also suggest that peaceful and stable international relations depend crucially on consensual agreement by officials in different countries on states' positions in the interstate hierarchy, the rules governing trade and use of force, the demarcation of spheres of influence, and common procedures for managing territorial changes.

Arguably, there has recently been an erosion, if not a complete breakdown, of consensus on those restrictive rules and norms conducive to international peace and stability. The US invasion of Iraq and NATO's attacks on Serbia, Libya, and other countries without UN authorization contributed to this weakening of principles governing the legitimate use of force by great powers. The Western countries' promotion of regime changes and color revolutions abroad also played a role in undermining the rules and norms of a restrictive international order based on the longstanding principles dating back to the Treaty of Westphalia in 1648 concerning reciprocal recognition of the legitimacy of ruling elites and noninterference in other countries' domestic affairs. Of course, the expansion of NATO and the European Union (EU) to include former Soviet satellite countries in Central and Eastern Europe and even former republics of the Soviet Union right up to Russia's border presents yet another challenge to one of the basic tenets of a restrictive international order requiring reciprocal recognition of and noninterference in another great power's traditional sphere of influence. In the next chapter (chapter 5), I will discuss another case that ended in peaceful resolution of a dangerous encounter—namely, the Cuban Missile Crisis of 1962. One of the chief reasons that US leaders were upset about the installation of Soviet missiles in Cuba was, of course, their perception that it was an aggressive intrusion by Moscow in Washington's backyard.

Russia's invasion of another sovereign country—namely, Ukraine—also represents a violation of international order in that it seeks to alter borders and territorial control by force. Of course, increasing US disengagement from international organizations and withdrawal from international accords—especially during Donald Trump's first administration when Washington withdrew from the World Health Organization, the Trans-Pacific Partnership, the Paris Climate Accord, the Iran nuclear deal, and quite a few others—are also damaging to a consensual and restrictive international order. Finally, to the extent that economic interdependence represents a pillar of the Kantian (Immanuel Kant's) tripod for peace (the other two pillars are democratic institutions and international organizations; see Russett and Oneal 2001), antiglobalization sentiments in the West and United States and their policies seeking to decouple economically from Russia and China are also concerning. Recent elections in established democracies also show a surge of support for right-wing political parties and politicians—some of them openly avowing their opposition to liberal values and democratic institutions (Norris 1999, 2011; Norris and Inglehart 2019).

In conclusion, the subject of this chapter—the peaceful nature of Anglo-American leadership transition—illustrates hindsight bias, problems with analyses that select on the dependent variable, and a proclivity to engage in post hoc explanation, reflecting a revisionist and distorted presentation of history. Neither democratic institutions nor cultural affinity can satisfactorily account for the evolution of Anglo-American relations from being tense, turbulent, and occasionally overtly hostile to being cordial and friendly. The changing balance of power between Britain and the United States offers a more persuasive explanation than their shared democracy and culture. In this respect, the traditional realist perspective—including power-transition theory's emphasis on power shifts as a determinant of international relations—trumps liberal interpretation of history assigning priority to democratic peace and cultural affinity.

I have argued in the preceding discussion that prevailing US explanations or characterizations of the Peloponnesian War, the two world wars, and the Japanese attack on Pearl Harbor are unconvincing. They distort history and are ideational constructions contrived to fit a political script being propounded and propagated with a clear ideological subtext and policy agenda. Whether consciously or unconsciously, they serve the purpose of mobilizing public support and legitimating government policies to confront ostensible foreign nemeses. Ancient Athens, Wilhelmine and Nazi Germany, and imperial Japan were aggressive and ambitious states. However, the depiction of Germany and Japan as cocky, overconfident rising states itching for a fight to claim the mantle of global dominance from an established hegemon represents revisionist history. Information about ancient Athens is more limited and ambiguous, but the attempt to match it with contemporary China is a stretch for anyone with some passing knowledge about these two polities. There is no direct evidence that I am aware of to indicate that Sparta's fear of Athens's rise was responsible for the outbreak of the Peloponnesian War, nor is there any direct evidence showing power shifts were in fact occurring between these two ancient Greek city states.

Moreover, I have argued that the so-called lesson of Munich tends to be simplistic. It neglects alternative explanations of this episode, and it fails to recognize contrarian evidence, such as that which is suggested by Japan's decision to attack Pearl Harbor. The injunction against appeasement also overlooks the possible deleterious consequences suggested by the experience of Philip IV's Spain fighting multiple opponents with the intent of establishing a reputation for firmness and resolve and thereby deterring possible future challenges to its authority and power (I will discuss this case briefly in this book's conclusion). This policy mired Madrid in perpetual conflict, exhausting it financially and militarily (Treisman 2004). It set Spain on a steady course of decline that it was never able to recover from. In contrast, Britain engaged in selective appeasement. It accommodated the United States and conciliated with France and Russia to enable it to focus its attention and resources on Germany in the years before 1914 (Friedberg 1988; Vasquez 1996). The outcome of World War I would have been very different if London had not undertaken these policies. Those who cite the lesson of Munich would not have approved or endorsed London's concessions to and compromises with the United States, and Britain would have been put in a worse situation if its leaders had listened to their advice.

Finally, in this chapter, I have introduced evidence suggesting that history has been misrepresented in an effort to explain the peaceful transfer of the world's leadership position from Britain to the United States. Descriptions of these two countries as democracies during the nineteenth century indicates "conceptual stretching," and their cultural affinity does not appear to be a sufficient condition to ensure peace since many countries with similar affinities have fought in the past. Moreover, as already pointed out, cultural affinity did not prevent war between Britain and the United States in 1775 and 1812. It is unlikely that this factor is even a necessary condition for peace since countries with different heritages have gotten along. A prime example comes from the member states of the Concert of Europe in jointly managing European relations to keep peace after the defeat of Napoleonic France in 1815. If cultural affinity were a necessary condition for peace, the world would be in trouble because obviously it is impossible for all countries to share the same cultural heritage. My remark does not deny that cultural affinity may be a facilitating condition for peace when it works in conjunction with other favorable factors.

Instead of democratic institutions and cultural affinity, fortuitous timing and the accident of geography appear to be more important factors in explaining the peaceful nature of the Anglo-American leadership transition. As I will argue in the book's conclusion, the United States was fortunate that it was located in a region where it did not have to face another country that could stand up to it and contest its dominance. At the same time, the European countries were too busy competing with one another to bother it. Both France and Britain even thought that they could recruit the United States as their ally, and they were often wary of antagonizing Washington for this reason. Timing was important because, as already mentioned, in the late 1800s and early 1900s, Britain faced challenges and competition from several rising powers, including Japan, Germany, and Russia, in addition to the United States. To lessen its strategic overcommitments and to concentrate its resources on a nearby threat coming from Germany, Britain decided to accommodate a more distant United States.

These reasons, in addition to the shifting balance of power between Britain and the United States, inclined London to accommodate US interests and demands in the Western Hemisphere. As a result, the United States was able to establish its hegemony over its home region. It was also given the rare opportunity to concentrate on its own growth without having to be distracted by allocating economic resources and policy attention to fend off foreign threats. No other country has thus far been able to achieve the same feat. Germany, Japan, and the USSR's bids for regional hegemony encountered stiff resistance, and they were turned back largely due to US efforts. An abiding principle of US foreign policy has been to prevent another regional hegemon from emerging in Europe, Asia, or the Middle East.

In conclusion, the historical evidence introduced by prevailing discourse to support various explanations about why war broke out or why peace was kept appears rather problematic in my view. There appears to be a tendency to shoehorn historical episodes to fit the theoretical formulations or empirical propositions being advanced. Sometimes history is deliberately bypassed, such as when power-transition theory excludes the United States from its analyses of the two world wars. As a result of this omission, it was able to portray the two world wars as an Anglo-German contest for world domination. Of course, by 1914 and certainly by 1938, the United States had already overtaken Britain to become the world's most powerful country. There is also the supreme irony that in the one and only case in modern history indicating a transition of world leadership from one country to another (namely, the Anglo-American transfer of the leadership position), war did *not* happen as proponents of power-transition theory and Thucydides's Trap would have predicted. Of course, the proponents of these formulations either conveniently overlook this case or they give short shrift to the one overriding variable that they champion in explaining other large armed conflicts—namely, the shifting power balance between Britain and the United States. This practice reminds one of the saying "To have one's cake and eat it too."

FIVE

The Parallels between the Cuban Missile Crisis and Contest over Taiwan

The world came closest to the brink of a nuclear war during the Cuban Missile Crisis in 1962 (Allison 1971; May and Zelikow 1977). This crisis ended when Nikita Khrushchev agreed to withdraw Soviet missiles from that island. It is remembered by most Americans as an example of successful crisis management by John F. Kennedy's administration and as a "win" in the conduct of coercive diplomacy (George, Hall, and Simons 1971). It is lauded as an instance of successful compellence even by scholars who have otherwise been critical of US decision processes in cases such as the Bay of Pigs fiasco, the failure of strategic intelligence to warn about Japan's impending attack on Pearl Harbor, China's decision to enter the Korean War, and misguided policies in the Vietnam debacle (including Operation Rolling Thunder, an air campaign carried out by Lyndon B. Johnson's administration to coerce North Vietnam to accept Washington's terms to settle the war), for which the same "best and brightest" officials, except the president (John F. Kennedy had been assassinated in the meantime and succeeded by Johnson), were responsible (e.g., Janis 1982a).

Compellence is distinct from deterrence because it seeks to force the other party to stop or reverse doing something that it has already undertaken, whereas deterrence is about preventing this counterpart from doing something that it may do but has not yet done. The success of compellence is supposed to be much more difficult to achieve than that of deterrence (Schelling 1966). If for nothing else, it is more humiliating for the other side to back down or cease its objectionable behavior in the face of a public threat than to eschew a course of action that it has not yet initiated and can thus limit any damage to its reputation by plausibly denying that it had ever intended to act in the proscribed way. Jack S. Levy (2008a, 542) explains the difference between these two concepts in terms of prospect theory. Compellence involves the other actor incurring an actual loss, whereas deterrence implies abstinence from a possible gain.

A lesser-known and relatively unpublicized part of the Cuban Missile Crisis suggests that Washington was not as successful in having its way in this episode as is sometimes popularly believed. A secret deal was reached, whereby the USSR would remove its missiles from Cuba, and the United States would reciprocate by removing its missiles from Turkey and refrain from invading Cuba again (Allison and Zelikow 1999, 356–66; Mearsheimer and Rosato 2023, 166–67). Naturally, US officials told their Soviet interlocutors that they would deny the existence of such a deal if it ever became public. We know, however, that the United States did remove its missiles from Turkey within half a year after the USSR removed its missiles from Cuba and that the United States did not attempt to invade Cuba again, as it did at the Bay of Pigs in 1961. The latter episode was significant because Moscow's public rationale for introducing missiles to Cuba was ostensibly to deter another attack by the United States against that island, as it had done previously in training, organizing, and coordinating the invasion by Cuban exiles at the Bay of Pigs. According to the Kremlin's narrative, having successfully defended Cuba, the presence of its missiles was no longer required on the island.

The Cuban Missile Crisis is interesting in part because, even years after its occurrence, it is still difficult for experts to reach definitive conclusions about US and Soviet motivations and how well these countries' policies had performed. As just mentioned, the Soviets claimed that their installation of missiles in Cuba represented an instance of successful deterrence, whereas popular interpretation among Americans suggests that it was an instance of successful compellence.

For the purpose of this chapter, however, my main interest is in how an analogy may suggest itself quickly and even naturally to some people, but it may not occur at all to others. For the present purpose, it is important to note that rarely do Americans use Cuba as an analogy when they think about or comment on Taiwan, nor do they, if you will, put themselves in the shoes of the Chinese in imagining how the feelings, calculations, and motivations in the Cuban Missile Crisis might also apply to the Chinese regarding Taiwan's contested status. There is a Chinese saying enjoining people not to do to others that which they do not wish others do to them (*Ji suo bu yu, wu shi yu ren* 己所不欲, 勿施於人). In English, the word "empathy" comes to mind.

The initial response of some US officials to the news of Soviet missiles in Cuba was nonchalant. Robert McNamara was supposed to have dismissed their presence in Cuba with something of an equivalent of a shrug, suggesting that a missile is a missile regardless of where it is based. After all, the United States had learned to live with Soviet submarines armed with nuclear weapons cruising up and down its eastern seaboard. That Cuba is located only about ninety miles from the United States does not affect the material fact that Washington commands an overwhelming nuclear advantage over the USSR and in the Caribbean, an overwhelming edge in conventional forces as well.

The real danger posed by the Soviet missiles had more to do with US domestic politics, specifically the expected political fallout should the president fail to act decisively or be perceived to lack resolve in addressing the presence of Soviet missiles in America's backyard. Republican right-wing politicians were expected to create a political firestorm by charging the president for being weak in confronting Fidel Castro's Cuba and its sponsor, the Kremlin. Kennedy and his advisors were also concerned about inaction or irresolute action adversely affecting the electoral prospects of the Democratic Party's candidates running for office in the then-impending congressional elections. Even the idea that the president might be impeached if he did not appear resolute and effective in dealing with the missile crisis had come up in private conversations at the White House (Allison 1971, 184–85). In short, the presence of Soviet missiles in Cuba might not have imperiled US national security, but it did place the president in political jeopardy.

Although resort to analogy is a common practice in policymaking, it is odd that, to my knowledge, published research by international relations analysts (at least those who are Americans) has not brought up some obvious parallels between US policies toward Cuba and Chinese policies toward Taiwan.

Of course, there are also fundamental differences between these two cases. Above all, Washington did not see Cuba as part of its territory, and irredentism was not a relevant motivation for it in its relations with this Caribbean nation. In contrast, Beijing sees Taiwan as a breakaway province, and its status is a matter of China's domestic affairs. To finally conclude China's civil war by reuniting Taiwan with the Chinese mainland has been declared publicly and consistently by Beijing as its top policy priority and its core national interest.

Of course, I do not mean to argue that Cuba offers parallels to Taiwan only in terms of their respective physical locations and distances vis-à-vis the United States and China, respectively, although these geographic facts are naturally pertinent. There are other considerations that make them similar, as we shall see in the next chapter's discussion of the Falklands/Malvinas War. In addressing these cases, I have in mind also emotional and cultural distance, domestic political salience, and the strategic implications for the parties' respective national security. As to be discussed further in chapter 6, it is striking that neither Britain nor Argentina had wanted a war over the Falklands/Malvinas, and for London, the economic and military value of these contested islands was low. Yet these countries found themselves at war due to domestic reasons, which I see to be a more important similarity for the three cases.

Returning to the idea of Cuba presenting an analogue to Taiwan, this analogy serves as a useful reminder for Americans about how they felt about Cuba when they comment on the controversy over Taiwan's status. This analogy is useful because it invites Americans to think about what was at stake for the United States in the Cuban Missile Crisis and how dangerous a crisis can escalate despite the fact that the emotions of nationalism and the cause of national reunification were not involved in that case. To put matters in a different way, what was at stake for the United States in the Cuban Missile Crisis to warrant its escalation of the crisis to the brink of a nuclear confrontation? After all, the United States had itself installed missiles abroad during those years, including in Turkey, which was located next to the then USSR, and, one suspects, also in South Korea and Taiwan, which are next to China.

If Americans felt so strongly about Cuba, would it be possible for them to imagine that the Chinese feel equally strongly—if not more—about Taiwan being aligned with a hostile extraregional power? One would surmise that the Chinese feel even more intensely about Taiwan, and the political, economic, and strategic stake involved in this island's status is even greater for them since nationalism and national reunification are added to the dangerous mix of factors that can make a crisis more combustible (Chan, forthcoming-c).

If John F. Kennedy could not afford to back down in the Cuban Missile Crisis in view of US domestic politics, how would this situation be different for Chinese leaders in a crisis involving Taiwan? If they want to hold on to power and protect themselves from their domestic critics, can Chinese leaders afford to appear "spineless" when dealing with Taiwan? One implication from this line of reasoning is immediately clear: one should avoid words and deeds that would put the leaders of the opposing side in an even more difficult domestic bind. In-your-face diplomacy and rhetoric intended to humiliate and embarrass one's foreign counterparts would only make a dangerous situation even more dangerous. During the Cuban Missile Crisis, President Kennedy was quite aware that Khrushchev might have been facing opposition from Soviet hard-liners opposed to his decision to deescalate the crisis. He asked his subordinates not to gloat publicly over what were to be presented as Soviet concessions. This observation reminds us of Thomas C. Schelling's advice, mentioned earlier, that if we cannot back down, we should help our counterpart to do so. After all, they also have their reputation to protect.

Ceteris paribus, the closer a conflict is located to a country's home turf, the greater is its stake in a dispute's outcome, the more intense its preferences, and the firmer we can expect it to stand its ground. Interstate conflicts are as much a contest of will as they are a match of capabilities. In the Cuban Missile Crisis, the United States was more motivated than the USSR, even though the balance of power was also operating in Washington's favor. In a possible crisis involving Taiwan, there will again be an asymmetry in motivation. Will this asymmetry be offset by an asymmetry in capabilities so that a more powerful United States can still deter a Chinese invasion of Taiwan, even though Beijing may have more intense preferences? China has, in recent years, closed the military gap that separates it from the United States, although perhaps Washington still presently enjoys an edge. But what about in a decade or two decades from now? Some Americans are advocating that the United States should change its Taiwan policy from strategic ambiguity to strategic clarity, banking on the belief that the United States still holds the military upper hand—for now.

Naturally, US officials are not in the habit of publicizing the domestic partisan reasons for their choice of foreign policy. *Pensons-y toujours, n'en parlons jamais*: always think about it; never talk about it. The public justification for US objection to Soviet missiles in Cuba was that, with the island being located only some ninety miles away from the continental United States, Soviet *offensive* missiles from the island would reduce the warning time available to US authorities and thus present an unacceptable risk to US national security (never mind what constitutes the difference between offensive and defensive missiles that US officials had in mind when they objected to Soviet missiles in Cuba). Of course, the same reason would apply to Chinese military planners as Taiwan is located about one hundred miles from the Chinese mainland.

Taiwan in fact occupies a much more strategically important position for China than Cuba does vis-à-vis the United States. In the words of General Douglas MacArthur (2005), Taiwan is an "unsinkable aircraft carrier." It holds the key to China's front door (Chan and Hu, forthcoming-b). In the hands of a hostile power, it can be used as a launching pad to stage offensive operations against the Chinese mainland (Wachman 2007). Taiwan's location is such that it can be used to interdict and interfere with China's north-south traffic and communication. It is a dagger pointed at China's soft underbelly—its eastern seaboard, where its economic and demographic center of gravity lies. In his testimony to the US Senate, Assistant Secretary of Defense Ely Ratner (2021, 1) explained, "Taiwan is located at a critical node within the first island chain, anchoring a network of U.S. allies and partners—stretching from the Japanese archipelago down to the Philippines and into the South China Sea—that is critical to the region's security and critical to the defense of vital U.S. interests in the Indo-Pacific."

In plain English, Taiwan is the pivot for the US containment policy in East Asia. China's navy and merchant marine have to pass through several "choke points" on their oceanic voyage to or from the mainland, with the Strait of Malacca being perhaps the most obvious one. Chinese shipping is vulnerable to US naval interdiction, and as Aaron L. Friedberg (2011, 228) points out, there is nothing that Beijing can do about this vulnerability—at least up to now. More recently, Brendan R. Green and Caitlin Talmadge (2022) discuss in detail Taiwan's strategic importance in bottling up China's navy. Chinese submarines, for example, have to transit through narrow channels before they can reach the open Pacific, and they are therefore vulnerable to being tracked and interdicted. In the hands of an unfriendly power, Taiwan denies the Chinese navy easy and safe access to the world's oceans. Conversely, if Beijing should gain control of Taiwan, it will have broken out of the first island chain created by Washington to restrict China's maritime reach. Beijing will also thereby have gained an important asset in oceanic surveillance, extending its defense perimeter more than one hundred miles eastward.

Parenthetically, the so-called first island chain runs from the Kurile Islands and the Japanese archipelago to the Ryukyu Islands and Taiwan and then to the northern Philippines and eventually Borneo. Taiwan is the linchpin in this chain. The second island chain extends from Japan's Bonin Islands to the Mariana Islands, then the western Caroline Islands, and finally to western Papua New Guinea. Guam occupies the pivotal position in this second island chain, just as Taiwan does for the first chain. The United States has built and maintained a series of military installations and alliances in these maritime networks to contain China. Should China gain control of Taiwan, it will have broken through the first island chain.

Importantly, even a casual glance at a map indicates that Taiwan commands far greater strategic importance for China than Cuba does vis-à-vis the United States. Located in the Caribbean, Cuba cannot possibly interfere with US shipping, which has unimpeded access to the Atlantic and Pacific Oceans from its eastern and western seaboard, respectively. At best, Cuba in hostile hands would pose a problem for the United States in the Caribbean and the Gulf of Mexico. As just mentioned, however, it cannot threaten to bottle up the US Navy and merchant marine, as Taiwan can to China. Moreover, unlike China's financial, industrial, and demographic centers, which are concentrated on its eastern seaboard, those for the United States are much more dispersed geographically. Given Taiwan's strategic importance to China—compared to that of Cuba to the United States—one can again imagine the significant stake that Beijing feels it has in Taiwan's status. If Washington is willing to risk a nuclear confrontation over Cuba, how much risk is Beijing likely to accept in a showdown over Taiwan?

Just like Japan's attack on Pearl Harbor discussed in chapter 3, the Cuban Missile Crisis and a potential conflict over Taiwan are examples of extended deterrence, except that the role of the defender is reversed in these cases. As we have seen, in 1941, Washington's threat to intervene on behalf of the European colonial powers motivated Japan to attack Pearl Harbor. In a potential conflict over Taiwan's status, Washington would again be in the role of a protector for a junior partner to deter an attack by China. It has evidently not occurred to many Americans that in the Cuban Missile Crisis, the USSR was acting to deter a US attack on its protégé Cuba. Similarly, the Chinese intervention in the Korean War can be seen as an instance of Beijing attempting extended deterrence to protect North Korea, except that in this case, this attempt failed because the United States ignored Beijing's warnings, and General MacArthur marched his troops north to unify Korea under a pro-US regime, the so-called home-by-Christmas offensive (Chen 1994; Whiting 1962).

As I explained in chapter 3, Washington's deterrence threat against Japan in 1941 worked in convincing Tokyo that it could not attack the European colonial powers in Southeast Asia without having to also fight the United States. Washington's attempt at extended deterrence thus backfired in directing Tokyo's armed hostilities to itself, as the Japanese would naturally have much preferred not to fight the United States. The parallel suggested by this episode to a possible conflict over Taiwan should be obvious: the United States is again undertaking extended deterrence in attempting to protect a third party—in this case, Taiwan. It is interjecting itself in China's civil war from Beijing's perspective. Deng Xiaoping, China's paramount leader during the late 1970s and 1980s, was blunt in telling US officials that in Chinese eyes, the Taiwan issue is fundamentally a US issue—without Washington "having Taipei's back," Taiwan's reunification with China would have been resolved much more quickly and easily.

As discussed earlier, if we take the Kremlin's word at its face value, then Soviet extended deterrence in Cuba worked. The installation of missiles in Cuba achieved its ostensible purpose of extracting a US pledge not to invade Cuba again. Naturally, this interpretation of history is not widely accepted in popular US narratives about this crisis. We cannot be sure of what exactly motivated Khrushchev to introduce missiles to Cuba (Allison 1971), but we do know that the United States has not tried to invade Cuba again or to seek the overthrow of Castro's regime by military means since the Cuban Missile Crisis in 1962. Counterfactual reasoning would prompt us to ask whether the United States would likely have invaded Cuba again in the absence of Moscow's gambit and the rumored secret deal that it had reached with the USSR for Moscow to withdraw its missiles. James D. Fearon (1997) tells his readers that in order for a deterrence threat to be made credible to its intended target, a country must run risks and bear costs that a bluffing country would not be willing to accept. By taking on these risks and costs, the country making the deterrence threat shows that it is sincere, thus separating (or distinguishing) itself from one that is merely bluffing and engaged in "empty talk."

We know that prior to 1962, the USSR had never installed nuclear weapons outside of its boundaries—not even on the soil of its Warsaw Pact allies in Eastern and Central Europe. Cuba was *the* exception that broke the rule. One might agree with the Kennedy administration that the introduction of these weapons to Cuba was a rather audacious, bold, reckless, or, if you will, risky and costly gambit. According to Fearon's logic, this action demonstrated Moscow's resolve or its serious commitment to defend Cuba. The nonoccurrence of another US invasion of Cuba or an attempt to overthrow Castro's regime since 1962 suggests that Moscow's extended deterrence worked. As remarked earlier, analysts do not pay nearly enough attention to the nonoccurrence of events, especially events that could have been expected otherwise.

There is, however, one problem with the above interpretation—namely, the USSR had tried to conceal the presence of its missiles in Cuba. If it had wished to demonstrate its resolve to defend this protégé, it should have publicized the introduction of these missiles to show its commitment to Cuba. Perhaps it was not publicized because Khrushchev did not want to force Kennedy's hand by causing a domestic uproar in the United States. We do not know. Yet the whole point of deterrence is to demonstrate—and publicize—one's resolve by committing one's reputation publicly to a course of action that could not be reversed easily without causing one to suffer serious political costs. Tomás Diez Acosta (2002) reports that in July 1962, Havana and Moscow had signed a defense treaty, including the deployment of Soviet missiles on the island (Operation Anadyr). Yet, according to him, Nikita Khrushchev had insisted that this treaty be kept secret. If so, this behavior does not conform to what one would expect from a committed defender. After all, a treaty is supposed to communicate to other states the defender's serious intention to intervene on behalf of its protégé in the event of war. A sincere defender would have publicized its commitment to this protégé in order to lend credibility to its declared commitment. The public nature of this declaration would mean that it could not easily retract its commitment without suffering serious reputational damage. This prospective damage thus makes its pledge to defend its protégé more credible because an insincere defender would not have taken on this cost. Only a determined defender would deliberately create this cost for itself because it does not expect itself to renege on its promise to defend its protégé. By locking itself in a commitment that it could not reverse without significant cost, the defender demonstrates its resolve and separates itself from an insincere defender.

For the same reason, Washington's heretofore policy of strategic ambiguity toward Taiwan—a posture that essentially refuses to precommit the United States to the defense of this island—is suspect. Fearon argues that extended deterrence involves a binary choice: to commit or not to commit to another state's defense. A declaration that "I *may* fight you, if you cross the redline" is inherently not credible because the target of this deterrence threat expects that a serious and sincere defender would have said "I will *definitely* fight you, if you cross the redline." Of course, concerns about moral hazard may incline the defender to hedge its support for the protégé lest this associate should undertake provocative actions that cause the target of deterrence to attack—precisely what the defender wants to prevent in the first place (Benson 2012). As mentioned earlier, Taipei may be emboldened to declare independence and thereby cause Beijing to attack if it is confident that Washington is irrevocably committed to its defense.

Berlin only realized just before the outbreak of war in 1914 that Britain would join the fight against it. Perhaps it was false hope or wishful thinking on its part that Berlin did not come to this realization earlier. Perhaps, British diplomacy had also played a role. London had been hesitant to come out definitely in support of Paris because obviously it would—and should—have been concerned that France might use Britain's commitment to provoke Germany for its own purposes. Moral hazard would then have inclined London to send more ambiguous signals to Berlin and Paris than it would otherwise have done.

If one accepts for argument's sake that the outcome of the Cuban Missile Crisis represented an instance of successful US compellence, what could account for it? What could explain the USSR's decision to back down? A plausible explanation would argue that Washington cared more about this issue and was more determined to have its way than Moscow—so much so that it was willing to run the risk of a nuclear confrontation with Moscow. Moreover, the United States held a stronger military hand than the USSR. Transferring this reasoning to a Sino-American conflict over Taiwan's status, Beijing presumably has a more intense preference, a larger stake in this dispute, and hence a stronger resolve than Washington. What can offset this asymmetry in motivation? Presumably, the answer is an asymmetry in military capabilities in favor of the United States. How much of an advantage must the United States have to override the asymmetry in motivation? We cannot be sure, although we do know that the military balance has shifted in recent years so that Washington's military advantage has eroded significantly. Perhaps the question boils down to whether Washington feels so strongly about Taiwan's status that it is willing to run the risk of a nuclear confrontation, as it had evidently felt this way about Soviet missiles in Cuba—whether for domestic political reasons or considerations of national security. Conversely, does Beijing feel so strongly about Taiwan's status that it is willing to run this risk? It has obviously so far decided not to run this risk. Conversely, will Washington eventually decide that the game is not worth the candle? According to the popular US narrative of successful compellence in the case of Cuba, an asymmetry in motivation caused Moscow to back down—that is, Khrushchev decided that Soviet missiles on that island did not warrant the risk of nuclear escalation.

For the sake of argument, let us say that a major difference in the US role in Cuba and Taiwan is that Washington was engaged in compellence in the former case and has been engaged in deterrence in the latter case. As mentioned earlier in reference to Levy's remark about prospect theory, it is more challenging to undertake successful compellence than successful deterrence because the former forces a counterpart to accept an actual loss, whereas the latter tries to prevent it from making a potential gain. Here is then another asymmetry in motivation—one that has apparently worked thus far in keeping peace in the Taiwan Strait.

But Beijing's patience is not infinite, and Chinese leaders have said that the Taiwan impasse cannot be passed forever from generation to generation without a resolution. As China closes the gap that separates its military capabilities from that of the United States, Washington's deterrence threat—that it has such a large stake in Taiwan's status that it is willing to run the risk of a nuclear confrontation—becomes less credible. Charles de Gaulle's apprehensions about relying on US nuclear deterrence, mentioned earlier, again comes to mind. An anonymous Chinese general has supposedly questioned Washington's resolve: "You [the United States] care more about Los Angeles than Taiwan!" (quoted in Cabestan 2024, 91).

Among other conclusions, the discussion in this chapter reminds us that some historical parallels or analogies come more readily to mind than others and that people from different backgrounds and political perspectives recall or reach for different historical episodes in attempting to illuminate their respective decision situations and search for policy options. Evidently, some historical memories come to people more naturally than others—and for understandable psychological reasons. They are more likely to remember or retrieve some past incidents than others, especially those that are vivid, traumatic, recent, and that have happened to them personally or to those close to them. Analogous situations that place them in an unfavorable or unflattering light are less likely to be brought up, and as I will discuss later in connection with attribution theory, people tend to apply different logic to explain similar actions by themselves and by others. Finally, this chapter's discussion points to the importance of empathy. Officials and scholars alike should try to put themselves in the shoes of other people and imagine how they would see or react to a situation from other people's vantage point. Buzan and Goh (2020) remark that people need to apply the same standards that they use to judge others to evaluate their own conduct. There is a Chinese saying about knowing yourself and knowing your counterpart and thereby becoming invincible in all battles (*Zhi ji zhi bi, bai zhan bu dai* 知己知彼, 百战不殆). Introspection would also have a good therapeutic effect as it helps to curb one's sense of self-righteousness.

SIX

The Falklands/Malvinas Conflict and Lessons for Taiwan

The war fought by Argentina and Britain in their dispute over the Falklands/Malvinas in 1982 does not usually come up in conversations about China's rise and narratives about a possible armed clash between this country and the United States. Yet this case strikes me as very pertinent to the ongoing dispute about Taiwan's status, which is the most likely source for Beijing and Washington exchanging blows. Among other things, the Falklands/Malvinas conflict was an unwanted war, a conflict that neither Argentina nor Britain had sought and one that both would have liked to avoid. It offers several important parallels to the tension across the Taiwan Strait for analysts and officials to reflect on.

The Falklands/Malvinas are located about three hundred miles from the southern coast of Argentina, but they are separated from Britain by about eight thousand miles. This geographic fact also applies to Taiwan, which is about one hundred miles from China's coast but over 7,600 miles from the US mainland. The United States has military bases and installations in South Korea, Japan, and the Philippines, but in a possible conflict over Taiwan, China will still be operating in or near its "home court." This asymmetry makes a large difference in the relative capabilities between the prospective belligerents because of what Kenneth E. Boulding (1962, 262) calls "the loss-of-strength gradient." The farther away a country has to fight from its homeland, the greater will be the diminution of its fighting capabilities. In all these cases, protectors of the Falklands/Malvinas, Taiwan, and, one might add, Cuba (from the USSR's perspective, see chapter 5) can "go home" as war exhaustion sets in, leaving their respective protégés to their own devices to live with a large, powerful neighbor. This observation, of course, also applies to the ongoing Russo-Ukrainian War, which will be the subject of the next chapter's discussion. One may question my argument by pointing out that Britain in the Falklands/Malvinas and China in the Taiwan case are not foreign third parties in the dispute in question because, after all, both see the islands being contested to belong to their respective sovereign jurisdictions. As discussed in chapter 5, extended deterrence involving a foreign third party applies more accurately to the USSR's role as a protector of Cuba in 1962, China's role as a protector of North Korea in 1950, and, of course, the US role in Taiwan and South Vietnam.

Distance not only points to physical separation but also signifies emotional attachment and historical ties. It can be a reasonable surrogate to indicate the relative stake, the relative resolve, and the relative salience of a dispute for the parties involved. Which side is more committed to its cause, more determined to stand its ground, and more willing to endure the hardships and privations caused by war? In this respect, US support for Taiwan and Ukraine appears to be more vulnerable to reversal than that for China and Russia, which are more likely to outlast their opponent in a protracted conflict politically and psychologically, if not also necessarily physically in the "burn rate," or the rate at which stocks of war materiel are drawn down. The same logic applies to the "attrition rate" with respect to war-related casualties. Which country is more able and willing to accept combat casualties? It stands to reason that a country fighting for itself would be in a stronger position, politically and psychologically, to sustain this loss than one that is fighting for someone else. One of the ostensible conclusions drawn from Washington's experience in Lebanon in the wake of a suicide bomber's attack on the US Marine barracks in Beirut in 1983, its encounter with Somali National Alliance under the control of Mohammed Farah Aidid in the Battle of Mogadishu in 1993 (depicted in the movie *Blackhawk Down*), and naturally also its wars in Korea, Vietnam, and Afghanistan is that Washington has an allergy to body bags returning home from foreign conflicts. Although Americans are likely to rally initially to support their government's military actions abroad, this support tends to fall precipitously as a conflict becomes protracted.

As shown in those episodes mentioned above and others, such as the US invasion of Iraq, patience, stamina, perseverance, and endurance—and not just raw muscle power—also matter in influencing the outcome of armed conflicts. These differences on the part of the disputants as well as differences in their respective abilities to extract, mobilize, and deploy resources and their respective willingness to tolerate pain and suffer hardship for their cause are intangible but nevertheless important factors affecting how lopsided conflicts in the past have ended in the Davids prevailing over the Goliaths (Arreguin-Toft 2005; Kugler and Arbetman 1997; Kugler and Domke 1986; Mack 1975; Merom 2003; Record 2007). That the United States has sought to fight foreign wars without accepting the risk of domestic political backlash by raising taxes to fund these undertakings or resorting to conscription to meet its needs for military personnel speaks volumes. Of course, military draft has been unpopular and contributed to the domestic opposition against the Vietnam War, for example. In a prospective war against China, it is more difficult to imagine that Washington could expect to have a victory "on the cheap."

Compared to studies of some other armed conflicts, such as the two world wars, the Falklands/Malvinas episode has received much less academic attention. It offers, however, in my view, some important implications for the danger of a Sino-American clash over Taiwan's status in addition to the role of geography suggested just now.

First, in situations of pivotal deterrence (also known as dual deterrence), Washington is supposed to be in a better position to discourage a war from happening between its two allies, and if an armed conflict nevertheless breaks out, it is also supposed to be in a uniquely advantageous position to mediate a truce and enforce a settlement between these allies (Crawford 2003). In contrast to other situations such as when the disputants are backed by competing great powers (e.g., recurrent crises over Berlin and Korea during the Cold War and several wars between India and Pakistan and between Israel and its Arab neighbors; Chan, forthcoming-a), situations of pivotal, or dual, deterrence are characterized by the fact that both disputants are US allies, and they cannot realistically turn to another great power for help (Crawford 2003). The border disputes between Ecuador and Peru and the conflict between Greece and

Turkey over Cyprus belong to this class of events. In these situations, Washington is in a uniquely influential position to discourage the disputants from fighting and, should fighting nevertheless occur, to stop it quickly and impose a ceasefire and settlement.

However, in contrast to the two cases just mentioned, US diplomacy was less effective in preventing armed conflict over Falklands/Malvinas between two of its allies, Argentina and Britain. Not only was Washington unable to stop large-scale combat from happening, but its subsequent attempts to mediate a settlement also encountered significant resistance from both Buenos Aires and London (Lippincott and Treverton 1988). Washington's relations with Buenos Aires became especially strained and tense. Not only were the Argentines seriously disappointed that their supposed special relationship with the United States did not produce the expected support—or at least neutrality—from Washington, but also they learned that Washington was actually secretly supporting London, such as by providing intelligence about Argentina's military to the British (Buenos Aires had thought that having played a special role in assisting the United States in waging a "dirty" covert war against Latin America's leftists, especially Nicaragua's Sandinistas, it had earned a special status in US eyes). The larger point of this discussion, however, is that it is much more daunting for Washington to head off a conflict between China and Taiwan compared to the Falklands/Malvinas case, in which war still broke out even though neither belligerent had wanted to fight. The Falklands/Malvinas war should have been an "easy test" for Washington's deterrence policy. The fact that war was not averted in this case highlights how stopping a potential Sino-American crisis over Taiwan's status from escalating—creating a conflict in which the United States itself would be directly involved—is an even greater challenge.

It is relevant to interject an important caveat at this juncture—namely, the difficulty in being definitive about whether a deterrence strategy has succeeded. Some people may argue that a war over Taiwan has not occurred thus far indicates that Washington's deterrence against a possible attack by Beijing on that island has worked. One has certainly often heard similar assertions during the Cold War, such as NATO's supposed success in deterring a Soviet attack on Western Europe. Yet it is inherently difficult to explain the nonoccurrence of events—a phenomenon that can be due to many different plausible reasons. That Beijing has not attacked Taiwan and that Moscow did not invade Western Europe do not necessarily mean that US or NATO deterrence has succeeded. We could only make this assertion if we knew for certain that they would have done so in the absence of US or NATO deterrence efforts. But we actually do not know what their intentions would have been in the absence of these efforts. Former US secretary of state Henry Kissinger has said, "Since deterrence can only be tested negatively, by events that do *not* take place, and since it is never possible to demonstrate why something has not occurred, it became especially difficult to assess whether the existing policy was the best possible policy or a just barely effective one. Perhaps deterrence was even unnecessary because it was impossible to prove whether the adversary ever intended to attack in the first place" (quoted in Danilovic 2001, 9; italics in original). I am reminded of the following story. A boy in Brooklyn would come out of his house every day at noon, jumping up and down and screaming. One day a neighbor finally approached him and asked about his bizarre behavior. The boy answered that he was trying to scare away marauding elephants from invading the neighborhood. When the neighbor remarked, "But there are no elephants in Brooklyn," the boy responded, "You see, it worked."

I do not mean to suggest by this anecdote and my earlier remarks that China would not attack Taiwan in the absence of a US deterrence threat. It might, but a more likely scenario is that without Washington "having its back," Taipei would more likely succumb to Beijing's pressure and reach a negotiated settlement with Beijing, thus removing the need for Beijing to undertake a military invasion to seize the island. Of course, as suggested by Paul Krugman's remark that I have introduced earlier, social scientists cannot undertake controlled experiments as in the natural sciences. We cannot unwind history and determine to our satisfaction how it would have turned out differently if we were able to alter some key conditions that, in our view, were responsible for the occurrence or nonoccurrence of events.

Several pertinent points should be introduced at this juncture. First, as I have mentioned briefly in the earlier discussion, Washington has practiced a policy of strategic ambiguity with respect to Taiwan's status (Bush 2005, 2013). Beijing has thus far eschewed direct military coercion against this island. It has instead adopted largely a "soft" policy emphasizing trade and investment to enhance cross-strait economic interdependence and to influence Taiwan's public opinion in favor of its goal of national reunification. This "soft" approach, however, has thus far not paid off as Taiwan's people have shifted over time to a self-identification as Taiwanese rather than Chinese (Kastner 2022). Thus, as mentioned earlier, Beijing has increasingly indicated its impatience and frustration, warning that the resolution of this island's status cannot be postponed indefinitely from generation to generation. We encounter a similar situation in the case of Falklands/Malvinas. Responding to the Reagan administration's last-minute attempt to head off war between its two allies, the head of Argentina's military junta Leopoldo Galtieri replied, "Listen, we've been negotiating with these guys for donkey's years. They don't want to do anything. It is politically mandatory that we take action" (quoted in Lippincott and Treverton 1988, 16).

Second, an important lesson of the Falklands/Malvinas War—one that has often been overlooked or at least not accorded enough emphasis—is that an armed conflict can occur even though both sides in a dispute are reluctant to go to war. Neither London nor Buenos Aires had wanted war. They had been engaged in protracted diplomatic talk lasting several decades. During this time, various proposals to resolve the islands' status were considered (such as some form of joint administration and leaseback to British administration after acknowledging Argentina's sovereignty), but there was no breakthrough to overcome the impasse. London's position can perhaps be best described in the words of its Foreign Office Undersecretary for the Falklands, David Scott, who told his Argentinian counterpart, Ambassador Juan Carlos Beltramino, "While Britain would not countenance the rape of the Falklands, it would actively encourage their seduction" (quoted in Lippincott and Treverton 1988, 4). Buenos Aires had undertaken different "soft" means to woo the islands' residents (the Kelpers) to accept Argentina's sovereignty, including various proposals and measures to contribute to the improvement of their physical infrastructure (such as funding roads, schools, and television) and air service to travel to the mainland. None of these gestures yielded positive results from Argentina's perspective. Why? This takes us to the third lesson from this episode.

Third, once London accepted that the Kelpers had a role in negotiating with Buenos Aires, in effect framing this dispute as a matter of self-determination and thus a case in which the Kelpers had a vote, this decision pretty much foreclosed the possibility of a definitive settlement. Although the Kelpers would naturally welcome economic largesse and other kinds of goodwill gestures from Argentina (e.g., travel documents and airline flights to visit

Argentina), they preferred not to succumb to its rule. Their position is understandable. They wanted to have the benefits of access to Argentina (which, as already mentioned, is much closer to them and thus more relevant to their daily lives) *and* also the continuation of British protection. They wanted to have their cake and eat it too. By in effect giving the Kelpers a veto on the resolution of the islands' political status, London had ensured that its dispute with Buenos Aires would be perpetuated. Not to put too fine a point on it, the Kelpers—whose number was about 1,800—were put in the driver's seat once the problem was defined by London as a matter of self-determination—hence a tale of the tail wagging the dog.

This framing of the issue as one of self-determination was naturally contested by Argentina, which advanced its cause as a matter of sovereignty and recovery from the indignities of colonialism. This situation of competing definitions of the dispute is also reflected in other cases where one of the disputants claims the right of self-determination and the other asserts the principle of sovereignty. These contesting views characterize the dispute over Taiwan's status and other controversies regarding the right of secession, such as by the Bosnians, Kosovans, Bengalis, Kurds, Crimeans, and the residents of Ukraine's Donbass region.

In objecting to Crimea's breakaway from Ukraine and its annexation by Russia, Washington has argued that these actions were contrary to international law because they did not comply with Ukraine's constitution nor were they approved by the entire Ukrainian population—in direct contradiction to its policy of supporting Taiwan's de facto independence. Here, again, we encounter the phenomenon that some historical parallels are more likely to be recalled or applied than others. The more "inconvenient" ones are usually overlooked, sometimes inadvertently but also sometimes deliberately, by political entrepreneurs in constructing their narratives to frame policy agenda and mobilize public support for their favored policy course. For example, US commentators and pundits rarely bring up Israel's annexation of Palestinian land or the failure of successive US governments to take effective action against this annexation when they criticize Russia's annexation of Ukrainian territory. Of course, Washington was quick to resort to military force to reverse Iraq's annexation of Kuwait. But it has reacted differently to Israel's annexation of Palestinian land and Iraq's seizure of Kuwait. Perhaps one of the reasons for this difference is oil, or more precisely, Washington did not want to have Iraq controlling a commanding amount of oil exports from the Middle East.

As talks between Britain and Argentina about Falklands/Malvinas dragged on, Buenos Aires began to feel increasingly frustrated as its negotiations with London and its friendly gestures toward the Kelpers failed to produce any tangible progress. Richard Ned Lebow (1985, 104) writes, "[Buenos Aires] came increasingly to believe, and not without reason that they were behaving like the proverbial donkey, tricked into pulling the cart by a carrot on a stick dangled before him." In the words of one US State Department official, the Argentinians felt that "the British were stringing them along and jerking them around" (quoted in Lippincott and Treverton 1988, 7).

Readers who are familiar with Taiwan's hugely asymmetric dependency on trade with and investment in mainland China can immediately see the parallel. Taipei wants the benefits of its economic ties with the Chinese mainland while continuing to resist Beijing's entreaties urging political reunification. Bilateral talks had produced some progress during Mao Ying-jeou's administration, when both sides agreed on the so-called One China Consensus—a formulation that was deliberately vague to allow each side to define what "China" means (to the Nationalists, or the Kuomintang, on Taiwan's side, China means the Republic of China, whereas to Beijing, it refers to the People's Republic of China). Even this superficial agreement, however, has since become unglued after candidates of the pro-independence Democratic Progressive Party came to power in successive presidencies and denied either the existence or the validity of this accord.

What had prevented an agreement to resolve the impasse over the status of the Falklands/Malvinas? Besides the Kelpers' role, domestic politics in Britain were important. Every time London came close to a settlement with Bueno Aires, conservative backbenchers in the parliament cried "sellout." The Falkland Islands Emergency Committee was a powerful lobby on behalf of the islanders, and the local press was also actively involved in arousing public and parliamentary indignation with headlines such as "The Islands That Britain May Give Away" (Lippincott and Treverton 1988, 3). The Falkland Islands Association continued to mobilize support for the Kelpers' right to decide their own future. Racism was obviously a factor. While self-determination was invoked for co-ethnics in the Falklands/Malvinas, this issue was brushed aside in other cases such as the repatriation of Hong Kong to China. While its dispute with Argentina lingered on, the British government was actively discussing passing a Nationality Act for the purpose of restricting the right of people of its former colonies—mostly black, brown, and yellow people from Africa and Asia—to come to Britain and become British citizens.

Returning to the topic about Britain's domestic politics and its policy-making process, there never appeared to be a good time to settle the dispute with Buenos Aires. When Argentina raised the temperature to force a deal, it was argued that Britain should not yield under pressure. During times when things were calm, the excuse was if it ain't broke, don't fix it. The Falklands/Malvinas dispute did not then rise to the top of London's agenda, requiring a sense of urgency to resolve what could be a ticking time bomb. The predisposition was always to kick the can down the road. Here again, the parallel with Taiwan should be evident. From Beijing's perspective, it has been waiting for over seventy-five years. As already mentioned, its leaders have indicated that their patience is not infinite, and the Taiwan issue cannot be postponed forever. In fact, seen from Beijing's perspective, it has been precisely Washington's aim to perpetuate the Taiwan impasse. This impasse serves US aims better by being kept alive rather than resolved, thus giving Washington bargaining leverage with Beijing over other matters—and working as a thorn in Beijing's side to irritate it occasionally (Chan, forthcoming-a, forthcoming-c). Of course, should Taiwan be annexed by China, Beijing's gain would further exacerbate the ongoing power shift to Washington's detriment. This consideration did not apply to the Falklands/Malvinas because possession of these islands would not have mattered for Britain's security. Argentina's gain would not have put Buenos Aires in a position to threaten Britain.

Evidently, maintaining the current situation—that is, Taiwan remaining a separate political entity from China and thus retaining its de facto independence (but refraining from declaring its de jure independence)—is just fine from Washington's perspective. This situation avoids the liabilities of having Beijing taking over the island—a change that would only further improve China's power position (see my previous discussion of Taiwan's strategic importance to China in chapter 5) and, at the same time, help reduce the danger of a war with China. But as time passes and the military balance becomes less unfavorable to Beijing, why should it put up with the perpetuation of Taiwan's de facto independence in exchange for the US promise to oppose its de jure independence—precisely what Washington's policy of dual deterrence is supposed to be about all along? This policy, also described as strategic ambiguity, seeks to prevent any "unpeaceful" resolution of Taiwan's status, meaning that the United States opposes Beijing resorting to force to reunify with Taiwan and, at the same time, opposes Taiwan formally declaring its independence. Like the Kelpers, the Americans want to have their cake and eat it too.

Of course, all sides know fully well that it has been Washington's backing of Taipei that has created the current deadlock, which, however, as just pointed out, is more appealing to Washington when considering the alternatives. To put the matter even more bluntly, from the US perspective, keeping the Taiwan controversy alive is more advantageous to it than settling it as this dispute continues to enable Washington to play the "Taiwan card" in negotiating with Beijing.

The same logic applies to Washington's bottom line—shared by Beijing and Tokyo—that a divided Korea but one whose tension is kept from boiling over suits its purposes just fine. This is another way of saying that all three would prefer to see Korea continue to be divided rather than unified for Realpolitik reasons of divide and rule. Of course, we do not expect their officials to say so publicly. Another implication of this line of reasoning is that, ironically, Washington, Beijing, and Tokyo have more in common in their basic views and interests than they care to admit with respect to Korea.

Returning to the Taiwan issue, as just mentioned, why should Beijing put up with a situation that subjects Taiwan's status deliberately to perpetual limbo or impasse, especially considering that this issue gives the United States a constant bargaining lever to gain concessions from Beijing and to irritate Beijing by "pushing its buttons" on this sensitive issue? There is, of course, an important difference between London's policymaking process regarding the status of the Falklands/Malvinas and Washington's policymaking process regarding Taiwan. Whereas in London's case, a definitive settlement of the islands' status escaped top-level attention due to a crowded agenda, the constant distraction to attend to other pressing matters, and its resolution encountering repeated objections from the political opposition and adverse public opinion, Washington's attitudes toward Taiwan disclose a deliberate attempt to "play for time" and to "gum up the works." Again, not to put too fine a point on it, it is preferable for Washington that the Taiwan issue remains unsettled rather than resolved as long as it does not boil over as it gives the United States an important lever in bargaining with China. Neither a Taiwan reunified with China nor a war over its status would be in Washington's interest. The dispute over Taiwan's status is worth more to Washington if kept alive than buried. Kicking the can down the road by maintaining the current situation suits its interests best.

Washington's public statements, of course, deny this motive, claiming that its interest is in defending democracy and Taiwanese people's right to self-determination. Beijing sees these claims to be disingenuous. US support for Taiwan was strongest when the island was ruled by an authoritarian regime and martial law prior to its recent democratization. Naturally, a critical part of Washington's heretofore policy of strategic ambiguity has been to deny the island's de jure independence as a quid pro quo for Beijing not to invade it—whether its people are in favor of it or not. That the United States opposes Taiwan's de jure independence even if the majority of its people favor it belies its declared commitment to their right to self-determination.

There was evidence of miscalculation and wishful thinking in the leadup to war in the case of Falklands/Malvina. As already indicated, Argentina's leaders had believed that Washington would take its side in its conflict with Britain—or that the United States would at least remain neutral in this conflict. They were mistaken in this belief. General Leopoldo Galtieri indicated after the war that he would not have started it had he known that Washington would oppose Argentina and support Britain (Paul 1994, 159). Argentina's foreign minister Costa Mendez had also acknowledged that Buenos Aires had banked on Washington's support or at least its neutrality. As already indicated, in these officials' view, Argentina enjoyed the status of a "privileged ally" in Washington because it had done some of the dirty work for the United States in fighting leftists in Latin America. Moreover, Argentina's leaders had hoped for a quick invasion and seizure of the disputed islands, thus presenting a fait accompli to the British, who, in their eyes, would be reluctant to use force to reverse this situation. On this important point, they were again seriously mistaken. In the words of one US State Department expert, "The Argentines just could not believe that the British were going to send their fleet 16,000 miles [round trip] to recover land that was obviously more important to Argentina than it was to Britain, at least in the view of the Argentines" (quoted in Lippincott and Treverton 1988, 14).

Indeed, even US officials had their doubts about Britain's resolve, with one of them expressing the view that "the idea that the Brits would seriously launch an invasion from eight thousand miles away seemed rather ludicrous and the stakes seemed so piddling, way down there in the windswept South Atlantic" (quoted in Lippincott and Treverton 1988, 11). Even after the British flotilla had departed for the Falklands/Malvinas to retake these islands from Argentina, Buenos Aires continued to believe that London was bluffing and that Washington was assisting London in this ruse. They were mistaken because they had overlooked the dynamics of domestic politics in Britain. Prime Minister Margaret Thatcher was under tremendous pressure not to let Argentina's aggression stand. A British Cabinet member had supposedly confided to a reporter, saying, "To be frank, I don't see how she [Margaret Thatcher] can survive [politically] if she shrinks from a military showdown" (quoted in Lebow 1985, 117). This view was basically confirmed by British ambassador Nicholas Henderson, who told US secretary of state Alexander Haig, "Argentina must withdraw; anything less would mean the fall of the Thatcher government" (quoted Lippincott and Treverton 1988, 12).

Domestic politics also played a decisive role in the Argentinean leaders' decision to resort to arms at the time when they did. Their campaign of terror against real and suspected leftists in their own country and their dismal economic performance increased their incentives to restore their legitimacy in the eyes of their public by asserting their nationalist credentials in a classic case of diversionary theory of war (Abeledo 2016; Lippincott and Treverton 1988). Responding to Haig's entreaties and threats demanding that Argentina withdraw its armed forces from the Falklands/Malvinas, Galtieri confided in him that "he [Galtieri] could not withdraw both his military and his administrative presence from the Malvinas and last a week" (quoted in Lippincott and Treverton 1988, 19).

These remarks point to the importance of domestic incentives to start or continue a foreign conflict—something that is generally overlooked in some prevailing theories of international relations, which tend to privilege structural factors, such as the interstate system's polarity or changes in the interstate distribution of power. One would assume that the stakes for Chinese leaders in a crisis involving Taiwan would be no less than for British leaders in the Falklands/Malvinas case—even if we disregard Taiwan's much greater strategic and symbolic importance for Beijing.

I have quoted Thomas C. Schelling (1966) earlier to emphasize that the other party in a dispute also has its reputation and prestige to consider, and it is therefore important to always create or provide an exit option for one's foreign counterpart to disengage without losing face rather than backing it into a corner to choose between accepting national humiliation and lashing out in a desperate gamble, as Japan did in December 1941. John F. Kennedy was aware of and sensitive to this consideration during the Cuban Missile Crisis. He ordered his subordinates not to embarrass Khrushchev over his decision to withdraw Soviet missiles. In fact, the secret deal he reached with Khrushchev appealed to the latter's incentives to accept a compromise and avert further escalation of the conflict.

Parenthetically, the timing of the Falklands/Malvinas war also stemmed from the Argentineans' miscalculation. They were forced to initiate military invasion (Operation Rosario) of the Falklands/Malvinas before they were fully prepared because when London ordered its marines to evict Constantine Davidoff, an Argentinean merchant of scrap iron, from the South Georgia island in March 1982, Buenos Aires was forced to respond—a contingency that it had not anticipated before Davidoff's landing. If they had waited for the British icebreaker *Endurance*, with its contingent of twenty-five marines, to leave the South Atlantic, as it was scheduled to do, and postponed their invasion of the Falklands/Malvinas for six months, when winter would have returned to the Southern Hemisphere and impaired the British military response, the outcome of the war could have been different.

As indicated earlier, Britain was quite willing to "unload" the Falklands/Malvinas if a face-saving, "dignified" way could be found to concede to Argentina's sovereignty claim. This inclination, however, was frustrated repeatedly by domestic partisan politics. The war that did happen was an unwanted war; if only the two sides could have found a way to finesse the situation, it could have been avoided. The Falklands/Malvinas are barren, wind-swept, thinly populated islands located far away from the British Isles and lack any strategic or economic value to London. As such, their importance lied mostly in their symbolic importance in Argentinean and British domestic politics. These countries went to war largely for this symbolic reason in the context of their respective domestic political situations.

The final lesson that I draw from the Falklands/Malvinas case is that Britain's victory in retaking these islands from Argentina was a Pyrrhic one. Even though, as suggested earlier, London was willing to compromise with Buenos Aires for a settlement over these islands' status—although timing never seemed right for this settlement to take place, and objections from the Kelpers and their backers in Britain always turned out to be insurmountable obstacles to this settlement—now, more than ever before, Britain is "stuck" with the defense and maintenance of this distant possession with a small population and little strategic or economic value. How long is London willing to sustain this situation? How long before this situation becomes untenable? It is difficult to defy the harsh geographic reality that these islands lie much closer to Argentina than Britain, with all the ensuing implications regarding the contestants' asymmetric economic and military leverage with the passage of time.

Why do I dwell on the relevance of the Falklands/Malvinas case for Taiwan? In addition to the various considerations already introduced, it is highly pertinent to share Singapore's former prime minister Lee Kuan Yew's thoughts on this topic. Lee was asked at a public forum for his opinion on whether the United States would intervene in a war against China over Taiwan. Lee's answer was quick and succinct. He said no (Lee 2013). His reason was simple. The United States might win the first time. But what about the next time? And the time after that and so on and so forth? In other words, how do Washington's patience, endurance, and perseverance compare with Beijing's? Presumably, their differences in these respects reflect their relative stakes in this dispute. One would presume that the side with a larger stake would more likely stand its ground and have a higher threshold for bearing costs and enduring privations in order to have its way. The outcomes of the Vietnam and Afghan Wars appear to confirm this proposition. Lee's point is, of course, that if US leaders take a long-term view, they will likely decide that the game is not worth the candle. Better not get into a morass in the first place. Naturally, leaders in Taipei are not so dense or oblivious to overlook this consideration. The United States may become impatient, distracted, or exhausted and go home, but they will still be "stuck" with their larger neighbor. How the "end game" will evolve must have surely also occurred to Ukraine's leaders, whose war with Russia I will turn to in the next chapter.

This chapter offers several takeaways. First, even when countries are initially inclined to come to a settlement to avoid war, they may still find themselves fighting in the end. The main reason for this phenomenon stems from domestic politics. Partisan considerations may impede and prevent a compromise even when leaders on both sides realize that their countries would be better off reaching a deal to avoid war. In other words, the rational unitary model, which analysts often apply to explain foreign policymaking, may be seriously flawed to the extent that it overlooks the importance of domestic political influences in leaders' decision calculations.

Second, states often find themselves fighting for intangible or symbolic reasons—reasons that are nevertheless important to their respective officials. Compared to almost all other recent interstate conflicts or disputes, the Falklands/Malvinas appear to offer little, if any, strategic or economic advantage to the contesting sides. Yet Argentina and Britain found themselves at war. Third, and paradoxically, my references to the impasse over Taiwan (and briefly to the situation regarding a divided Korea) also argue that states, especially major powers, may have an incentive in keeping local feuds alive rather than helping to resolve them. Fourth, self-determination is, of course, a laudable goal, but it is also a principle that has often been overlooked or deemphasized when major powers find its application to be inconvenient or contrary to their Realpolitik interests. The Falklands/Malvinas episode, however, also points to the danger of trapping oneself in a cul-de-sac. Having defined the matter as one over which the Kelpers would have a veto, London practically ensured that this dispute would linger rather than be resolved. London should have realized that the Kelpers would be reluctant to accept Argentinean sovereignty as long as they could expect continued British protection.

Fifth, by siding with Britain and helping London retake the Falklands/Malvinas, the United States belied its own Monroe Doctrine seeking to exclude European influence from the Western Hemisphere. It also undermined the idea of establishing a zone free of nuclear weapons in Latin America. Michael Barletta and Harold Trinkunas (2004, 346) write, "In Buenos Aires, rumors circulated that Britain had made nuclear threats against Argentina, and British news reports 'confirmed' these threats after the conflict. London was widely seen as having violated the Treaty of Tlatelolco, that aims to make Latin America a nuclear-weapons-free zone. South American policymakers viewed U.S. support for British reconquest of the islands as an abrogation of the inter-American defensive alliance, voiding the U.S. security guarantee to Latin American states against extra-regional incursions."

Finally, myopia often takes precedence over long-term thinking. As Lee Kuan Yew's answer to the question of whether the United States would intervene militarily in a contingency involving Taiwan indicates, consideration of the long-term implications of this involvement would discourage Washington from intervening. It is often easier to start a war than to conclude it. If leaders think about how they will end a war that they are about to initiate, they will perhaps be more reluctant to start it. This was, of course, the fatal mistake made by the Japanese leaders when they decided to attack Pearl Harbor. They should have considered much more thoroughly the "end game" to conclude their war against the United States. Of course, had British leaders thought about long-term consequences, it would seem that they would probably have reconsidered their decisions in the Falkland/Malvinas dispute—especially if in the long run, Britain would still be unable to hold on to these islands even if they wished to. This conjecture would seem reasonable, but I would not wager on it because politicians typically think in the short term, especially when the next election is just around the corner. Thus, political expediency often inclines officials to emphasize the short-term consequences of their decision—especially if they are the ones who will have to pay the political price for the immediate repercussions of their policy, whereas their successors will be the beneficiaries in the long run, or, at least, these successors will be spared the costs stemming from short-term expediencies based on domestic partisan reasoning.

SEVEN

Ukraine Today, Taiwan Tomorrow?

Russia invaded Ukraine in February 2022. Since then, there has been much talk of "Ukraine today, Taiwan tomorrow" (Taiwan Policy Centre 2022). This quote was the title of a 2022 study issued by Britain's nonprofit organization the Taiwan Policy Centre. It was also the title of a featured seminar sponsored by the Belfer Center of Harvard University's Kennedy School; moreover, the German Marshall Fund has issued a study on this topic (Parello-Plesner 2023). In addition, Chairman Michael McCaul of the Foreign Affairs Committee of the US House of Representatives participated in a discussion on the ABC (American Broadcasting Company) network, with the pointed title "Ukraine Today—It's Going to Be Taiwan Tomorrow" ("Chairman McCaul" 2023). These are just a few examples showing that people are reminded of possible parallels between these two cases or situations.

In a similar vein, Japanese prime minister Fumio Kishida, who was visiting the White House in April 2024, said, "Ukraine today may be East Asia tomorrow" (White House 2024). Those who mention Ukraine and Taiwan in the same breath probably have in mind that we have—or can have—in both situations an authoritarian government invading a smaller, peaceful, and democratic neighbor. They would be right in pointing to this similarity, even though they also often overlook other parallels between these two cases as well as dissimilarities between them (Chan 2022; Chan and Hu, forthcoming-b). "There is often little reason why those events that provide analogies should in fact be the best guides to the future . . . because outcomes are learned without careful attention to details of causation, lessons are superficial and overgeneralized . . . decision-makers do not examine a variety of analogies before selecting the one that they believe sheds the most light on their situation" (Jervis 1976, 281–82). Therefore, Richard E. Neustadt and Ernest R. May (1986b) urge their readers to be explicit when invoking analogies in their analyses, writing down the likenesses and differences between a current situation and a past instance that is being used to offer decision guidance. Some scholars (e.g., Rich, Banerjee, and Tkach 2023) have already called attention to some important differences between Ukraine and Taiwan. I will discuss these differences later.

Let us first turn to the idea of empathy. It is always a good idea to imagine our reaction if the shoe is on the other foot. I have already called attention to some parallels between Cuba's relations with the United States and Taiwan's relations with China, notwithstanding important differences that set them apart. In judging Russia's motivations leading to its invasion of Ukraine, we might consider a *Gedanken* experiment or a counterfactual mental exercise to consider what any US president would have done if Russia or China had sought to promote regime change in Mexico, seeking to install a pro-Russian or pro-Chinese government in Mexico City and recruit it to join an international coalition led by Moscow or Beijing. Judging by the Reagan administration's invasion of Grenada in 1983—a tiny Caribbean country, which cannot by any stretch of imagination be said to present a threat to the national security of the United States—the answer seems quite clear. The US government claimed that its invasion of this island was intended to protect the safety of some six hundred US medical students living on the island—a pretext that hardly anyone believed. The real purpose of the US invasion was to overthrow this island's rulers with a Communist sympathy. Ronald Reagan had characterized Grenada as a "Soviet-Cuban colony" and claimed that the invasion had happened "just in time," presumably to prevent a Communist takeover.

Kenneth N. Waltz (2000a, 31–32) muses, "Any country finds it difficult to understand how another country feels. Americans should, however, be able to imagine what their fears would be if they had lost the Cold War and Russia expanded the WTO [Warsaw Treaty Organization] into the Americas, all the while claiming that it was acting for the sake of stability in central America with no threat to the United States implied." We already know how Beijing would react to the prospect of a pro-US government being installed right on its border. This prospect was the proximate reason for China's intervention—or rather counterintervention in the wake of US intervention—in the Korean War. Russia's reaction to a comparable situation was also predictable. The US response to Soviet missiles in Cuba was additionally instructive.

One can debate endlessly about "who started it" in the case of the ongoing war in Ukraine (e.g., Massie 2014; McFaul, Sestanovich, and Mearsheimer 2014). In a series of articles, John J. Mearsheimer (2014, 2022a, 2022b, 2023) warns about the danger of the West's persistent effort to extend the European Union and NATO eastward right up to Russia's border. He did not mince words, as one of his articles was entitled "Why the Ukraine Crisis Is the West's Fault" (Mearsheimer 2014). He pointed out that Russia would view Ukraine joining NATO as an existential threat, arguing that the Kremlin's response was defensive in resisting this Western encroachment on its traditional turf. Therefore, the West, in his view, bears considerable responsibility for the ongoing war between Ukraine and Russia. Elsewhere, Vladimir Putin was quoted saying,

> With NATO's eastward expansion the situation for Russia has been becoming worse and more dangerous by the year. . . . We cannot stay idle and passively observe these developments. This would be an absolutely irresponsible thing to do for us. . . . For our country, it is a matter of life and death, a matter of our historical future as a nation. This is not an exaggeration; this is a fact. It is not only a very real threat to our interests but to the very existence of our state and to its sovereignty. It is the red line we have spoken about on numerous occasions. They have crossed it. (Mearsheimer and Rosato 2023, xi–xii)

Mearsheimer was not the only one to have warned about Russia's pushback. George F. Kennan (1997), the architect of the US containment policy after World War II, was also opposed to NATO expansion, warning, "Expanding NATO would be the most fateful error of American policy in the entire post-cold-war era." Note that Kennan's warning was made in 1997, some twenty-five years before Russia invaded Ukraine. William Burns (2019, 233), former US ambassador to Russia, also issued a warning in 2008, long before Russia's invasion of Ukraine in February 2022, writing, "Ukraine's entry into

NATO is the brightest of all red lines for the Russian elite (not just Putin). In more than two and a half years of conversations with key Russian players, from knuckle-draggers in the dark recesses of the Kremlin to Putin's liberal critics, I have yet to find anyone who views Ukraine in NATO as anything other than a direct challenge to Russian interests. . . . I can conceive of no grand package that would allow the Russians to swallow this pill quietly." John J. Mearsheimer and Sebastian Rosato (2023, 127) write, "In June 1997, fifty former senators, cabinet secretaries, ambassadors, and foreign policy specialists sent an open letter to President Bill Clinton, declaring that the current US-led effort to expand NATO . . . is a policy error of historic importance." They also cite Michael Mandelbaum (1997), who had warned that "the Clinton plan [on NATO expansion] is therefore perfectly non-sensical. NATO expansion isn't just pointless. It's also dangerous." Kenneth N. Waltz (2000a, 31) points out that NATO enlargement would have the effect of bringing Russia and China closer, remarking, "To alienate Russia by expanding NATO and to alienate China by pressing it to change its policies and lecturing its leaders on how to rule their country, are policies that only an overwhelmingly powerful country could afford, and only a foolish one be tempted, to follow." Other adjectives regarding US views on Russian and Chinese concerns such as arrogant, ambitious, hubristic, and dismissive, even contemptuous, also come to mind. The prevailing US narrative nowadays arguing that Russia's invasion of Ukraine was an "unprovoked" war overlooks important details and disregards warnings from US academic experts and former government officials, not to mention Russian sources.

The West had precipitated the Russo-Ukrainian War by encroaching on Russia's traditional sphere of influence, even though Moscow had made unilateral and consequential concessions both before and after the USSR's collapse and disintegration. As Charles A. Kupchan (2010, 397) points out, "From Moscow's perspective, Russia for successive years made a series of concessions to the West, including accommodating NATO expansion, reacting with restraint to democratic revolutions in its 'near abroad,' and facilitating strategic access for the United States in Central Asia and Afghanistan." Moscow not only accepted the dissolution of the Warsaw Pact, the dismantlement of Communist rule in its former satellite countries in Eastern and Central Europe, and the secession of former constituent republics of the Soviet Union (including the Baltic states), it also consented to NATO membership for a united Germany. Although William Perry, former US secretary of defense in the Clinton administration, blamed Russia's actions in Ukraine, Syria, and elsewhere for the recent deterioration of Russo-American relations, he acknowledged that "gains [made shortly after the Cold War's end] were initially squandered more as a result of US than Russian actions" (quoted in Borger 2016). He, too, had opposed NATO's expansion, and he had even considered resigning over this issue. He described those US officials favoring NATO expansion as being contemptuous of a weak Russia. "Who cares what they think? They're a third-rate power" was their reply to Perry's objection to NATO expansion (Borger 2016).

The year 2008 was especially an important turning point. The NATO summit meeting in April 2008 declared that this alliance would welcome Georgia and Ukraine to join it. This announcement was preceded by Western countries' support of Kosovo's secession from former Yugoslavia and their recognition of it as an independent, sovereign state. Vladimir Putin warned, "We view appearance of a powerful military bloc on our borders . . . as a direct threat to the security of our country. The claim that this process is not directed against Russia will not suffice. National security is not based on promises" (quoted in Toal 2017, 125). His concerns appeared to be confirmed when Georgia's president Mikheil Saakashvili, encouraged by the precedent presented by Kosovo, provoked a war with Russia in the summer of 2008 (Kofman 2018). Kosovo also had an impact on Russian thinking as indicated by Putin's following indignant statement: "If someone thinks that Kosovo can be granted full independence as a state, then why should the Abkhaz or the South-Ossetian people not also have the right to statehood!" (quoted in Toal 2017, 154).

The United States and its NATO allies did not take Russia's protests and warnings seriously—or those of their own experts or officials, like Mearsheimer, Mandelbaum, Waltz, Burns, Kennan, and Perry. In December 2021, Moscow proposed a treaty to guarantee Ukraine's neutrality and a pledge of no further NATO expansion. Vladimir Putin was most concerned that Ukraine would be armed with nuclear weapons, and he had wanted Western assurance against this possibility (Roberts 2022). The United States rejected flatly this Russian proposal. In the words of Secretary of State Antony Blinken, "There is no change. There will be no change" in US position to maintain NATO's "open door" policy (US Department of State 2022). Geoffrey Roberts (2022) describes Russia's invasion of Ukraine as a classic example of preventive war intended to forestall Kyiv's NATO membership—this membership being seen by the Kremlin not necessarily only in terms of Kyiv joining this alliance in name but also in it becoming a NATO member in fact (i.e., a de facto member), a membership that is already in the process of being incorporated into NATO's military planning and infrastructure.

Just prior to Russia's invasion of Ukraine, the United States turned down Russia's proposed treaty. At a press conference on January 26, 2022, the following exchange took place between a journalist and Blinken in regard to a US document apparently responding to this Russian proposal:

> QUESTION: Hi. Thank you, Mr. Secretary. I realize that you don't want to get into the specifics of what is actually in this document and—although I'm sure I and my colleagues will continue to try to get them. But can you say more broadly—when you say that there are core principles that you're committed to and to uphold and defend, does that mean that in this document you told the Russians point blank in writing that "no" is the answer to their demand for a formal bar on the expansion of NATO, the permanent exclusion of Ukraine, and the withdrawal of certain forces and equipment from Eastern Europe? Is that what this says? Can—is there anything different in this document than what we have heard publicly over the course of the last couple weeks?
>
> SECRETARY BLINKEN: Again, without going into the specifics of the document, I can tell you that it reiterates what we've said publicly for many weeks and, in a sense, for many years: that we will uphold the principle of NATO's open door, and that's, as I've said repeatedly in recent weeks, a commitment that we're bound to. And so the document, as I said, makes very clear some of the basic principles that we are standing by, committed to, and will uphold, much of which has been stated in public, including by me in recent days and weeks. And that goes to NATO's "Open Door" policy. (US Department of State 2022)

From a rationalist perspective (e.g., Fearon 1995; Powell 1999), the occurrence of war means that there has been a bargaining failure. According to the rationalist logic, war is inefficient, meaning that it is a costly and risky endeavor in which the combatants not only expend resources in battle but also take on great risks of war turning out adversely for them, potentially entailing the loss of their country's territory and even sovereignty, their domestic popularity, their political fortune, and even their lives (witness the fate of Adolf Hitler, Benito Mussolini, Hideki Tojo, and Saddam Hussein, just to mention a few), for example. Therefore, if the leaders of belligerent states could foresee how their wars would turn out, they would prefer to settle them on that basis and thus spare themselves the costs and risks of fighting. When a fight breaks out, it suggests that the combatants have discrepant expectations of how the war will end because, for each side to choose war, they evidently expect to do better on the battlefield than their opponent gives them credit for. Even though they realize war's inefficiency (i.e., its costs and risks), they cannot agree on a settlement because of these divergent expectations. What can cause this disagreement about how a given war will end, which would thus lead to a bargaining failure to avoid war? Fearon, Powell, and other rationalist scholars point to the leaders' private information, their difficulties in making binding commitments, and the indivisibility of that which they are contesting about (that is, the object of their dispute cannot be easily divided, such as national sovereignty).

A person following the rationalist logic would conclude that war happened because bargaining between Kyiv and Moscow had broken down. The two sides obviously had discrepant views on how a war would turn out for them. Each of them evidently believed that they would do better on the battlefield than what their counterpart was willing to concede to them without war. Hence, they went to war to demonstrate by their battlefield performance that they had deserved a better deal from their counterpart than it would have offered in the absence of war. An outside observer would infer that typically the weaker side of a lopsided contest would prefer not to fight a much stronger opponent unless it has reason to believe that this unfavorable balance in their relative capabilities would somehow be offset, such as when a foreign ally helps it to overcome this disadvantage. If a foreign ally "has its back," the weaker contestant is more likely to resist pressure from its stronger counterpart and to hold out for better terms of settlement (Benson 2012; Chan, forthcoming-a, forthcoming-c). Of course, the leaders of the weaker contestant may also refuse to compromise because of domestic considerations, such as when they are wary of losing their legitimacy or power in view of the prevailing public opinion even if they know or believe privately that it is better for their county to come to terms with its larger and stronger neighbor. As discussed previously, this domestic political consideration was an important factor in the Falklands/Malvinas War—a war that neither Argentina nor Britain had wanted initially. Ukraine and Taiwan also present similarities in these important respects.

As with the Cuban Missile Crisis (for the USSR) and the Korean War (for China), the war in Ukraine and tension across the Taiwan Strait (for the United States) can be interpreted as instances of extended deterrence, whereby a major power seeks to protect a junior partner against aggression by another major power. The Biden administration was quite clear from the outset of the Ukraine conflict that direct US military intervention on behalf of Kyiv was "off the table." This being the case, its threat to deter Russia from attacking Ukraine was obviously weakened. That US "boots on the ground" in Ukraine was not in the cards communicated to Moscow that Washington did not perceive Ukraine's status as equivalent of its NATO allies—a view that is, of course, not unexpected. Indeed, even after Russia had launched its invasion of Ukraine, Washington, on several occasions, has signaled its reluctance to provide Kyiv with certain weapons systems, such as advanced combat aircraft and rockets that could reach targets in Russia's interior—a decision that was modified by Biden on May 30, 2024, to allow US weapons to be used by Ukraine to strike targets inside Russia just across the border from Kharkiv, Ukraine's second largest city, which has been attacked by Russian drones and missiles.

In view of more recent delays in US congressional action to authorize funding to aid Ukraine, it has become more apparent that the United States was not necessarily seeking a Ukrainian victory as much as forestalling its defeat at the hands of the Russians. This conflict has taken on the appearance of a war by proxy, whereby the Western powers are seeking to tie and wear down Russian forces. As remarked earlier, it is inherently difficult to convince the target of one's extended deterrence, that one is serious in being willing to bear the necessary costs, including shedding blood, on behalf of another country (the protégé). Charles de Gaulle's remark questioning the reliability of Washington's "nuclear umbrella" to protect France reflects this inherent difficulty. Even before his inauguration for a second presidential term, Donald Trump has signaled publicly that he will pressure Kyiv to settle its war with Russia.

Obviously, conflicts in Ukraine and over Taiwan are similar in that they are occurring on Russia's and China's doorsteps, respectively, or in their respective traditional spheres of influence—thus similar in this way to the Cuban

Missile Crisis for the United States. Moreover, people on opposing sides in the Ukraine and Taiwan disputes share long historical ties and deep cultural affinity. Geographic location and distance are relevant because they can serve as proxies indicating the relative stakes that the contesting parties and their partners have in a dispute. Ceteris paribus, the closer a dispute is located to a country's home turf, the more it has a stake in its outcome and therefore the more resolved it is to stand its ground. Ukraine and Taiwan are important to Moscow and Beijing, respectively, for strategic and symbolic reasons (e.g., Chan and Hu, forthcoming-b). As already mentioned earlier, Kenneth E. Boulding (1962) also points to another geographic consideration: a country's capabilities become more attenuated the farther it has to fight from its home base.

Ukraine is the traditional gateway for invaders from Russia's west—most memorably, those led by Napoleon Bonaparte and Adolf Hitler. Its strategic importance has been underscored by classic geostrategic writers (e.g., MacKinder 1904, 1919, 1943; Spykman 1942, 1944), who argue that whichever state controls this corridor, or more specifically Eastern Europe, would be able to dominate the Eurasian heartland, and whichever country controls this heartland would be able to dominate the World Island, or, in other words, the Eurasian landmass.

Taiwan also has paramount strategic importance to China. It is, in General Douglas MacArthur's (2005) words, "an unsinkable aircraft carrier," which can be used to disrupt China's north-south communications and threaten its eastern coast, representing China's economic and demographic center of gravity and hence its soft underbelly, as well as the pivot in the first US-constructed island chain to bottle up China's navy. In hostile hands, Taiwan can serve as a launching pad to attack China, and conversely, if Beijing gains control of this island, its merchant fleet and navy would gain access to the open Pacific, thereby greatly attenuating China's current vulnerability to a military blockade and choke points, represented by shallow channels, which would allow the United States to track and interdict Beijing's submarines in the event of armed hostilities (e.g., Chan, forthcoming-c; Chan and Hu, forthcoming-b; Green and Talmadge 2022; Wachman 2007).

Even stripped of the island's symbolic value for China's national reunification, one can imagine Taiwan's importance in Chinese strategic planning if we pause briefly to ponder how the United States acted vis-à-vis Cuba and especially Washington's reaction to the installation of Soviet missiles on that island in 1962. Of course, Cuba does not command nearly the same strategic importance to Washington as Taiwan does to Beijing—after all, a glance at the map tells us that Cuba can hardly impede US shipping on either coast facing the open Atlantic and Pacific Oceans.

This discussion brings us to important differences between Ukraine and Taiwan: the matter of sovereignty and the right of secession and self-determination. Western discourse comparing Ukraine to Taiwan almost never brings up these points. Stated plainly, all countries in the world recognize Ukraine as an independent, sovereign country, but only about a dozen microstates have diplomatic relations with Taiwan. They are Belize, Guatemala, Haiti, Vatican City, Marshall Islands, Palau, Paraguay, Saint Lucia, Saint Kitts and Nevis, Saint Vincent and the Grenadines, Eswatini, and Tuvalu—tiny countries that most people would have great difficulty locating on a map.

Even the United States itself does not recognize Taiwan as an independent, sovereign state. Washington's joint communique with Beijing in 1972 states plainly, "The United States acknowledges that all Chinese on either side of the Taiwan Strait maintain that there is but one China and that Taiwan is a part of China. The United States Government does not challenge that position. It reaffirms its interest in a peaceful settlement of the Taiwan question by the Chinese themselves" (Taiwan Documents Project, n.d.). Washington clearly did not contest that the people on both sides of the Taiwan Strait are Chinese, and it did not claim that there was a Chinese nation on one side of this strait and a Taiwanese nation on the other side. As just stated, the United States has officially acknowledged that "all *Chinese* on either side of the Taiwan Strait maintain that *there is but one China* and that *Taiwan is a part of China*" (italics added). The meaning of this language is quite clear, although Washington has changed its official position over the years, leading Beijing to charge that the United States has reneged on its commitments, which is, of course, one of the major reasons why it is difficult for states to settle a dispute without fighting. As James D. Fearon (1995) argues, mistrust in another state's promises—that is, the difficulties in enforcing the terms of a contract or to force another state to honor its commitments—impedes states' efforts to reach a settlement to avoid war, even though they realize that wars are inefficient.

The profound difference distinguishing the Ukrainian and Taiwanese conflicts is that whereas an overwhelming majority of states see Russia as an aggressor that has invaded another sovereign state, an equally overwhelming majority of states see Taiwan's status as China's internal matter, and they would be skeptical of Taiwan's right to secede from China. In fact, the United States has itself taken the position that Crimea's secession from Ukraine and those oblasts in Ukraine's eastern Donbass region (the oblasts of Donetsk, Kherson, Luhansk, and Zaporizhzhia) that have broken away from Kyiv represent illegal acts contrary to international law. Washington has refused to recognize the legitimacy of their plebiscites and argued that their secession must comply with Ukraine's constitution and be approved by the entire Ukrainian population. Of course, as Ralph Waldo Emerson (n.d.) writes, "A foolish consistency is the hobgoblin of little minds." Washington's policies on various independence movements, or secession attempts—such as in the cases of Biafra, Bangladesh, Croatia, Bosnia, Kosovo, South Vietnam, Taiwan, and now Crimea—have shown great variation. The important point in this discussion, however, is that a basic difference between Ukraine and Taiwan is usually overlooked—or deliberately obfuscated—in current discourse prevailing in the United States. Washington's position on Taiwan is problematic even in the views of former US officials, such as Henry Kissinger, who has remarked, "For us to go to war with a recognized country . . . over a part of what we would recognize as their country would be preposterous" (quoted in Tyler 1999, 225).

There are other important differences between Ukraine and Taiwan that caution us against facile analogies. Simply put, China is not Russia, and East Asia is not Europe. China is far more embedded in the global economy than Russia, and it would be much more challenging to coerce Beijing by economic denial than Moscow. Even in the latter case, Moscow managed to dampen inflationary pressure and maintain its economic growth in the face of a trade boycott and financial blockade mounted by Western countries. Russia's economy actually grew over 3 percent in 2023, and after shooting up to a high level of about 18 percent in February 2022, its inflation has settled down to an annual rate of about 7 percent (Zakaria 2024). Western countries' efforts at economic coercion turned out to be less effective than expected because countries such as India, Brazil, Saudi Arabia, Turkey, and, of course, China have continued to do business with Russia. It would be far more difficult for Western countries to coerce China economically in a contingency involving Taiwan without imposing severe pain on themselves because of China's deep and extensive involvement in the global economy. In contrast to the Europeans' economic relations with Russia, China is the top trade partner for practically all its neighbors, hence suggesting that it would be even more challenging to overcome the problem of collective action (Olson 1965) to undertake effective economic sanction against Beijing.

Unlike the USSR during the Cold War, China is not waging an ideological campaign to compete with the United States. It is not seeking to export its economic model or political system, nor is it trying to recruit other countries to form a military alliance. The United States, rather than China, has been promoting its brand of capitalism and democracy abroad and instigating regime changes and color revolutions. It has also been more active in forming an incipient coalition to contain China in the form of the Quadrilateral Security Dialogue (the Quad). This comment does not, of course, deny that China and Russia have had a recent rapprochement. Yet their bilateral relationship is far from the alliance system headed by Washington. Although China obviously seeks influence in other countries, it is not trying to compete with or supplant the United States in its traditional spheres of influence in the Western Hemisphere, Western Europe, and the Middle East. Again, this comment does not deny that Beijing has acquired a more active and prominent profile in the Middle East, which can be seen in its recent facilitation of a rapprochement between Tehran and Riyadh. Nevertheless, Beijing is not seeking local clients in other parts of the world, as Moscow used to.

For a variety of political and historical reasons, there is no equivalent to NATO in Asia (Cha 1999, 2016; Hemmer and Katzenstein 2002). The US alliance network in Asia has taken bilateral forms, even though Washington has tried recently to organize more "minilateral" arrangements, like the Quad, consisting of the United States, Australia, India, and Japan. Having eschewed direct military intervention in the Russo-Ukrainian War, it is questionable that Washington would decide to interject itself directly and militarily in a conflict with Beijing over Taiwan's status—even though, as mentioned earlier, there is an ongoing debate in Washington about whether to change its policy of strategic ambiguity to declare publicly its commitment to defend Taiwan in a possible war. I will refrain from presenting an extended discussion here on the shifting military balance between China and the United States; suffice it to say that there is general agreement that China is militarily stronger than Russia. Fareed Zakaria (2020, 68) reports that "the Pentagon has reportedly enacted 18 war games against China over Taiwan, and China has prevailed in every one." Richard Bernstein (2020) and Jean-Pierre Cabestan (2024, 83–86) make similar observations.

China, Russia, and the United States have been involved in indirect conflicts, or wars by proxy. The Vietnam War is such an example, showing Moscow and Beijing's efforts to tie down US forces, deplete its resources, and sap its energy. After the USSR invaded Afghanistan, the United States reciprocated by arming and supporting the mujahideen to resist this foreign occupation. Of course, this effort subsequently "boomeranged" in that these Muslim fighters later morphed into the Taliban, which was the target in the subsequent US invasion of Afghanistan. Recent episodes in the Middle East also indicate Tehran's use of its proxies—such as Hamas, the Hezbollah in southern Lebanon, and the Houthis in Yemen—to harass and attack Israeli and American targets. The war in Ukraine offers another instance of the United States and its Western allies seeking to exhaust the Russians without getting directly into a fight with them. Should Washington decide to intervene directly in a contingency involving Taiwan, it would constitute a departure from this model of proxy wars, and the question naturally arises as to what would or could motivate it to alter its longstanding strategic practice and its avowed lesson from the Korean and Vietnam conflicts to never again fight a land war in Asia. There must be some important difference between Ukraine and Taiwan to warrant this change in US policy, recalling that the Biden administration had made it publicly very clear that a situation of US "boots on the ground" was off the table before Russia invaded Ukraine.

There are other differences between Ukraine and Taiwan. For instance, Ukraine shares a land border with Russia and other countries; some of them are sympathetic to Kyiv's cause. This geographic fact means that it was easier for Russia to invade Ukraine, but it is also easier for other friendly neighbors to supply aid to Kyiv. In contrast, Taiwan is an island, which makes it much more difficult both for Beijing to invade it due to the "stopping power of water" and for friendly countries to supply aid to Taipei (Mearsheimer 2001, 44, 77, 83–84, 114–28, 136, 141, 264–65, 418, 444).

There are, however, two plausible parallels between these two cases—ones that have rarely been brought up by those who use Ukraine today as an analogy for Taiwan tomorrow. We all know that the United States invaded Iraq because the George W. Bush administration had declared that Baghdad had weapons of mass destruction or was about to have these weapons. We also know that in his attempt to avoid Saddam Hussein's fate, Libya's Muammar Qaddafi invited international inspection to prove that he did not have these weapons or a program to develop them. Having established these facts, NATO still waged a war on his regime, which ended in his gruesome death. Ironically, the two other members of the axis of evil—North Korea and Iran, one of which definitely has nuclear weapons and the other of which almost certainly has a program to develop these weapons and can acquire these weapons on short order—have not been attacked. What do these episodes have to do with Ukraine and Taiwan?

Ukraine had given up the nuclear arsenal left by Moscow on its soil in exchange for security guarantees from Russia, the United States, and Britain in the so-called Budapest Memorandum of 1994. Under US pressure, Taiwan terminated its nuclear program on two occasions, thus putting itself also at the mercy of Washington's protection. The parallel in these two cases is, of course, whether Kyiv and Taipei would have been better off today if they had made a different decision on nuclear weapons. Would Kyiv have been better able to deter Russia's invasion if it had these weapons? And similarly, would Taipei be in a more effective position to head off the military threat from China if it had acquired these weapons? Although these questions do not get nearly the amount of public attention that they deserve, officials in other countries in a comparable security situation must be watching intensely and pondering seriously about these questions—with obvious implications for the nuclear nonproliferation regime in the future.

Another plausible or possible parallel for Ukraine and Taiwan has to do with how the West, especially the United States, practiced restraint during the Cold War in encroaching on Russia's traditional turf, or what the Russians describe as their near abroad. Washington exercised significant prudence in its previous encounters with Moscow and Beijing that had a potential for conflict escalation, even though it held a significant military edge over the latter two Communist states (Chan, forthcoming-b). Although, as discussed earlier, the United States had insisted that the USSR remove its missiles from Cuba in the 1962 crisis, the Kennedy administration chose a quarantine (a euphemism for blockade, used because a naval blockade would have been an act of war) over a surprise air attack as its opening gambit. It also made a secret deal with Moscow, making a quid pro quo to enable a compromise to avert an escalation of their conflict. Moreover, even though Washington provided rhetorical support for the people of Central and Eastern Europe in their resistance to Soviet domination, it did not give them direct, tangible help, such as during the Hungarian uprising in 1956 and the Prague Spring in 1968, both of which were crushed by Soviet military intervention.

Remembering China's counterintervention in the Korean War, US leaders also took precaution to avoid a repetition of this episode in the Vietnam War (Khong 1992). Of course, Washington treated the USSR and China differently during the Cold War. While tacitly recognizing a Soviet sphere of influence, it recruited allies and built military bases right up to China's borders, actions suggesting that it was unwilling to accord to China, in contrast to the USSR, a cordon sanitaire, or, in other words, buffer states, or a zone of Chinese influence. Three major wars fought by the United States were quite literally on China's doorsteps—that is, in countries contiguous to China: Korea, Vietnam, and Afghanistan. There were, of course, also several crises involving Taiwan and other smaller offshore islands from the Chinese mainland, such as Quemoy and Matsu.

Since Russia's precipitous decline ending in its collapse and the end of the Cold War, the United States and its NATO allies have behaved more aggressively, such as by attacking Serbia, recruiting former Soviet allies and even former republics of the USSR to join NATO, and promoting an agenda of regime change and supporting various color revolutions abroad, including in areas adjacent to Russia. As discussed earlier, Washington appears to have reversed—or is in the process of reversing—its policy on Taiwan, undertaking a "pivot to Asia," promoting the new concept of the Indo-Pacific to replace the Asia-Pacific, and finally reinvigorating the Quad—all pointing to a more concerted and transparent effort to contain China's rising influence.

So what? Washington pushed for NATO expansion, including inviting Georgia and Ukraine, two former republics of the USSR, to join the alliance. Contrary to its practice of prudent statecraft during the Cold War in avoiding infringement on the USSR's traditional sphere of influence, Washington's policy after the Cold War's conclusion has been less cautious, more aggressive, and more confrontational. The reason for this change in US conduct is the perception that a weakened Russia can be pushed around; as reported earlier, former US secretary of defense William Perry has remarked that warnings of Moscow's likely adverse reaction to NATO's enlargement had gone unheeded due to US officials' dismissive attitude toward and even contempt for a diminished Russia. "Who cares what they think? They're a third-rate power" (Borger 2016). Stated plainly, Russia's invasion of Ukraine was not entirely "unprovoked" as Western, including American, media usually portray it.

Few commentators and scholars in the West, including in the United States, suggest that this episode indicates that weakness can incline other countries to become more aggressive in advancing their agenda. Moreover, this characterization will inevitably raise the uncomfortable question of whether Russia has actually been playing defense, while the West, offense. In this case, power-transition theory would be right—except that when the side that was already ahead gains even more power, it can destabilize international relations. In this reasoning, the widening power gap between the United States and the West more generally, on the one hand, and Russia, on the other hand, would be a source of instability. Few pundits and academics present this proposition, even though the rising power of the West, especially that of the United States (relatively speaking, compared to Russia), would have supported their premonition of a more unstable world—except, of course, not exactly along the lines of the typical script being propagated in these countries concerning the danger posed by a rising China.

My reference to Washington's tendency to adopt an increasingly hard-line policy toward Beijing raises another awkward issue. In this case, a stronger China—in contrast to a weaker Russia—has also invited more harsh treatment from the United States. In other words, interstate power shifts—whether strengthening Washington's hand relative to Russia or weakening its hand relative to China—did not make a difference in US policy toward them. In both cases, the United States has adopted a more bellicose posture. One can almost hear objections from some readers arguing that the US policy has been a response to a more aggressive Chinese (or Russian) policy. This objection can be settled by checking which country has undertaken more military actions abroad, say, in the last four or five decades, including their frequency of armed interventions, militarized disputes, air attacks (including those by unmanned drones) on suspected terrorists and even foreign officials (such as Iran's general Qasem Soleimani in Baghdad in January 2020), covert military operations (such as mining Nicaragua's ports), and outright invasion of other countries (such as Grenada, Panama, Iraq, and Afghanistan).

In quantitative analyses of international relations, researchers usually control statistically the influence of other intervening variables in order to determine the "true" impact of an independent variable (say, a country's democratic institutions or its economic interdependence with other countries in the world) on a dependent variable (say, the frequency of its involvement in foreign wars). Because territorial disputes and disagreements about borders are the most common reasons for states to go to war (Vasquez 1993, 2009), the incidence of US and Chinese involvement in foreign armed conflicts would be cast in even sharper relief if this consideration is taken into account (the United States has fewer neighbors than China and, ipso facto given the logic just presented, should have fewer instances of being involved in foreign armed conflicts).

The major point that I am trying to make in referring to almost ritualistic invocations of "Ukraine today, Taiwan tomorrow" is that such statements recall a similarity between these two cases, albeit one that is not usually intended by those who use Ukraine as an analogy for Taiwan—namely, they both reflect more "in-your-face" diplomacy to expand or maintain Western and US influence in Russia's and China's near abroad. We can endlessly debate about which side is the revisionist seeking to alter a status quo—and the answer depends on one's reference point, such as whether it refers to Ukraine's status in 1988 or Taiwan's status in 1948, and these benchmarks for establishing the status quo or status quo ante make all the difference in our views. Here again, different people may have very different views about where to place the benchmark, and history in itself cannot settle their differences.

People may disagree with my general sense that Washington's support for Ukraine has waned recently and that it appears rather limited and lukewarm. This sense stands in contrast to Biden's recent statements with respect to Taiwan. On at least four different occasions (August 2021, October 2021, May 2022, and September 2022), he answered yes when asked whether the United States would intervene on Taiwan's behalf should China attack this island (e.g., Kanno-Youngs and Baker 2022; Wingrove 2022a, 2022b). On each occasion, his answer was unequivocal and sounded very much like a radical departure from the traditional US posture of strategic ambiguity. Biden's public statements could hardly be gaffes or slips of the tongue—certainly not when he repeated the same answer on each occasion, even though officials in his own administration have tried to "walk back" his words each time, claiming that official US policy on Taiwan has not changed and that it still abides by the one-China principle. When combined with recent US actions such as high-level officials' visits to Taipei (such as that of former house speaker Nancy Pelosi) and arms sales to its government, these reassurances can hardly convince Beijing that Washington's policy has not changed. There has clearly been a shift in US policy indicating greater commitment to Taiwan, although whether Washington intends to or will follow through on its support for Taiwan when push comes shove is still an unknown. Regardless, US rhetoric—including Biden's words—implies that it may be more determined to defend Taiwan than Ukraine. Of course, Taiwan has a larger economy than Ukraine, and it has much more trade with the United States. Its semiconductor industry is also of greater strategic importance than Ukraine's export of grain. Therefore, it is not surprising if Washington sees more at stake, strategically and economically, in Taiwan's status than Ukraine's.

What is more surprising, however, is how Taiwan's public opinion has been influenced by recent events involving Ukraine. Comparing polling results before and after Russia's invasion of that country, people in Taiwan have expressed *less* confidence in the prospect of the United States coming to their aid in the event of a war against China, and this shift has occurred even *after* Biden's statements. For example, a poll conducted by the Taiwanese Public Opinion Foundation in March 2022 shows that 10.5 percent of the respondents firmly believed that the United States would intervene militarily on Taiwan's behalf in a war against China, 24 percent somewhat believed in this prospect, 26.5 percent did not quite believe in this prospect, 29.4 percent did not believe at all in this prospect, and 9.6 percent did not indicate an opinion (Liao 2022). Compared to a similar poll conducted in October 2021 (i.e., before Russia invaded Ukraine), those who believed firmly that the United States would intervene on Taiwan's behalf fell from 26.7 percent to 10.5 percent, while those who did not believe at all that the United States would do so increased from 11.4 percent to 29.4 percent. These changes are significant, and the major intervening event between these two surveys was Russia's invasion of Ukraine.

Another survey undertaken by Taiwan's Institute for National Defense and Security Research, an affiliate of its Ministry of Defense, in March 2022 also indicates a significant drop in the number of its respondents believing that the United States would or could come to Taiwan's defense should China attack this island. It reports that 14 percent expressed the opinion that the United States would do so, and 26 percent believed that this would be a possibility. Combined, these two categories suggest about two-fifths (or 40 percent) of the survey's respondents had some expectation of US intervention. Compared to the results of an earlier survey undertaken by the same institute in September 2021 (thus, prior to the war in Ukraine), this figure indicates a substantial drop in the number of respondents who believed that there "would be" or "could be" US military intervention to help Taiwan. The same combination of these two groups was about three-fifths, or more precisely 57 percent, in the earlier survey. There was thus again a rather steep decline of 17 percent in a relatively short interval, showing a major loss of confidence on the part of Taiwan's people in the reliability of the US commitment to help. The organizers of these surveys attribute this shift to the effect of the Russo-Ukrainian War ("Public Less Confident" 2022). Having seen the level of support Washington has shown to Kyiv, people in Taiwan now have less confidence in US support.

A recent analysis by T. Y. Wang and Su-Feng Cheng (2024) confirm the results of these surveys of Taiwan's public opinion. They report that "since Biden's pledge, Taiwanese citizens' confidence in Washington's security commitment has not risen but fallen," and "the public's confidence in America's defense commitment did sink between 2021 and 2022. The average probability of 'no confidence' rose by 5%, while that of 'full confidence' fell by 6%" (T. Wang and Cheng 2024, 62, 64). There is typically a pattern such that those Taiwanese favoring independence tend to have higher expectations that the United States would come to the island's aid, and conversely, those who do not favor independence (at least not now) tend to be more skeptical of the prospect of US intervention on Taiwan's behalf. These correlations are natural and to be expected because people have a strong preference for consistency in their beliefs, not to mention also the influence of motivated bias.

However, recent polls in Taiwan have contradicted these usual patterns. "After controlling for the effects of other confounding variables, independence supporters' confidence in America's defense support fell between the two surveys. The average probability of 'no confidence' rose by 4%, while that of 'full confidence' fell by 5%"; moreover, "independence-leaning citizens historically have a strong belief that the US would come to Taiwan's aid should China attack Taiwan. But contrary to this expectation, Taiwanese citizens' confidence in Washington's security commitment did not rise but fell after Biden's security pledges and the war in Ukraine, and pro-independence respondents' conviction fell even more" (T. Wang and Cheng 2024, 66). These authors conclude that "one possible explanation for the decline in [Taiwan people's] confidence is that the Russo-Ukrainian war has demonstrated Washington's reluctance to become directly involved in overseas military conflicts" (70). Here, therefore, is a dramatic example of how American people's perception of having extended strong support for and large amounts of assistance to Ukraine—at least judged by the rhetoric of many of their leading officials and politicians—appears *not* to be shared by popular beliefs and opinions on the part of a foreign audience.

The above survey results are informative. Those Americans who are advocating stronger US support for Taiwan often profess that they want to protect the island's democracy and its people's right of self-determination, although obviously these are not their only reasons. Ironically, there has been a drop in Taiwanese people's confidence in the US pledge to defend them in the wake of the Russo-Ukrainian War and after Biden's repeated public commitment to intervene on Taiwan's behalf in the event of an attack by China. The people of Taiwan remember that they were treated shabbily and cavalierly when Washington abruptly and unilaterally abrogated its defense treaty with Taiwan and switched its diplomatic recognition from Taipei to Beijing. They had felt abandoned and betrayed. They are not so forgetful of this experience or so dense as to overlook the fate of US allies in Saigon and Kabul. They have a realistic understanding that they are a pawn caught in the rivalry between Washington and Beijing. Their importance to Washington is secondary rather than intrinsic—that is, the United States cares about their status because China cares about it. Or, in other words, their importance to the United States is derivative of China's importance to the United States, and thus, they are *not* intrinsically important to Washington even though American rhetoric about supporting democracy and self-determination may suggest otherwise. The people of Taiwan appear to have an intuitive understanding that "contrary to the popular narrative, the West has supported democracy only when that support has been reinforced by material interests, and rarely, if ever, when it has posed a threat to such interests" (Grigoryan 2020, 158).

Given this understanding, an overwhelming majority of Taiwan's people prefer to maintain the status quo—if necessary, for an indefinite period. China is important, even vital, to the health of Taiwan's economy. The majority of Taiwan's people would prefer not to roil relations with the mainland, even though Washington might use their status to occasionally ratchet up tension with China to show its displeasure with Beijing, to gain a bargaining advantage, or simply to irritate the Chinese. Taiwan's people understand clearly that they can be the biggest casualty in this game between two great powers and that they would suffer the most if there should be war. Judging by the fact that about ten million Ukrainians have left their country, thus voting by their feet, and in the face of signs indicating increasing fractures in Western support for Kyiv, political dynamics inside Ukraine may yet change. The secession by Crimea and the four oblasts in the Donbass region have changed the domestic political balance inside Ukraine because these more pro-Russian parts that formerly belonged to Ukraine no longer play a role in this country's domestic politics. Their exit has, of course, been offset by the mass exodus of Ukrainians escaping the war, as just noted.

Of course, all wars must come to an end sooner or later. But as indicated in the last chapter's conclusion, leaders sometimes fail to anticipate the "end game" to bring a war to its conclusion. It is even more difficult for outside observers to predict how the Russo-Ukrainian War would terminate. After the lack of progress from Kyiv's vaunted offensive in the spring of 2024, there have already been rising voices in Washington advocating that Kyiv should consider negotiating a peace deal with Moscow. It is obvious already that the people of Ukraine have suffered the most from the war and that reconstruction after the war would be an arduous and costly endeavor. Perhaps the people of Taiwan have seen and understood this situation more quickly and clearly than other observers of this war, explaining their majority's preference to maintain the current situation and to refrain from "rocking the boat."

Survey results on Taiwanese people's public opinion show an interesting, significant, and unexpected phenomenon. Although US officials and the American public probably believe sincerely that they have extended strong and generous support to Ukraine's resistance against Russia's aggression, this belief is not necessarily shared abroad—or is at least not shown in the case of Taiwan's public opinion for now. Here is then an example that there can be a serious discrepancy between one's self-perception and others' perception of oneself. It is possible and even likely and convenient for Americans to forget or at least choose not to remember their Vietnam fiasco, "Kabul moment," and hasty withdrawal from Lebanon and Somalia, but other people may not be so forgetful. The refrain "Ukraine today, Taiwan tomorrow" may very well resonate differently for different people, depending on whether they find themselves in Ukraine, Taiwan, or the United States.

EIGHT

The Suez Crisis, *Mayaguez* Affair, and Other Historical Legacies

There is little doubt that officials, like the rest of us, frequently use analogies to choose and/or advocate for policies (e.g., Khong 1992; Neustadt and May 1986b). Washington's decision processes about the Korean and Vietnam Wars, for example, were profoundly influenced by the so-called lessons of the 1930s suggesting that a failure to resist aggression would subsequently cause a wider and more devastating war. These lessons refer to the dire consequences of inaction in the face of Germany's rearmament program and *Anschluß* with Austria, Italy's aggression against Ethiopia, Japan's invasion of China and its seizure of Manchuria, and especially the 1938 Munich Conference remembered for Britain's and France's appeasement of Adolf Hitler's demand that Czechoslovakia cede the Sudetenland to Germany. According to these supposed lessons, passivity and, even worse, accommodation of aggressors will only whet their appetite and encourage them to become even more aggressive.

US officials in the Truman and Johnson administrations were motivated to intervene in the Korean and Vietnam Wars, respectively, heeding to what they understood to be the lessons of the 1930s and especially that of Munich—specifically their interpretation of the momentous events of those times to mean that appeasement or a failure to resist aggression would only embolden aggressor states, raising the danger of a larger and more costly war in the future. Events in the 1930s and Munich occurred during the formative years or earlier careers of these US officials, but the influence of these events' legacy continues to be felt even after this generation has passed from the scene. Thus, George W. Bush had claimed that Saddam Hussein was "another Hitler." This characterization was obviously a caricature and an exaggeration. As Janice Gross Stein (2023, 399) remarks, "Whatever Saddam was, it is difficult to argue that he was comparable to Hitler either in his intentions or his capabilities: the scope of his ambition or the number that he had killed did not compare to Hitler nor did his relative military capabilities." Bush was engaging in hyperbole to inflate the threat posed by Saddam Hussein, and in this sense, he was trying to use a historical analogy to justify his policy to attack Iraq and also to mobilize public support for this policy.

Margaret MacMillan (2008, 157) warns that "analogies from history must, of course, be treated with care. Using the wrong one not only can present an oversimplified picture of a complex situation in the present but can lead to wrong decisions." George W. Bush was not the only one to exaggerate. MacMillan cites the example of Norman Podhoretz, who equated the campaign against international terrorism after the 9/11 tragedy to World War IV (the Cold War was World War III according to Podhoretz). How meaningful is such an attempt to invoke history and forge analogies? In this case, the intent appears to be to sensationalize, to sound the alarm, and to mobilize support for a political cause.

Americans are not the only ones whose views on foreign policy have been shaped by events in the 1930s. These events and the prevailing understanding of the disastrous consequences of democracies' failed policies in the 1930s were also on the minds of French and British officials during the 1956 Suez Canal crisis. They equated the actions of Egyptian president Gamal Abdel Nasser to nationalize the Suez Canal with that of Adolf Hitler and Benito Mussolini (Fry 1989, 7, 10). Rose McDermott (1998c, 148) writes, "It is clear that the Munich analogy influenced [British prime minister Anthony] Eden's and [French prime minister Guy] Mollet's analysis of the Suez Crisis. Eden really did see Nasser as a latter-day reincarnation of Hitler. Eden believed that concessions to Nasser would only lead to greater aggression on Nasser's part throughout the rest of the Middle East." US ambassador to France C. Douglas Dillon wrote in his cable to his boss, Secretary of State John Foster Dulles, describing similar views held by France's top official and reporting Guy Mollet's disappointment due to his perceived lack of US support, stating, "He [Mollet] felt that the US was embarking on the same course of error by appeasement that had been followed toward Hitler in the 1930s. . . . He said he had never been so disturbed and worried for the future and was certain that if we did not take action to stop Nasser now we would be faced with the same problem 3, 6, or 9 months hence, only the Western position by that time would have greatly deteriorated" (quoted on 153).

These views were shared by Anthony Eden, who writes in his memoirs these words: "Success in a number of adventures involving the breaking of agreements in Abyssinia, in the Rhineland, in Austria, in Czechoslovakia, in Albania had persuaded Hitler and Mussolini that democracies had not the will to resist, that they could march with the certitude of success from signpost to signpost along the road which led to world domination. . . . As my colleagues and I surveyed the scene in those autumn months in 1956, we were determined the like should not come again" (quoted in MacMillan 2008, 160). Eden's analysis was, of course, an exaggeration, and coming from the leader of a country that used to be the world's dominant power, it also comes across as ironically self-referential and self-serving. Of course, his use of analogy equating Nasser with Hitler was a hyperbole. As MacMillan (160–61) remarks, "Nasser was no Hitler intent on conquering his neighbors. Rather, he was a nationalist who badly needed resources to develop his own country and to stake out a position of leadership in the Middle East. The British position in collusion with the French and the Israelis to seize the Suez Canal was not only badly conceived; it rallied the Egyptians and the wider Arab world to Nasser's side. Furthermore, it infuriated the Americans, who, far from seeing a repeat of the 1930s, worried about the moral impact on other Third World countries." Indeed, to borrow from a Chinese saying, Britain and France's action in this case was tantamount to thieves crying "theft"—that is, complaining loudly about the very transgression that they were themselves guilty of. MacMillan's observation quoted above also suggests that close allies sharing similar political and cultural heritage may not agree on the appropriateness and relevance of an analogy from the past for a current situation.

Egypt's takeover of the Suez Canal from the Franco-British company that was managing it was perceived by British and French leaders as international aggression, and they were determined to force Nasser to "disgorge" the fruits of his aggression. London and Paris conspired with Israel in planning Operation Musketeer. By prearrangement reached at the French town Sèvres on the outskirts of Paris, the leaders of these countries agreed to invade Egypt. Israel attacked Egypt on October 29, 1956, and it succeeded in taking command of the Sinai by November 2 of that same year. "On 30 November, Britain and France issued their discriminatory ultimatum to Egypt and Israel and on 31 October bombed Egyptian airfields" (Fry 1989, 19). British and French paratroopers were dropped at Port Said and Port Fuad on November 5, and they carried out an amphibious landing at Port Said on November 6. In this episode, the lessons of the 1930s and Munich not only played a role in influencing British and French policymaking but also were deployed to mobilize public opinion, rally US support, and legitimate these countries' aggression—that is, historical analogies in this and other cases have been used to advocate and justify policies rather than just to define a problem and search for a solution. The Suez Canal crisis abated when the United States pressured the British and French to withdraw their forces from Egypt.

There is also the possibility that historical parallels or precedents are invoked in a way to reassure oneself that the decision reached is the correct one. Historical analogies can thus be deployed to lend comfort or confidence to decision-makers. In other words, they can serve as a security blanket psychologically and induce confirmation bias and lead to a premature closure of decision-making. Some policy choices that do not resonate with the particular historical episode recalled or that are thought to even contradict it do not get the proper amount of attention that they deserve. For example, in US policymaking processes leading to decisions to intervene in both the Korean and Vietnam Wars, there was scant consideration that these conflicts were civil wars rather than cases of international aggression in which one country's soldiers crossed an international boundary to invade another. This view continues to this day in US discourse about Taiwan, taking it for granted that the ongoing dispute over this island's status is one between two sovereign states rather than parties to a civil war. Naturally, the representation of this dispute and of the Korean and Vietnam Wars in this light makes all the difference in the world, lending legitimacy to US intervention as opposition to a foreign aggressor invading another independent country. Unsurprisingly, most Americans do not think of General Ulysses Grant's troops crossing the Mason-Dixon Line in the same light. In discussing Xi Jinping's intentions regarding Taiwan, they also do not ponder why Abraham Lincoln is held in such high regard in US history.

Moreover, in their decisions to intervene in the Korean and Vietnam Wars, US leaders assumed from the outset that they were dealing with a probe or challenge from a monolithic international Communist bloc. They thus perceived Kim Il-sung and Ho Chi Minh as stooges or surrogates acting at the behest of Beijing and Moscow. They saw these leaders for North Korea and North Vietnam, respectively, as Communists rather than nationalists. Subsequent events showed that they were hardly puppets of either the Chinese or the Russians. Had any of these assumptions been met by vigorous challenge and debated thoroughly, the very premise on which US leaders acted to undertake and justify their decision to intervene in these conflicts would have been seriously undermined. Significantly, these assumptions endured even after they were invalidated by events. Thus, US leaders held onto these same views after the Korean conflict in their policymaking about the Vietnam conflict, and the idea that they are dealing with a possible case of interstate aggression has persisted to this day in their pronouncements about Taiwan. It would, of course, never occur to any one of them that it would be ludicrous to describe Union soldiers crossing the Mason-Dixon Line in the same way.

To the extent that an analogy is shared strongly by members of a decision group, it can have a chilling effect on open and free deliberation. Yuen Foong Khong's (1992) analysis of US policymaking during the Vietnam War suggests that historical analogies can even have a perseverance effect, contributing to resistance to alternative explanations and disconfirming evidence, as just suggested in the preceding paragraph. Their effect on decision-makers can last long after the episode remembered has lost its contemporary relevance. In other words, historical analogies can become entrenched and thus difficult to dislodge even when circumstances have changed to make their application to the contemporary world problematic.

The recent popularity of the Peloponnesian War as a result of Graham T. Allison's (2017) warning of Thucydides's Trap comes to mind. After all, many things have happened in the interim since this war was fought among ancient Greek polities, including nationalism and nuclear weapons, which can affect and alter officials' decision calculations. However, once a particular interpretation of a historical episode has gained widespread support, this settled consensus appears to be quite resistant to challenge from dissident views presenting an alternative perspective. The so-called lesson of Munich also comes to mind as an example. It becomes almost a sacrosanct dogma. There is hence the danger of groupthink (that is, conformist reasoning, concurrence-seeking behavior, and a reluctance to buck against group consensus) in these circumstances (Janis 1982a). The fact that people hang on to outdated beliefs reflects in part their strong preference for consistency and their tendency to discount information contradicting their existing beliefs, hence the persistence of their outdated beliefs despite empirical disconfirmation.

Although groupthink is a common phenomenon (Janis 1982a), it is not inevitable. There are times when policymakers disagree strongly with one another, and the process leading to Jimmy Carter's decision to launch a military operation to rescue American hostages held by Iranians in Tehran provides an apt example. "It is clear that historical analogies were very powerful forces in establishing the relevant frames for central decision makers" (McDermott 1998b, 51), although different historical episodes were salient for Carter and his top advisors. The *Pueblo* incident provided this framing for Secretary of State Cyrus Vance, whereas the Bay of Pigs invasion and Israel's successful raid on Entebbe, Uganda (to rescue Israeli hostages held at the airport there), were the prism through which Zbigniew Brzezinski, Carter's national security advisor, saw the problem facing the administration. Carter's position was closer to Brzezinski's. After the rescue mission had failed (S. Smith 1985), he requested a copy of the speech given by John F. Kennedy after the debacle at the Bay of Pigs to formulate his own communication to the American people. As prospect theory would have predicted, Carter's perception that his administration was in the domain of loss inclined him to accept considerable risk, choosing the option (namely, to use military means to extricate US hostages held in Tehran) that promised the greatest immediate payoff but the least probability of success. All the key participants in this case realized that the rescue mission involved significant risk, with an estimate that 60 percent of the hostages might perish in this operation (McDermott 1998b, 70).

Unlike his colleagues, Vance was not willing to accept this level of risk and dissented strongly against the use of military force to rescue the hostages. After he was overruled, he resigned over this issue. As events turned out, he was right in advocating doing nothing rash and waiting for Iran's domestic politics to take its course, leading to the eventual peaceful release of the hostages. Parenthetically, in knowingly opting for a policy (the use of military force to rescue the hostages) with a large payoff but very low odds of success, US officials in this episode behaved in a similar way as Japanese leaders did in 1941 when they wagered a huge gamble in deciding to attack Pearl Harbor. Vance's resignation also reminds us that some high-ranking officials have a strong sense of integrity, courage, and principle to buck against the group consensus. As mentioned earlier, William Perry, the defense secretary in Clinton's administration, had also considered resigning over NATO's expansion—a policy that he strongly disagreed with.

Operation Musketeer (the joint attack by Britain, France, and Israel on Egypt under false pretenses in the 1956 Suez Canal crisis) was one of those episodes indicating that democracies are quite capable of initiating war and, indeed, engaging in collusion and fabrication of reasons to undertake or escalate armed hostilities. Besides this case, doubts have been raised about the justification given by the Bush administration to invade Iraq, the Gulf of Tonkin incident(s), which the Johnson administration used to ask Congress to approve its intervention in the Vietnam War, and the Kennedy administration's public denial of a US role in the Bay of Pigs invasion of Cuba. The public rationale given by the Bush administration for invading Iraq was that Saddam Hussein had or was developing weapons of mass destruction and that he had connections with Al Qaeda (Mearsheimer and Walt 2003; Kaufman 2004). Both of these claims have since been shown to be false, and the US invasion and occupation of Iraq turned out to be quite unpopular despite the administration's claim of "mission accomplished" (Miller Center, n.d.; Ricks 2006; Woodward 2006). The Johnson administration had claimed that the North Vietnamese had attacked US destroyers in the Gulf of Tonkin on two occasions in August 1966, using these alleged incidents to ask for a congressional resolution to authorize its decision to intervene in and expand the Vietnam War. We have learned subsequently that the text for the requested congressional legislation had been prepared prior to these alleged incidents and that at least the second incident did not in fact happen (Hallin 1986; Moise 1996; Wells 1994). Moreover, the US Navy was involved in supporting South Vietnamese raids against North Vietnam at that time. The Kennedy administration had also initially lied when it denied the US role in the Bay of Pigs invasion, even though the Central Intelligence Agency was deeply involved in the training of the Cuban exiles participating in this invasion and in the planning and execution of this invasion. Kennedy only acknowledged the US role when public disclosures of

Washington's involvement in different facets of this episode had made denial impossible (Janis 1982c; Wyden 1979).

This behavior of initial denial and subsequent retraction has occurred before. In the U-2 affair during the Eisenhower administration, a US spy plane flying over the USSR was shot down, and Washington lied about the nature of this flight, claiming that it was a civilian NASA (National Aeronautics and Space Administration) aircraft that had strayed off course only to retract this cover story when Moscow indicated that the pilot was captured and still alive (McDermott 1998e). Going back farther in history, Franklin D. Roosevelt's administration claimed disingenuously that a US naval vessel, the USS *Greer*, had been attacked by a German submarine in 1941, when in fact the United States had already been undertaking covert hostile actions against Germany (Mearsheimer 2011, 46–49; Schuster 2010).

The list can go on. Bill Clinton (2020) publicly denied that he had an affair with a White House intern, telling news correspondent Jim Lehrer that there "is no sexual relationship with Monica Lewinsky." During his administration, the US Air Force bombed the Chinese embassy in Belgrade, Serbia, killing three Chinese nationals. Washington claimed that this attack was an innocent mistake, but the Chinese were incredulous. Western media reported that this attack was in fact deliberate and not an accident (Sweeney, Holsoe, and Vullimany 1999; "Truth behind America's Raid" 1999), and the controversy over this episode continues to this day (Allsop 2024).

The US bombing of China's embassy in Belgrade serves as a useful reminder that memories of the past can differ for different people. Although many Americans probably do not remember or know about this incident, the Chinese have not forgotten about it (Allsop 2024). Far more Americans are likely to recall Iranians taking over the US embassy in Tehran and seizing US diplomats as hostages than the US bombing of China's embassy in Belgrade. The Iran hostage affair made a deep impression on Americans, and the failed mission to rescue US captives held in Tehran was arguably one of the main contributing causes for Jimmy Carter to lose his bid for a second presidential term (e.g., McDermott 1998b; S. Smith 1985). The attack on the US consulate in Benghazi, Libya, by Islamic militants in 2012 and the terrorist bombings of the US embassies in Kenya and Tanzania in 1998 also made a deep impression on Americans, and they were a topic of presidential campaigns and often mentioned in US media narratives on combatting international terrorism. In contrast, the US bombing of China's embassy in Belgrade has had far less saliency.

This disparity points to the tendency for people to recall much more easily, readily, and vividly those dramatic experiences that they themselves have had in comparison to the experiences of others. That some historical precedents or parallels may cast one in an unflattering or unfavorable light may also have a psychological influence in the ease with which we recall the past. Thus, Americans do not typically juxtapose their role in the Cuban Missile Crisis with the Chinese position in the Taiwan Strait, and they do not realize or notice inconsistencies in opposing Crimea's secession from Ukraine, on the one hand, and their support for Kosovo's independence and Taiwan's de facto separation from China, on the other hand. As a further example, the downing of Korean Airline flight 007, which had strayed into Soviet airspace in 1984, by a Soviet interceptor received a great deal of press coverage at that time in the West. Two hundred and forty-six passengers and twenty-three crew members perished in this tragedy. There was much less awareness that missiles fired by the navy's USS *Vincennes* shot down a civilian airliner from Iran in 1988. The downing of Iran Air flight 655 killed 290 people on board.

There may be a psychological explanation for these tendencies. Attribution theory suggests that people resort to different reasons to explain their actions and others' actions (e.g., Mercer 1996). When I miss or am late for an appointment, I point to circumstances beyond my control, such as my alarm clock malfunctioning, my car not starting, or the bad luck of running into a string of red lights or being delayed by a traffic accident. But when another person is tardy or fails to show up for an appointment, I tend to question this person's reliability (a personality flaw) and sometimes even entertain the thought that this person wants to deliberately stand me up (an intentional insult or slight). Thus, Americans perceived Soviet missiles in Cuba to pose an offensive threat, but US missiles in Turkey were thought to not be provocative to the USSR and to be necessary for the defense of an ally. Attacks on US embassies proved the terrorists' evil designs, but the US bombing of China's embassy was an error in target identification. The downing of the Korean airliner indicated Soviet callousness, but the downing of the Iranian airliner was due to confusing radar signals. We tend to see other people's or countries' actions to be more coherent, coordinated, and purposeful than our actions. Thus, it is not unnatural for us to be more inclined to apply the unitary rational-actor model to explain another country's actions and often see our own actions to be a function of bureaucratic pulling and hauling (Allison 1971). Of course, the unavailability of data about the other country's bureaucratic politics can also account for this difference.

One can benefit from studying missteps committed by the same country on different occasions but over similar issues. After he was overthrown by a popular uprising led by Ayatollah Ruhollah Khomeini, the shah of Iran, Mohammed Reza Pahlavi, sought refuge abroad. Jimmy Carter and his advisors debated long and hard about whether to admit him to the United States. After much delay, great hesitation, and heavy lobbying by the shah's influential American friends, Carter finally relented and agreed to issue a visa for him to go to New York for medical treatment in October 1979 (Daugherty 2003; McDermott 1998a). This decision set off a cascade of events leading to the storming and seizure of the US embassy in Tehran in November and the imprisonment of US diplomats as hostages by radical Iranian students. Events in the wake of Carter's decision to allow the shah to enter the United States became the most serious challenge to his presidency domestically and internationally, arguably contributing to his failed bid for a second presidential term.

In May 1995, the United States issued a visa to Taiwan's president Lee Tenghui, who was known for his pro-independence leanings. This decision represented a break from Washington's longstanding policy of banning high-ranking officials from Taiwan from visiting the United States (except for refueling stops for their aircraft in transit to another country). Obviously, Beijing was greatly upset by this decision—more so because it occurred just weeks after US secretary of state Warren Christopher had reassured his Chinese counterpart, Foreign Minister Qian Qichen, that the US government would not issue an entry visa to Lee (Sheng 2001, 26), who went on to visit his alma mater Cornell University and gave, in Beijing's view, an inflammatory speech there. The United States often seeks to explain away such incidents by pointing to bureaucratic snafus or congressional pressure.

However, Chinese officials are inclined to see such incidents as reflecting more coordination and intentionality. They tend to perceive their US counterparts' actions to be more purposeful, often representing a charade of "good cop, bad cop." That is, in their view, the US executive branch often points to congressional pressure as an excuse or alibi, stressing the domestic political constraints facing it to argue that its hands are tied and to explain why it could not sometimes deliver on promises made to the Chinese. In other words, domestic factors, such as congressional lobbying and public opinion, are used to gain bargaining leverage and extract concessions from Beijing, putting the Chinese on a perpetual treadmill, whereby they have to run faster just to keep up.

Robert Jervis (1976) points out the human tendency to see the other side's actions to be more deliberate and organized than warranted. Robert D. Putnam (1988) has introduced the idea of two-level games to illuminate how domestic constraints faced by officials in a democracy—specifically their need to submit international deals for domestic ratification—can be used as a lever to negotiate more favorable terms in bargaining with their foreign counterparts. Because domestic veto players restrict the policy space available to democratic leaders—that is, domestic groups limit the range of acceptable deals for democratic leaders—their authoritarian counterparts can be more easily "pushed around" to make concessions since they face less severe domestic constraints and hence more leeway to make foreign deals.

To return to Lee Tenghui's visit to the United States, Beijing ordered a series of military exercises in Taiwan's vicinity to demonstrate its displeasure. In response, Bill Clinton sent two US carrier battle groups led by the USS *Nimitz* and USS *Independence* to the Taiwan Strait. This US display of military force made a deep impression on Chinese officials, who were powerless to act against this contemporary equivalent of gunboat diplomacy. This embarrassment has served as a powerful motivation for China to modernize its military, especially its navy. It appears that in this case as well as that of the shah's admittance to the United States, domestic politics and congressional lobbying played an important role, thus suggesting that Chinese officials have exaggerated the element of deceit or duplicity in US actions. In both cases, the decision to issue an entry visa to the United States had serious long-term effects.

As already discussed earlier, the Korean War affected US officials' thinking and deliberations about the Vietnam War—whether the lesson from that conflict was supposed to be that the United States must never again fight a land war on the Asian continent or that it must not alone bear the burden of fighting China. The "Vietnam syndrome" had in turn affected subsequent US policy debates, such as Washington's support for Nicaragua's contras and its military actions against Serbia and Iraq. In a similar way, the bombing of the US Marine barracks in Beirut, Lebanon, in 1983 appeared to have had a sobering effect on Washington's interventions abroad in areas of peripheral interest to the United States (D. Kennedy 1988; Scott 1991). It is likely to have influenced a quick reversal of US policy when Bill Clinton's administration recalled US troops from Somalia in the wake of American casualties, depicted in the movie *Blackhawk Down* (Menkhaus and Ortmayer 1995).

The so-called Somali syndrome in turn influenced Clinton's subsequent decision *not* to intervene to stop genocide in Rwanda in 1994 (Power 2001, 2002). Former US deputy special envoy to Somalia Walter Clarke was quoted saying, "The ghosts of Somalia continue to haunt US policy. . . . Our lack of response in Rwanda was a fear of getting involved in something like a Somalia all over again" (Clarke, n.d.). The reverberations of the US experience in Somalia went beyond policymaking circles. When Washington considered intervening in Haiti to restore the presidency of Jean-Bertrand Aristide and to stem the exodus of Haitian refugees heading for Florida in 1993, Haitians opposed to this intervention protested at the dock in Port-au-Prince against the arrival of the USS *Harlan County*, chanting, "Somalia, Somalia!" Clinton subsequently decided to recall this vessel intended to transport Americans and other nationals to train Haiti's military and police (Ortmayer and Flinn 1997, 20–21).

Implicit in the various episodes just referenced is the importance of domestical political considerations in influencing officials' formulation and choice of foreign policy options. There is sometimes a tendency to treat foreign policymaking as if it can be easily segregated from domestic politics, thus addressing them as separate compartments. For example, in his influential study of groupthink in various US foreign policy episodes, Irving L. Janis (1982a) hardly mentions any domestic consideration in US officials' deliberations on foreign policy. Similarly, criticisms of Neville Chamberlain for committing the sin of appeasement do not usually take into account public and elite opinions in Britain and the member states of the British Commonwealth at the time.

Yet we all know that in reality, officials make their foreign policy very much with an eye on its domestic ramifications, such as the prospect of electoral defeat for the Democratic Party and even that of impeachment of the president in the Cuban Missile Crisis and the effects of public opinion and the impact of escalating the Vietnam War on Johnson's domestic Great Society program (Berman 1982). That US leaders in the Vietnam War chose a course of action that sought neither military victory (which would have provoked Chinese intervention) nor withdrawal (which would have engendered domestic criticisms of being soft on Communism and having "lost" a country to Communism during the incumbent officials' watch) had a great deal to do with their consideration of domestic politics. According to Daniel Ellsberg (1972) and Leslie H. Gelb (1971), this consideration motivated successive US administrations to pursue a stalemate in this conflict. Their primary motivation was not to win the war but rather not to lose South Vietnam to the Communists while they were in office, staving off defeat and playing for time until they could pass on this problem to the next administration.

Surely, McCarthyism and the political controversy regarding "who lost China" had a profound effect on US policymaking in the Korean and Vietnam Wars, and Republican criticisms of Truman's "mess" in the Korean War was also an important factor in subsequent US domestic politics and foreign policy (Thomson 1973). Thomas J. Christensen (1996) writes about how the formulation of US and Chinese grand strategies have interacted with the mobilization of domestic political support. US officials may not explicitly discuss domestic politics in debating and formulating foreign policy, but public opinion and electoral competition are surely on their minds, as Rose McDermott (1998b) points out was the case in the Carter administration's deliberations on how to rescue US hostages held in Tehran. These officials were acutely aware of how the hostage situation was hurting Carter's popularity and his reelection prospects.

In addition to the thorough analysis by Yuen Foong Khong (1992) on the influence of the Chinese intervention in the Korean War and the supposed lesson of Munich on US policymaking in the Vietnam War, there are other instances showing that historical memory has affected the course of policy deliberations. Robert F. Kennedy is said to have told other members of the ExCom (Executive Committee) during the height of the Cuban Missile Crisis that he did not wish to have his brother John F. Kennedy remembered by history to have committed "Pearl Harbor in reverse"—that is, to have ordered a surprise US attack on Soviet bases in Cuba (Allison 1971, 132). His remark was apparently persuasive in convincing the rest of the group to switch their support from a surprise air strike to an announced naval blockade as the preferred option to address the presence of Soviet missiles on that island.

The example just introduced about the United States committing Pearl

Harbor in reverse is interesting because it shows that historical analogies or lessons can be invoked to call for some action and also to refrain from taking other action. In this case, the United States eschewed a course of action (namely, a surprise air strike against Soviet installations in Cuba). Similarly, the fact that the United States did not intervene in the Rwandan genocide in 1994—perhaps due to the lesson learned by the Clinton administration from the misadventure in Somalia (the Battle of Mogadishu in 1993)—is also informative. So-called lessons of Korea and Vietnam, of course, also enjoined US leaders to avoid a land war on the Asian continent. However, the general proclivity for people, including scholars in undertaking their research, is to explain why something has happened rather than why it did not—that is, the nonoccurrence of events. Analysts do not usually study nonevents or disasters avoided. In this sense, their work tends to be biased. Indeed, history tends to be biased in the sense that it only records what has happened but not those events that could have happened but did not.

My remark just now referring to the legacy of Chinese intervention in the Korean War on US policymaking about the Vietnam War requires a clarification or emendation. US leaders deliberately chose policies in the latter conflict that they knew to be less effective in coercing Hanoi for the sake of minimizing the risk of Chinese military intervention (Khong 1992). In doing so, they could have overcompensated for the risk of this contingency, thus resulting in suboptimal policies in fighting the Vietnam War. Therefore, that Chinese military intervention did not happen in the Vietnam War does not necessarily mean that the lesson of Korea had worked—or at least in all its ramifications.

Analogies can be beguiling and even irresistible, but they can also be misleading. A superficial resemblance between a past episode and a current situation can cause leaders to make mistakes in addressing the problem at hand. In facing the first major crisis of his presidency shortly after the US defeat in Vietnam in 1975, Gerald Ford had to deal with the capture of *Mayaguez*—a rusty forty-year-old freighter / container ship making regular runs between Hong Kong and Singapore—by the Khmer Rouge, or Cambodian Communists. He and his entourage immediately thought of the *Pueblo* incident in January 1965 when a US naval intelligence vessel was seized and held by the North Koreans (Lerner 2002), who only released the crew after the United States signed a written apology and an admission that this ship was spying on North Korea, promising that it would cease this action in the future (the

United States stated orally prior to signing this document, indicating that this pledge was only intended to gain the release of the ship's crew).

Ford was determined not to repeat the *Pueblo* experience—a long captivity for the crew members and the humiliation of having a US vessel impounded by the Cambodians. He ordered hasty military action, which ended up costing more American lives than the number of hostages released by the Khmer Rouge (Neustadt and May 1986a). In this case, the history of the *Pueblo* incident misguided US policy in handling the *Mayaguez* crisis. The parallel between these two cases broke down because whereas *Pueblo* was a naval intelligence vessel, *Mayaguez* was a civilian container ship. Furthermore, US officials failed to consider the possibility that the boarding and seizure of the *Mayaguez* could have been an unauthorized action undertaken by some lower-ranking members of the Khmer Rouge. Phnom Penh had actually wanted to return the ship and its crew to US custody before Ford started the fireworks.

Robert Jervis (1968, 474) points out that "a country's representatives may not follow instructions and so may give others impressions contrary to those the home government wished to convey." In the Cuban Missile Crises, US intrusion into Soviet airspace continued even though the president had directed all U-2 flights grounded. There is always someone who did not get the word or who did not wish to carry out an order. People tend to see other countries' foreign policy as "more centralized, disciplined and coordinated than it is . . . [seeing] others as more internally united than they in fact are and generally [overestimating] the degree to which others are following a coherent strategy" (Jervis 1968, 475).

Officials suffer routinely from information deficit. They often cannot wait to have all pertinent data become available before making a decision. Mearsheimer and Rosato (2023) call attention to this pervasive and enduring phenomenon challenging decision-makers. Therefore, researchers in the academy may sometimes be too critical when there is a policy failure. Amos Tversky and Daniel Kahneman (1974), two pioneers of prospect theory, introduce the ideas of availability bias, representativeness bias, and anchoring bias to point to people's common judgment errors when operating under uncertainty. Naturally, the influence of analogies is greater when the information available to decision-makers is more limited and more ambiguous. Like the rest of us, they fall back on analogies to help them to frame questions and search for solutions. Of course, recent, familiar, and traumatic and dramatic past episodes, especially those involving their own personal experience or that of people who are close to them, tend to be more easily recalled (availability bias). Moreover, past episodes that show superficial similarities with a current policy problem, such as the seeming parallels between the capture of US vessels by Communist countries—*Pueblo* by the North Koreans and *Mayaguez* by the Khmer Rouge—are more readily recalled (representativeness bias). Researchers writing about policy failures have the benefit of hindsight—a tendency that can incline them to believe these failures to be more predictable and thus more avoidable than at the time when officials had to make their decisions (Fischhoff and Beyth 1975). Finally, given the limited and ambiguous nature of information available to officials, it is natural and even prudent for them to make small, if any, adjustments to their existing beliefs or existing policies (anchoring bias). There can therefore be sound reasons for the phenomenon of policy stasis or changing policies slightly or incrementally.

The information available to officials can be compatible with competing hypotheses. As remarked earlier, at the time of the Munich Conference in 1938, it was still unclear whether Adolf Hitler had only limited demands or an insatiable appetite for aggrandizement. The critical piece of information pointing to the latter interpretation did not become available until he invaded countries without a large German-speaking minority. As another example, although US officials were aware that the Japanese fleet had left its home ports in December 1941, this information was compatible with the hypothesis that it was headed for Southeast Asia (then the dominant US expectation) rather than for Pearl Harbor (Wohlstetter 1962). Hindsight bias tends to influence people's thinking in retrospect. Moreover, we also tend to minimize the element of chance after knowing an event has happened, thus exaggerating its certainty or inevitability. The Japanese fleet had not been sighted on its long voyage to Pearl Harbor, with two refueling stops. Had its movement been detected, this contingency would have probably caused it to abort its mission. Conversely, in April 1980, Jimmy Carter had the misfortunes of US helicopters encountering mechanical problems on their way to rescue hostages held in Tehran and the collision at Desert One between one of these helicopters and an aircraft tanker tasked to refuel them (S. Smith 1985). These mishaps led to his decision to call off the mission.

Lest we forget, the limited and ambiguous information available to officials can be compounded or at least partly caused by an adversary's deliberate efforts to deceive them, what James D. Fearon (1995) has referred to as misrepresentation. The Japanese task force heading for Pearl Harbor was instructed to take precautions to cover their tracks, including a ban on dumping their trash at sea. Efforts by the Japanese to conceal their mission were also in part facilitated by the US decision to scale back monitoring posts out of a fear of causing an unwanted and premature confrontation. The biggest advantage enjoyed by those planning a surprise attack is that they control timing and location. Their attempt to disguise their intention is most likely to succeed when it works to reinforce the defender's existing bias, such as in Germany's invasion of the USSR in 1941 and the Yom Kippur War launched by Egypt and Syria against Israel in 1973 (Handel 1977; Shlaim 1976; Whaley 1973). In the former case, Joseph Stalin did not believe Hitler would attack Russia and thus bring about a two-front war for Berlin. There was also a general belief among Soviet leaders, one caused by their supposition based on precedents, that Berlin would not attack until after it had issued an ultimatum. In the latter case, the Israelis were as much misled by the Arab countries' ruses as by Tel Aviv's own so-called conception—that is, its civilian and military leaders' entrenched belief that their enemies would not dare to attack as long as Israel had command of the sky—a supposition that was nullified when Moscow provided air defense missiles to Cairo. In both wars, the attackers worked to reinforce the defenders' preexisting biases rather than trying to change their beliefs.

Finally, there is another point pertinent to the study of past cases of strategic surprise (Ben-Zvi 1976; Betts 1980–1981; Chan 1979; DeWeerd 1962; Wohlstetter 1965). The United States was surprised by China's decision to intervene in the Korean War. Although Beijing did try to warn Washington about its intention, its threat was not made more compelling or credible to Washington by disclosing China's military preparations and deployments. The reason is obvious: revealing this information will compromise Beijing's attempt to take advantage of the element of surprise. Thus, Beijing faced a choice in this situation (Slantchev 2010): to enhance the credibility of its deterrence threat to head off a US-led invasion of North Korea or to maximize its military advantage by disguising its troop readiness and deployment.

During the Vietnam War, some pundits and news commentators pointed to the French defeat at Dien Bien Phu to warn the United States about the battle of Khe Sanh Valley. The United States, however, commanded far more airpower than the French, and it was able to pound the Communist positions surrounding this US outpost and succeeded in breaking the siege, even though it subsequently abandoned the marine base there. Thus, although there are some similarities between these two situations, these similarities turned out to be superficial. This reference to Dien Bien Phu also serves as a useful reminder that some analogies may come more quickly and naturally to us than others. Prospect theory tells us that retrieval of past experiences is easier when these experiences are recent, dramatic, and/or have happened to oneself or someone close.

There may be another reason why we do not embrace some analogies readily. We are less likely to accept some analogies because they make us uncomfortable or can cast a negative light on our motives or actions. Thus, Dien Bien Phu made Americans uneasy because of its association with France's war to reestablish its colonial rule in Vietnam. Among the analogies that were applied by US officials in making policies on the Vietnam War, there was not much inclination to recall the French experience, perhaps because they were waging a colonial war and Americans were reluctant to see a parallel between French and US actions. Similarly, Americans do not perceive a parallel between Soviet action in the Cuban Missile Crisis and US action regarding Taiwan's status, even though both can be seen as instances of extended deterrence. If Moscow is seen to be engaged in extended deterrence to protect Cuba, this interpretation would naturally cast the United States in the role of an aggressor. Similarly, few Americans are likely to see a similarity between Crimea's secession from Ukraine and Taiwan's de facto breakaway from China or between US support for Kosovo's independence and its opposition to the separatist governments in the Abkhazia and South Ossetia regions of Georgia. Therefore, given differences in individuals' experiences, backgrounds, and perspectives, some historical parallels are more likely to occur to them or be accepted by them than others.

Other examples come to mind. In the discourse on China's authoritarian government and its suppression of its citizens' political rights, the Tiananmen Square crackdown in 1989 is often mentioned by Westerners, including Americans. Other comparable episodes—such as the killing of protestors at Tlatelolco, Mexico City, in 1960; in Kwangju, South Korea, in 1980; and in Rabaa al-Adawiya Square, Cairo, in 2013—are less often cited. Protests in Hong Kong during 2019–2020 received a great deal of press coverage in the

West, but they are not usually compared to other contemporaneous mass demonstrations in Bolivia, Chile, Colombia, Ecuador, France (*gilets jaunes*), Iran, Iraq, Lebanon, or the United States (Black Lives Matter), even though many of these latter political movements caused a large number of fatalities (no one died in the Hong Kong protests). Nor were the more recent Hong Kong protests compared to the events in 1967 under British colonial rule when the police crackdown was much more violent and brutal, causing more than fifty deaths (Ives and Chen 2019). Critics of China usually overlook Bloody Sunday in January 1972 when British paratroopers killed thirteen people taking part in a peaceful civil rights march in Londonderry, Northern Ireland. British commentators do not usually bring up these episodes, including the brutal suppression of the Irish people's demand for independence and London's colonial policies elsewhere, when discussing the protest movement in Hong Kong.

Of course, our selection bias can also operate in reverse—that is, we may exaggerate the likenesses between two cases while overlooking important differences that distinguish them. In the next chapter, I will discuss the extent to which Wilhelmine Germany serves as a suitable analogue for contemporary China. Reinhard Wolf warns China against repeating the *Kaiserreich*'s policies that led to Berlin's self-encirclement before 1914. He emphasizes that "concerns about national status strongly affected both the fateful escalation of the 1914 crisis and the growing antagonisms of the years preceding" (Wolf 2014, 185). He is referring to Berlin's quest for a battle fleet (*Hochseeflotte*) and overseas colonies as proximate causes for alienating and alarming its neighbors. Michelle Murray (2010) also writes about bellicosity born of Germany's sense of insecurity, and she argues that Berlin's declared ambition to build a strong navy and to acquire foreign colonies could not but concern its neighbors—especially Britain, which would clearly be the target of German naval armament. German admiral Alfred von Tirpitz's idea of developing a "risk fleet" that would cause London to hesitate to risk a naval confrontation was naturally alarming to the British. In Murray's view, Berlin's policies compounded rather than eased its international problems prior to 1914. Jack Snyder (1993, 66) is even more blunt, arguing that Wilhelmine Germany had embarked on a binge of "self-destructive aggression," which brought about a countervailing coalition that eventually led to its defeat.

John J. Mearsheimer and Sebastian Rosato (2023, 103–11), however, challenge these views, arguing that Berlin's grand strategy was in fact a rational response to the circumstances it faced before World War I. True, it did lose this conflict, but we cannot therefore infer from this outcome that its policies were self-destructive because of our hindsight bias. After all, sometimes rational processes fail to produce the desired outcomes, and irrational processes produce desired ones due to serendipity (we all have heard about some people winning large lottery prizes—a phenomenon that does not necessarily mean that their good fortune was due to rational behavior or refute the argument that they were mathematically challenged, referring to the prohibitive odds against winning). Robert Jervis (1976, xxiii) observes, "The world is probabilistic; it can be rational to pursue a policy that in fact turns out badly, much information is hidden from actors, and . . . the best-grounded inferences can turn out to be incorrect." Mearsheimer and Rosato (2023, 99) put matters this way: "Rational states can fail to achieve their desired outcomes because of exogenous constraints or unforeseen circumstances. Hence, it does not make sense to judge a state that tries and fails to reach some objective as nonrational. The converse is also true: a state that achieves its preferred outcome is not necessarily rational. Nonrational states can succeed for many reasons, including material superiority and dumb luck."

This is good advice. We cannot infer from an outcome that the process producing it is either sound or unsound. We should also guard against hindsight bias in another sense—namely, the tendency to see events to be more likely and outcomes more certain than they actually are. Moreover, although heuristics are useful as mental shortcuts to frame problems and search for solutions, they can also be misleading. Prospect theory reminds us that our decision-making can be biased or distorted due to the availability bias, representativeness bias, and anchoring bias, as Tversky and Kahneman (1974) point out. Moreover, Jervis (1968) reminds us that we tend to see others' actions as more coherent and intentional than they usually are, and we are also more inclined to interpret others' behavior as a response to us than as a result of other causes. Finally, attribution theory tells us that when another person or country does something we dislike, we tend to explain their action as an indication of their malevolent intention or inherent bad faith. Yet when we undertake similar actions, we tend to explain them away by pointing to circumstances beyond our control. Thus, we shuttle our logic so that we resort to dispositional explanations when others engage in actions we dislike but present circumstantial explanations when we act in a similar way (Mercer 1996).

NINE

Discourse on China's Rise and the Problem with Selective History

In chapter 2, I discussed power-transition theory according to which systemic wars are likely to be started by revisionist latecomers attempting to challenge and displace the incumbent leading state as the global hegemon. This theory argues that it is the combination of power shifts favoring an upstart and this state's revisionist impulses that produces the most destructive havoc to the world. Unfortunately, the concept of revisionism has been undertheorized, and much of the existing empirical literature on power-transition theory does not even include this variable in their analyses. The concept of revisionism has sometimes been used to refer to a state's attempt to alter the existing distribution of power, in which case, this concept comes close to duplicating power-transition theory's other variable—namely, power shifts—and it begs the question of which state in the world does not aspire to improve its power position in the international hierarchy, thus making the concept of revisionism practically meaningless.

The concept of revisionism has also been used to refer to a state's attempt to change the existing rules and norms of international order—a view that in turn begs the question of which state does not wish to see some of these rules and norms altered while preserving other rules and norms. In other words, all states in the world are in this situation, wishing to change some rules and norms while retaining others. States play both offense and defense. Some people's discussion of the concept of revisionism implies that the rules and norms of international order are somehow fixed, when in fact they are constantly evolving, being negotiated and renegotiated. Prevailing narratives in US scholarship often make attributions about revisionist and status quo orientations to states that seem to stand these ideas on their head.

Thus, for example, a country, like the United States, that openly promotes and advocates regime change, color revolutions, and exporting democracy and capitalism to the rest of the world is characterized as a status-quo state. Similarly, a state that introduces new doctrines such as "responsibility to protect," "preventive war," and "crimes against peace and humanity" is described as a defender of the status quo. At least rhetorically, Washington has unabashedly sought to "make the world safe for democracy." In contrast, a country like China that professes its adherence to traditional Westphalian principles of state sovereignty and noninterference in other countries' domestic affairs is said to be revisionist. Since the Maoist years, Beijing has abandoned its ideology to promote and instigate world revolution to overthrow capitalism. It has ceased its support for armed insurgencies abroad. The usage of the term "revisionism" in prevailing discourse in the West and the United States does not correspond to this word's customary meaning. This is one more example of how scholarship can be biased and used to promote a particular narrative or perspective that places one's own country in a favorable light. As I said before, scholarship cannot be separated from the real world of power politics, and it does not represent some neutral, objective, and value-free account of international relations.

Moreover, there is a definite bias in many of the current narratives, suggesting that somehow the status quo is to be preferred over change and, in some contexts, that the status quo is even sacrosanct. It is unclear why the rejection and abandonment of some longstanding institutions, practices, or ideas—such as slavery, colonialism, apartheid, and states' ostensible right to wage war—are somehow objectionable. Isn't the abolition of these norms and institutions a welcome development? And aren't more recent ideas and norms—such as crimes against peace and humanity, prohibitions against genocide, bans on chemical and biological weapons, and humanitarian intervention—novel principles and hence "revisionist"? In current practice, the concept of "revisionism" is often deployed as a code word to indicate an author's disapproval of another country's foreign policies rather than as an analytic variable. It is rarely defined conceptually or operationally, thus causing a great deal of confusion and obfuscation.

One thing appears to be clear, though. Revisionism is a label applied to former or current enemies (including lesser powers such as the "axis of evil"). It is an interesting fact that although alleged revisionist states are said to be responsible for starting wars of aggression, their ranks also prominently feature those that have been defeated in these wars—such as Napoleonic France, Wilhelmine and Nazi Germany, Fascist Italy, imperial Japan, and, of course, the USSR, albeit, in this case, in a cold rather than hot war. Current discourse pitting the United States and China in a possible war follows this well-worn script. It appears that revisionist states are especially prone to start wars but also to lose them. It is an interesting question whether a state is considered revisionist because it has started a systemic war or because it has lost this war. Scholars of international relations rarely examine how alleged revisionist states have acted differently from their opposite numbers—namely, the ostensibly satiated, satisfied established states that are supposed to be committed to the status quo.

My remarks above do not deny that there have been recent efforts to interrogate the idea of revisionism and to articulate this concept more self-consciously and systematically (e.g., R. Allison 2017; Chan 2004a, 2015, 2021a; Chan and Hu, forthcoming-a; Chan, Hu, and He 2019; Chan et al. 2021; Cooley, Nexon, and Ward 2019; Davidson 2006; H. Feng 2009; Foot and Walter 2011; Goddard 2018a; He et al. 2021; Hurd 2007; Johnston 2003, 2013, 2019; Kastner and Saunders 2012; Lind 2017; Murray 2019; Sample 2018; Schweller 2015, 2018; Thies and Nieman 2017; Ward 2013). Yet despite the impression that may be created by the number of citations just given on studies of revisionism, attempts to develop and apply this concept more analytically and systematically and to incorporate it in empirical research on war and peace have still not permeated the dominant discourse on an ostensible revisionist China threatening to undermine international order. The prevailing practice is to continue to deploy this concept rhetorically rather than analytically. Moreover, there is still a shortage of studies focusing specifically on China's conduct *in comparison* with that of other countries, such as the United States (e.g., Chan 2004a, 2015; Chan, Hu, and He 2019; Chan and Hu, forthcoming-a). In what ways has Beijing acted differently from Washington to warrant the designation of a revisionist state? Analysts and commentators often assert this designation without explaining their logic or offering systematic evidence.

There is a pervasive presumption in prevailing US discourse that rising states are somehow inherently aggressive and bellicose. I have already quoted Susan L. Shirk's (2007, 4) assertion that "history teaches us that rising powers are likely to provoke war." It is unclear where the evidence is for this claim and which states Shirk would include in her category of rising states. For example, was the United States once a rising state, say, in the latter part of the nineteenth century and the early part of the twentieth century? Would it qualify as a rising state again in the years following the USSR's demise—an event that elevated its status further to the point of becoming the world's undisputed unipolar power?

I mentioned earlier that on the occasion of the hundredth anniversary of World War I, several scholars wrote about whether and how Wilhelmine Germany can offer an instructive analogue for contemporary China lest Beijing repeat the same mistakes made by Berlin that contributed to the global conflagration ending in its defeat and ruin. It is interesting to note that the *Kaiserreich* is selected as a source for lessons that China can learn from history. Scholars and pundits alike do not appear nearly as disposed to refer to the United States during, say, the administration of Theodore Roosevelt as a basis for comparison with Xi Jinping's China. They have not tried to compare US foreign policy then with Chinese foreign policy now. That is, they have not bothered to ask which of these two countries has acted more like a revisionist state.

There are, of course, scholars, such as Barry Buzan (2004), who point out that there was a seismic transformation in US policy in dismantling the post-1945 international institutions that it had constructed and sponsored—long before the Trump administration. There was, of course, a time when US policies were more isolationist and Washington declined to be bound and constrained by international rules and institutions, as evidenced by its rejection of the League of Nations and the International Trade Organization (the Havana Charter). The United States has also participated in protracted negotiations involving the creation of the International Criminal Court, the Kyoto Protocol to limit the emission of greenhouse gases, and the UN Convention on the Law of the Sea only to subsequently refuse to join these international accords.

Barry Buzan and Michael Cox's (two British scholars) study (2013) offers a refreshing exception to my generalization (I quote them later)—but neither are American, which in turn tells us that some parallels are more easily recalled by some people than others even when the relevant parallels pertain to their own country's history. Similarly, Yuen Foong Khong (2001), a Singaporean who studied at Harvard, was the one calling attention to the contrasting experiences of a conformist Japan and a revisionist United States in the late 1800s and early 1900s. Similarly, Kishore Mahbubani (2020), whose observations I will introduce later, was Singapore's ambassador to the United Nations. Of course, in referring to these writers, I do not mean to suggest that there are no Americans who point to some uncomfortable historical precedents when comparing past US conduct with current Chinese practice. Graham T. Allison (2017), whose observations I will also introduce later, is one such rare scholar. There are also others, such as Richard Ned Lebow and Benjamin Valentino (2009), who call into question the extent to which power-transition theory offers a valid explanation of past international relations and its applicability to contemporary Sino-American relations, and Jennifer Lind (2017), who has written an article with the title referring to the United States as Asia's "other revisionist power." Other US scholars, such as Ivo H. Daalder and James M. Lindsay (2005), Randall L. Schweller (2015, 2018), and Stephen Walt (2005), also call out Washington's propensity to exercise "muscular" policy, resort to assertive unilateralism, and behave as a revisionist power in the post–Cold War era. There are still others who engage in empirical analyses to study whether China is a revisionist state and, if so, the extent of its revisionism (e.g., Johnston 2003, 2013, 2019; Kastner and Saunders 2012). Still others undertake comparison of the extent to which the United States and China have behaved as revisionist powers (e.g., Chan 2004a, 2015; Chan, Hu, and He 2019; Chan et al. 2021; Foot and Walter 2011). But these scholars are in a distinct minority compared to those who assert China's alleged revisionism without providing any systematic empirical evidence, especially in comparing Beijing's conduct with Washington's.

American scholars of international relations have also not generally shown much inclination to compare the policy agenda and conduct of the United States during the years of its ascent with those of imperial Germany and imperial Japan (although some, such as Zoltan I. Buzas [2013] and Jonathan Renshon [2017], discuss the blowback from Japan stemming from US racial discrimination against Japanese nationals). These countries were all rising powers during the latter part of the nineteenth century and the early part of the twentieth century. Which of these countries was the most expansionist and sought to make and propagate its own rules and principles, and which ones were more assiduous in following the norms and conventions of international relations prevailing at the time? Much of the current dominant discourse in the United States suggests revisionist history that overlooks important similarities and differences between Theodore Roosevelt's America, on the one hand, and its cohorts Wilhelmine Germany and imperial Japan, on the other hand.

Reflecting on Wilhelmine Germany's experience, Reinhard Wolf (2014, 187) counsels Beijing to be patient and to give the international community more time to adjust to its rise. His advice and observation regarding possible parallels between Germany then and China today seem to be sensible and well intentioned. However, his study also raises as many questions as it answers in the sense that compared to the United States during its ascent from the mid-1800s to the early 1900s, German actions then and Chinese actions now do not appear to be more egregious, aggressive, or destabilizing. There therefore appears to be a case of selecting on the dependent variable. Comparing China today to Wilhelmine Germany is based on the implicit premise that we should be concerned about the danger of war caused by an aggressive rising state—as we all know that the *Kaiserreich* ended in fighting and losing World War I.

If one had picked the United States of the late nineteenth century and early twentieth century as the counterpart for comparison with contemporary China, one's conclusion might be very different from Wolf's because, as noted already, Washington's actions did not precipitate a global war and the Anglo-American transition was peaceful, although the United States had threatened, fought, and come close to war on several occasions, as my earlier discussion indicated. There are indeed parallels between the *Kaiserreich* and contemporary China, and the most important one is that both of these latecomers are located in crowded neighborhoods, surrounded by other established and rising powers. This fact distinguishes them from the United States, which has been peerless in its home region and which was left alone to grow its power after London decided not to contest Washington's regional hegemony in the Western Hemisphere because the European powers were too busy competing with one another (Elman 2004). Unlike China, the United States had the good fortune of not having to attend to its national security and therefore had a favorable opportunity to focus on its economic growth without being saddled with a heavy defense burden or distracted by foreign threats (Y. Feng 2006). Moreover, as Barry Buzan and Michael Cox (2013, 118) remark, "The United States has been more fortunate in that its unity question was largely laid to rest after the Civil War, and did not much affect its peaceful rise. For China, the unity question is still not fully resolved, especially over Tibet and Taiwan. It plays significantly into China's international image, and therefore into its wider foreign policy and IR."

China's unity problem is, of course, the result of US intervention to prevent Beijing from taking over Taiwan, starting with Truman's order for the US Navy to intervene in the Taiwan Strait shortly after the outbreak of the Korean War. One can quibble with Buzan and Cox by pointing out that the US ascendance in international relations was not entirely peaceful. It had at least one major war, the Spanish-American War in 1898, numerous military interventions in the Caribbean and Central America, and several "close encounters" that could have ended in war with Britain. Moreover, if we look further back in history, there was also the war between Mexico and the United States in 1846–1848, not to mention numerous military campaigns and battles fought against America's indigenous peoples. That the United States waged war against these much weaker opponents does not, of course, mean that its ascent was peaceful—only that the targets of its aggression were more easily defeated.

During the time when the United States was a rising power, London was facing several rising powers. The United States was fortunate also in this respect. Britain decided to accommodate, conciliate, or associate itself with some countries (e.g., the United States, France, Russia, and Japan) in order to concentrate its finite resources on Germany. In this view, the accidents of location and timing had more to do with war occurrence than the rising states' conduct. The United States today is practically a resident country in East Asia with its many allies and military bases surrounding China. Unlike Britain, which withdrew from the Western Hemisphere, the United States has not left China alone. Of course, Britain's departure from the Western Hemisphere meant that the United States was left alone to dominate this region. London's accommodation of Washington enabled friendly relations between these two countries—one of its consequences being the US intervention against Germany, which made all the difference in the outcome of both world wars.

As just observed, there are important differences between the United States as a rising power then and China as a rising power now. Yet it is instructive that contemporary China is compared to Wilhelmine Germany and not to the United States, say, during Teddy Roosevelt's administration. As already mentioned, the implicit logic for comparing contemporary China and Wilhelmine Germany is that war broke out in 1914 leading to the *Kaiserreich*'s defeat and demise, and the analyst making this comparison wishes not to see China repeat Germany's mistakes and start another major conflict. As I have already noted, this rationale points to an instance of selecting on the dependent variable, or, in other words, picking a historical analogy that had produced a tragic disaster and asking what can be done to avoid this outcome again.

This approach, however, overlooks another possible inquiry, such as the comparison of the *Kaiserreich*'s conduct with that of Teddy Roosevelt's America. Did their foreign policies share similarities, or were these policies profoundly different, leading to different historical outcomes? For that matter, what are the historical outcomes of interest to us: whether war broke out or, rather, who won and who lost in this war? Could it be that Washington's conduct during the years of US ascendance was as egregious and aggressive as that of Wilhelmine Germany, but geographic location and accidental timing were more important factors, accounting not so much for these countries' involvement in foreign crises and wars but rather the different outcomes of these crises and wars for them, with one emerging victorious and the other vanquished? Why select Wilhelmine Germany rather than the United States during Teddy Roosevelt's administration as a mirror to study and comment on contemporary China?

I will return later to discussing US conduct during its years as a rising power. One can argue that this conduct was not any less aggressive or expansionist compared to Germany's, although there was one difference between them: the United States picked on weaker opponents, whereas Germany had the misfortune of having to fight against other major powers in its neighborhood. As noted earlier, the United States had the good fortune of being located in a region where it stood head and shoulders above its neighbors. After Britain withdrew from the Western Hemisphere, no other state in the Americas was in a position to stand up against the United States and block its ascent to become a regional powerhouse.

It is pertinent and important to recognize that prevailing US discourse on China's rise can be seriously warped. Washington accuses Beijing of intending to evict the United States from East Asia, even though it had propagated the Monroe Doctrine to exclude European influence from the Western Hemisphere. Stephen Walt (2005, 125) refers to "U.S. conduct in North America and the Western Hemisphere [when it was a rising power], where it proceeded to conquer a continent, subjugate the indigenous inhabitants, evict the other Great Powers, and openly proclaim its own hegemony over the region."

Similarly, Kenneth N. Waltz (2000b, 36; italics in original) comments forthrightly, "When Americans speak of preserving the balance of power in East Asia through their military presence, the Chinese understandably take this to mean that they intend to maintain the strategic hegemony they now enjoy in the *absence* of such a balance." Benjamin Schwarz (2005, 27) elaborates further,

> Hardliners and moderates [in the United States], Republicans and Democrats, agree that America is strategically dominant in East Asia and the eastern Pacific—China's backyard. They further agree that America should retain its dominance there. Thus U.S. planners define as a threat Beijing's efforts to remedy its own weak position in the face of overwhelming superiority that they acknowledge the United States holds right up to the edge of the Asian mainland. This probably reveals more about our ambitions than it does about China's. Imagine if the situation is reversed, and China's air and naval power were a dominant and potentially menacing presence on the coastal shelf of North America. Wouldn't we want to offset this preponderance?

In a similar vein, William H. Overholt (1993, 414) invites his readers to imagine a situation where China and the United States have reversed their roles: "If Beijing were demanding the independence of Alaska, sending emissaries to impose immediate change in the governance of New York, and giving advanced weapons to independence fighters in Puerto Rico, while voting in favor of economic war and having its foreign minister declare the transformation of the United States into a communist state a primary objective of Chinese foreign policy, Washington would be concerned."

People like Schwarz and Overholt are rare and in a distinct minority of people who have empathy for their counterpart by asking how it would feel if the shoe were on the other foot—a special gift to see and understand a situation from another person's perspective. Perhaps the most eloquent statement reflecting this gift and the ability to engage in introspection comes from the eminent Anglo-Irish statesman and philosopher Edmund Burke, who writes,

> Among precautions against ambition, it may not be amiss to take one precaution against our own. I must fairly say, I dread our own power and our own ambition: I dread our being too much dreaded. . . . It is ridiculous to say we are not men, and that, as men we shall never wish to aggrandize ourselves in some way or other. . . . [W]e say that we shall not abuse this astonishing and hitherto unheard of power. But every other nation will think we shall abuse it. It is impossible but that, sooner or later, this state of affairs must produce a combination against us which may end in our ruin. (Quoted in Layne 2006a, 204)

Reasoning from a different perspective, Waltz issues a similar warning. He argues that unipolar periods in international relations tend to be short. He offers two reasons for this expectation. First, when power is concentrated in the hands of one preponderant country, its misuse is more likely. Second, "even if a dominant power behaves with moderation, restraint and forbearance, weaker states will worry about its future behaviour" (Waltz 2000a, 23). Americans praise the wisdom of their nation's founders for instituting a system of checks and balances to mitigate the danger of power being abused when it becomes concentrated in the hands of any one individual or institution. Waltz asks rhetorically whether unbalanced or unchecked power presents similar perils in international relations. "Unbalanced power, whoever wields it, is a potential danger to others. The powerful state may, and the United States does, think of itself as acting for the sake of peace, justice and well-being in the world. These terms, however, are defined to the liking of the powerful, which may conflict with the preferences and interests of others" (24).

Waltz (25) concludes, "Concentrated power invites distrust because it is so easily misused." In a similar vein, Christopher Layne (2006b, 21) remarks, "Unipolarity substantially erases the distinction between balancing against threat versus balancing against power, because the threat inheres in the very fact that hard-power capabilities are overconcentrated in the hegemon's favor."

Colin Elman (2003, 16) concurs, noting, "It is possible that, when states are approaching capabilities of hegemonic proportions, those resources alone are so threatening that they 'drown out' distance, offense-defense, and intentions as potential negative threat modifiers."

These contemporary scholars of international relations echo Edmund Burke's and Pericles's warnings. I have introduced earlier Pericles's admonition to his fellow Athenians to be wary in the application of their overwhelming power. Introspection and empathy are not most people's strong suit. However, when they try to ask themselves how they would see, feel about, and react to a situation if the roles were reversed, they are undertaking the most effective and sensible form of reasoning by analogy. They would be comparing their own perceptions and motivations with those of a counterpart in their imagination.

I have mentioned earlier that US officials have often urged China to abide by a "rules-based international order," and Chinese officials have retorted by asking whose and which rules their US counterparts have in mind. The assertion that rising states disregard these rules and seek to upend the existing international order based on them is one of the two main factors advanced by power-transition theorists as an explanation for the occurrence of systemic war (e.g., Organski and Kugler 1980; Kugler and Lemke 1996). A latecomer's revisionist agenda—its attempt to challenge and replace the existing order—is a crucial variable for the occurrence of such war in addition to the phenomenon of power transition.

I have also mentioned earlier that it is unclear in what ways Wilhelmine Germany acted as a revisionist power, distinguishing its conduct from those of its predecessors and contemporaries. What specific norms and rules of international relations did Berlin violate that the other great powers have not? If it had prevailed in World War I, how would the norms and rules of the then-prevailing international order have been changed? This observation can also be made about imperial Japan. Although it had acted aggressively in China and Korea in its quest for foreign colonies, markets, and resources, its conduct was not different from the other colonial and imperial states at that time. Barry Buzan and Evelyn Goh (2020,76) write, "As a newcomer to the great power club, Japan evinced an intense desire to conform to the prevailing standards of social Darwinism in order to get recognition as an equal." As Yuen Foong Khong (2001, 40) also points out, "In the 50 years following its forced opening to the outside world in 1853, Japan proved an example par excellence in conforming its government institutions, legal system, and general international practices to the interests, rules, and values of 'civilized' international society, as prescribed by Western nations."

That is, Japan had adopted, imitated and followed Western institutions and conventions assiduously. Translated, it could not be characterized as a revisionist state if by "revisionism" we mean attempts to challenge the existing norms and rules of the then-prevailing international order. Yet Japan's quest for international recognition was blocked by Western powers. After a series of military victories, Japan forced China to cede the Liaotung Peninsula to it in the Treaty of Shimonoseki (1895). Even though Tokyo had acted according to the then-prevailing "rules of the game" in seeking territorial expansion in China, it was forced by Russia, Germany, and France to disgorge this conquered territory—where these very countries then claimed ports for themselves after Tokyo had turned it over to China. "No understanding of twentieth century Japanese nationalism is possible without some comprehension of the bitterness and sense of humiliation that swept the country in the wake of the Tripple Intervention" (Storry, quoted in Khong 2001, 41).

The Chinese also bitterly recall their experience at the hands of Western and Japanese aggressors during their "century of national humiliation" (Z. Wang 2012, 88; Wikipedia 2024a). During this time, foreigners were not subject to Chinese laws in China due to their "extraterritorial" privileges; they had their own laws and police to administer justice in foreign "concessions" in Chinese cities; they had unfettered access to trade and preach in all parts of China; they operated gunboats up and down China's rivers; they were in charge of China's customs; and, as every Chinese student is taught, there used to be a sign posted at the entrance of a public park in Shanghai reportedly announcing, "Dogs and Chinese not admitted," as indicated by the title of an article by Robert A. Bickers and Jeffrey N. Wasserstrom (2009). Such gratuitous insults and deliberate indignities were naturally infuriating and not easily forgotten. It is perhaps not too difficult to understand that sanctimonious preachings about norms and rules of international order did not play very well for the Chinese. Indeed, it would sound quite odd and even outrageous to modern ears that Britain could wage war on China based on the claim that it had been denied unfettered access to sell opium, a narcotic, in China in the name of free trade. This was the proximate cause of the Sino-British conflict known as the Opium War.

I have presented above Japan's and China's experiences to show the need for empathy and introspection, if you will, to analogize and imagine oneself in other people's shoes. When Americans tell the Chinese subtly and sometimes not so subtly that they should get over their feelings of victimhood, such as to stop harping on their "century of humiliation," they are compounding these feelings by showing a lack of sensitivity. How would Americans react to being told to get over the tragedy of 9/11 or Jewish people to forget about the Holocaust? Although research on historical analogies has not touched on the importance of empathy and introspection, these qualities are very much related to the use or abuse of history. As I have already said on several occasions, different people are apt to remember and interpret history differently. Although the application of history to decision-making is a universal practice, the meaning, salience, and recollection of particular episodes vary for different people because of differences in their experience and background. An appreciation of how one's counterpart sees and understands the past is therefore important in practicing sound statecraft and scholarship.

Feelings of grievances, as my earlier quote from John A. Vasquez argues, are the source of interstate disputes rather than changes in the interstate distribution of power. Jean-Marc Coicaud (2001, 92) remarks in this vein, pointing out that neither Europe nor China "is likely to challenge the United States for hegemony. They seek respect more than hegemony." Moreover, in the case of China, "equality in status, a fierce insistence on not bowing to foreign prescription, is for Chinese leaders not a tactic but a moral imperative" (94). The United States routinely lectures foreigners that they should adopt its values and model of governance. It is these patronizing and condescending attitudes that are so infuriating to the Chinese, who retort that it is not just up to the Americans to evaluate their political system, and indeed, even many Americans have serious reservations about how well their democratic institutions have been performing. Nearly one-third (30 percent to be precise) of Americans, for example, believe Biden was elected president due to voter fraud (Kamisar 2023), and a majority of them feel that their country has been heading in a wrong direction; hence, Donald Trump's rhetoric to make America great again resonates with many of them.

Even liberal US president Barack Obama, who is known for his support for the cause of justice and his sensitivity to the plight of the downtrodden, has stated unabashedly that "America should write the rules. America should call the shots. Other countries should play by the rules that America and our partners set, and not the other way around" ("Obama" 2016). In reaction to such statements, Chinese president Xi Jinping (2021) declared pointedly that "China welcomes helpful suggestions, but will not accept sanctimonious preaching." Americans' haughty disposition and evangelical zeal were captured nicely when, in 1940, Nebraska's senator Kenneth Wherry declared that "with God's help, we will lift Shanghai up and up, ever up, until it is just like Kansas City" (quoted in Carillet 2008). One wonders how he would compare Shanghai with Kansas City today.

Grievances are often fueled, compounded, and reflected by feelings that the rules of the game are rigged and that there are double standards. Status denial and a perception that other countries were trying to thwart their country's rise was a powerful motivation for Japan in the 1930s, and the same is true for China today. The irony is that the one country that had demonstrably created its own rules had a much easier time gaining acceptance by the then-dominant power, Britain. The United States unilaterally proclaimed the Monroe Doctrine, seeking to bar European influence from the Western Hemisphere, even though it claims that China is trying to do the same in East Asia. Otto von Bismarck, Prussia's chancellor, once remarked, "Monroe's epistle [was] 'a species of arrogance peculiarly American and inexcusable,' a 'presumptuous idea' that even Washington had been unable consistently to interpret and apply" (quoted in Herwig 1986, 196). He demanded that "Monroe's 'insolent dogma' be revoked 'in plain daylight,'" declaring that this unilateral US assertion "has not become an international law, to which the European nations are tied" (197).

Even British prime minister Lord Salisbury remarked that the Monroe Doctrine was not international law and "no nation, however powerful, [is] competent to insert into the code of international law a novel principle which was never recognized before, and which has not since been accepted by the government of any country" (quoted in Khong 2001, 44). Khong (49) emphasizes that paradoxically: "The cases of Japan and the United States illustrate opposing power transition scenarios: a relatively weak new power with limited regional ambitions conforming to a set of norms already agreed upon and held by others, compared with a strong new great power candidate with a well-defined regional dominance, increasingly trying to establish its own rules in competition with others, and to play its own game beyond its regional sphere.

Ironically, the first case led to war whereas the second did not." Zoltan Buzas (2013) writes about the "color of threat"—that is, how prejudice and discrimination have played a part in connecting race to threat perceptions (such as popular images of the "yellow horde" and Chinese coolies in motivating US laws banning Asian, including Chinese, immigration).

In view of Khong's observation, theories like that of power transition appear as ideational constructs propagating and legitimating the distinct views of a ruling hegemon. Rather than presenting a neutral description or explanation of world affairs, these theories need themselves to be deconstructed and explained. Graham T. Allison (2017, 90) reminds his readers that during the period when it was a rising power, "the US [had] declared war on Spain, expelling it from the Western Hemisphere and acquiring Puerto Rico, Guam, and the Philippines; threatened Germany and Britain with war unless they agreed to settle disputes on American terms; supported an insurrection in Colombia to create a new country, Panama, in order to build a canal; and declared itself the policeman of the Western Hemisphere, asserting the right to intervene whenever and wherever it judged necessary—a right it exercised nine times in the seven years of TR's [Theodore Roosevelt's] presidency alone." He cautions Americans in wishing China to behave "more like us." John J. Mearsheimer (2001, 238) quotes Henry Cabot Lodge in a similar vein, remarking that during the years of its ascendance, the United States had compiled "a record of conquest, colonization, and territorial expansion unequaled by any people in the nineteenth century." Compared to the United States, Wilhelmine Germany's territorial conquest would appear puny. The amount of territory that the United States had seized from Mexico alone comprised of all or parts of today's Arizona, California, Colorado, Nevada, New Mexico, Utah, and Wyoming.

Singapore's former ambassador to the United Nations Kishore Mahbubani is quoted saying that even during the relatively peaceful administration of Barack Obama, the United States had dropped twenty-six thousand bombs on seven countries in 2016 alone, whereas China has not fired a single shot across its border since 1979 when it fought its last war with Vietnam (Kang 2020, 140). These historical accounts are not reflected in reigning theories of international relations seeking to understand the causes of war and peace.

When considered in the context of Khong's study of the obstacles faced by imperial Japan in its quest for status recognition, rhetorical assertions about rising powers' ostensible revisionist intentions to upend the rules and norms of international order should also be taken with a large grain of salt. Even though, as Khong (2001, 44) argues, imperial Japan tried its best to conform to the then-prevailing "rules-based international order," its wish to be admitted to the elite club of great powers encountered serious resistance. This fact and other points made earlier suggest that today's ritualistic invocations of "rules-based international order" are in fact a canard.

Recall, as already mentioned, Japan was unable to get Westerners (especially Britons and Australians) to even acknowledge the principles of sovereign equality among states and the equality of races at the Versailles Conference in 1919 (parenthetically, this demand by Japan was, of course, revisionist in the sense that it sought to alter the then-prevailing order based on blatant racial discrimination and colonial aggrandizement—phenomena that in turn beg the question whether those people who decry revisionism would agree that it would be a good idea to retain these rules and institutions). Contemporary China declares that it would only recognize the UN Charter as the basis of international order but not the rules created by a handful of Western countries, or what Beijing calls Washington's "house rules" (*jia fa bang gui* 家法帮规; W. Wang 2021; Zhao 2022). Beijing argues that the most authoritative and representative voice of world order is the UN General Assembly. It is, of course, precisely the leading Western powers, Britain and the United States, that have been most often outvoted in this forum and that were the ones who were most resistant to calls to sanction the apartheid regimes in Rhodesia and South Africa, even though they are nowadays the most vocal proponents of human rights and the "responsibility to protect." When they were unable to obtain UN authorization, NATO members attacked Iraq and Serbia anyway.

It is, of course, not unusual to hear Americans and Westerners more generally to argue that the Chinese vision of world order based on Westphalian principles is outdated and that these state-centric rules and norms should be replaced with ones that give more emphasis to people's individual rights. Does this stance suggest that we should consider changing the voting protocols of the United Nations to reflect population size—even if this means Africans, Indians, and Chinese would then procure an even larger voice in deciding international rules and norms than their current voting majority?

Contradictions between historical practice and prevailing international relations discourse are a persistent phenomenon. Washington has routinely criticized Beijing's conduct in enforcing its sovereignty claims in the East China Sea and South China Sea as infractions of international law. It has called attention to Beijing's rejection of the International Arbitration Tribunal's authority to adjudicate a competing sovereignty claim filed by the Philippines concerning its assertion of ownership of parts of the South China Sea. However, the United States has not even signed the UNCLOS (United Nations Convention on the Law of the Sea), while China has joined this convention. Beijing's rejection of the tribunal's jurisdiction was based on its invocation of a special provision of this convention. Moreover, Washington has rejected the International Court of Justice's ruling finding that it had violated international law when it mined Nicaragua's harbors. Of course, Washington has refused to accept this ruling.

The United States led the prosecution of German and Japanese war criminals in Nuremburg and Tokyo after World War II. It has since then routinely accused other countries of violating the rules of war, including, for example, the "ethnic cleansing" carried out by the Serbs against the Bosnians. Washington was reticent in leveling such charges against the Israelis in their assault on Palestinians living in Gaza in 2024, which has thus far resulted in over fifty thousand fatalities. Thus, historical precedents and parallels are not always applied consistently. In 2020, during Donald Trump's first administration, Washington actually imposed sanctions on prosecutors working for the International Criminal Court (ICC) in order to block their investigation of alleged war crimes committed by Americans. The financial assets of these ICC personnel were frozen, and they and their families were banned from entering the United States (Human Rights Watch 2020a, 2020b). Moreover, the US government threatened to sanction anyone for cooperating with ICC investigators looking into allegations of war crimes committed by Americans in Afghanistan.

Although the Biden administration reversed these policies in 2021, Secretary of State Antony Blinken stated publicly that the United States continues to "strongly disagree" with the ICC's investigations in Afghanistan and Palestine and would "vigorously protect current and former United States personnel" from any ICC attempts to exercise jurisdiction over them ("US Lifts Trump Sanctions" 2021). As Allison (2016) reminds us, all major powers, not just China, have rejected international legal verdicts that are, in their view, contrary to their national interests. His observation calls attention to the frequent practice of referring selectively to historical episodes. His remark is again a reminder that people sometimes ransack history for evidence to support their favorite narrative.

Returning to a comparison of US and Chinese conduct, Barry Buzan and Michael Cox (2013, 118) state forthrightly, "Parallels could in fact be drawn between the ruthless military anti-secession and rejection of self-determination that underpinned the US civil war, and China's similar current attitudes towards Tibet, Taiwan, and Xinjiang. Abraham Lincoln and the Chinese Communist Party would perhaps have understood each other quite well on this question." In the spirit of my earlier remark about putting oneself in another person's or country's shoes, Senator Frank Church of Idaho pointed out, in a hearing on the Vietnam War, another unpleasant parallel that can be bothersome for many Americans: "Had England, which favored the South, adhered to the same principle that now seems to govern American policy, and had sent troops in the name of self-determination into the Confederacy, I think the English Government would have been hard put to convince Abraham Lincoln that there should be an election to determine the ultimate outcome of the war" (quoted in Khong 1992, 236).

The conclusion drawn by Khong (2001) about the ironically different outcomes between imperial Japan's and rising United States' statecraft is not only intriguing but also important—as the former state sought to conform to the then-prevailing international rules and norms, whereas the latter state introduced and flaunted its own rules and norms, even though both countries had engaged in aggressive, expansionist policies. One often hears nowadays US and British condemnation of China's commission of genocide against the Uighurs. To Chinese ears, these criticisms seem "over the top" (see also "Genocide" 2021) and again remind them of hypocrisy and double standards. When discussing Chinese transgressions, Americans often seem to have national amnesia about the forced eviction of Native Americans from their ancestral homes to enclaves called "reservations," the enslavement of African Americans, the expulsion of over one million Mexican Americans during the 1930s, and the "internment" of US citizens of Japanese ancestry in the 1940s.

As already mentioned earlier, attribution theory reminds us that when another party acts badly, we tend to attribute this behavior to its malevolent intention or inherent bad faith, or, in other words, see it as a reflection of a character flaw. We see its behavior to be dispositional. In contrast, when we engage in similar behavior that is objectionable to others, we resort to circumstantial explanation. That is, we are likely to point to a situational dictate (as opposed to personal volition) or factors beyond our control (e.g., "my hands are tied") to explain our conduct. Our memory of history and recollection of analogies from the past are therefore selective, and our interpretation of events also reflects the tendency to shuttle our logic of explanation depending on whether we are discussing our own conduct or that of others.

Western countries were quick to bomb Serbia for its acts of "ethnic cleansing" but slow to act against Israel's recent actions in Gaza. They condemn Beijing's intimidation of Taiwan, but they appear to forget their own recent history, such as Britain's brutal suppression of the Irish independence movement and similar actions taken by France in Algeria and Vietnam. In US eyes, those rioters who destroyed property, attacked bystanders, and stormed and ransacked Hong Kong's Legislative Council were "prodemocracy" protestors. US Democrats, however, call those who assaulted the Capitol on January 6, 2021, "insurrectionists" and "seditionists," while Republicans claim that they were engaged in "legitimate political discourse" (Cheney 2022). The list can go on. Suffice it to say that such rhetoric grates on the Chinese, especially when these charges are leveled against them by scholars who are supposed to be objective and impartial. As I have remarked earlier, some historical parallels come more easily to people's minds, while others are more readily forgotten or conveniently overlooked.

Perhaps this is understandable because scholars are after all human beings, and it is natural for people to see what they want to see or expect to see. They are quick to perceive information that is supportive of their preexisting beliefs or expectations even when this evidence is flimsy and slow to recognize information that disconfirms their beliefs or expectations even when a massive amount of such contradictory data exists (Jervis 1976). People are also information misers, who tend to hold on to information that is easily retrievable and simple—or rather, simplistic historical analogies—which enables them to make mental shortcuts in coping with complicated situations (Khong 1992). There are also the pressures of groupthink and political correctness, which foster conformist thinking and premature closure in defining the nature of a policy problem (Janis 1982a). This danger is the greatest when there is widespread acceptance of what are supposed to be important lessons of history, when the available information about a current situation is limited and ambiguous, and/or when contrarian perspectives and uncomfortable recollections are located in the remote past and the deepest recesses of our minds.

Returning to Reinhard Wolf's (2014) advice to the Chinese, he writes about the fear of status loss and the impending adverse power shifts inclining Austria-Hungary and Germany to take a hard line in the July Crisis of 1914. He assigns an important role to the alliance ties in prewar Europe in contributing to the dynamics of conflict escalation and contagion set off initially by the assassinations of Archduke Ferdinand and his wife in Sarajevo. The embedded and interdependent nature of the alliance ties in the European system caused this chain-ganging effect (Christensen and Snyder 1990; Tierney 2011). In this regard, there is obviously an important difference between then and now. China has only one formal ally (North Korea), and it is not entangled to nearly the same extent in these ties as pre-1914 Germany and the contemporary United States.

Indeed, Wolf's observation of entangling alliances and foreign ambitions—with their attendant risks of involuntary involvement in conflicts abroad and excessive overseas commitments (causing "imperial overstretch," as Paul Kennedy [1987] warns Washington)—is more pertinent to the United States than China. The dangerous brew that led to war in 1914 also consisted of recurrent crises and an intense armament race (Thompson 2003). At least until quite recently, there has been scant evidence that China's neighbors have been ramping up their defense spending in reaction to China's rise—not even Taiwan has been doing so (Kang 2025)—thus again suggesting a crucial difference between Europe then and Asia now. This situation, however, warrants continued monitoring as it may be changing.

Reflecting on Germany's situation then and China's situation now, Etel Solingen (2014) warns that we should not jump too quickly to accept superficial analogies as a substitute for careful analysis. In the years leading up to World War I, Germany's politics and policymaking were dominated by the so-called iron-and-rye coalition, consisting of conservative politicians, agrarian protectionists, leading industrialists, advocates of military (especially naval) programs, and proponents of colonial and imperial expansion. This coalition wanted to preserve a conservative monarchical order at home and pursue weltpolitik to elevate Germany's profile abroad. These interest groups engaged in logrolling to promote their agenda. In his book *Myths of Empire*, Jack Snyder (1993) describes in detail this connection between domestic politics and international ambition for both imperial Germany and imperial Japan, pointing to a common pathway to war that eventually ended in both countries' defeat and ruin.

Solingen points out that the iron-and-rye coalition dominating Wilhelmine Germany's politics and policymaking was an inward-looking and nationalist combination. The ruling coalitions of some other states at that time, especially in Serbia and Russia, shared a similar profile. In contrast, China today is far more embedded and integrated in the global economy, and it is located in a region where the ruling coalitions of other countries have also shown a strong preference for an open economy and free trade as a national strategy to achieve political legitimacy, as opposed to pursuing international rivalry and foreign conflict as a top priority. Solingen (2007) shows the stark contrast between the political economies of countries in East Asia and those in the Middle East. Although there are, of course, strident nationalists in China, its dominant ruling coalition has been internationalist in outlook since Deng Xiaoping's economic reforms in the late 1970s. Economic growth, rather than the quest for foreign influence and glory, has been Beijing's top priority up to now.

Again, the above comment does not deny that there are outspoken nationalists and inward-looking lobby groups in China. Rather, my remark refers to policy priority and the distribution of power and interests inside China, suggesting to me that those who are in charge still tend to put a premium on economic growth and international stability. In order to achieve a high rate of economic growth, Beijing needs a stable international environment to acquire the necessary capital, technology, and markets for its export-led model of development. It is the United States, especially during the Trump administrations, that has acted to decouple the country from China and the rest of the world.

There is more evidence to show that both the Trump and Biden administrations in the United States have increasingly turned away from a liberal regime of open economy and free trade, sometimes subsumed under the broad heading of globalization. In contrast, Xi Jinping has pledged China's continued commitment to globalization (Xi 2017; Timsit 2021). Of course, things are subject to change as well in China. A strong implication of this discussion is therefore the importance of monitoring any notable alterations in the nature and composition of China's ruling coalition and any significant shifts in its strategy to promote and sustain economic growth, such as a turn to a more inward-looking economic policy. In other words, we cannot assume that the same policy priorities or the same cast of political actors will continue to be dominant in the coming years. That said, the longer a ruling coalition has been in power and the more entrenched it is, the more difficult it is to dislodge it.

Although we obviously cannot rely only on a government's words to indicate its policy intentions and conduct, official rhetoric does disclose its legitimating strategy to justify its role and promote its image in international relations (Goddard 2018b; Miller 2021; Pu 2019). This rhetoric has an impact on how other states perceive a rising power. Prussia's chancellor Otto von Bismarck was skillful in elevating his country's international profile and increasing its power without causing its neighbors to rally against it. Conversely, rhetoric and conduct can be provocative in arousing anxieties, suspicions, and even alarms in other states, causing them to mobilize against a rising power. Thus, Susan L. Shirk (2023) writes about China's recent "overreach." The main point I want to raise in this discussion, however, is that bellicose statements and brusque diplomacy had an effect in causing the *Kaiserreich*'s self-encirclement, or self-isolation, by alienating the other European countries prior to World War I. In contrast, Beijing has tried to ease other countries' concerns about its rise by emphasizing concepts such as peaceful rise (*heping jueqi* 和平崛起) and peaceful development (*heping fazhan* 和平發展) and striving for a moderately well-to-do society (*xiaokang shehui* 小康社會). Without arguing that China's foreign audience will necessarily buy into Beijing's narratives and self-portrayal, there is a large difference between its diplomatic language and that of the *Kaiserreich*'s. There have, of course, been foreign criticisms of China's "wolf-warrior diplomacy" and its jingoist films, but Beijing's conduct in these respects is no more egregious than the many instances of "Rambo-like" practice in US diplomacy. Indeed, China's "wolf warriors" were clumsy attempts to imitate America's Rambo.

To sum up this chapter, I have asked why some historical analogies are applied to contemporary China but not others. The concept of revisionism has been invoked to characterize countries such as Wilhelmine and Nazi Germany, Fascist Italy, imperial Japan, and the Communist Soviet Union. Contemporary China is often included in this category of revisionist rising states, which are usually seen as a threat to international stability and peace. The *Kaiserreich*'s experience has in particular been used to warn China about mistakes that can bring about a country's defeat and ruin due to its reckless and aggressive policies. This focus, however, appears to have been influenced by our hindsight bias (Fischhoff and Beyth 1975)—that is, by our awareness that Germany fought in and lost World War I. It also represents an example of "selecting on the dependent variable"—namely, studying a case only if it shows a particular outcome that we are interested in, which in this case is the occurrence of a large, devastating war and a disastrous defeat in this conflict. An assertive, even aggressive, United States during the period of its ascendance in international relations has attracted less scholarly attention—in large part, I suspect, because, contrary to popular formulations about the effects of power transition, war did not happen in this case, or, in other words, because of the nonoccurrence of the expected. This comment in turn suggests a common tendency of people to search for evidence to confirm their expectation rather than attend to information that contradicts this expectation. This confirmation bias reflects and underscores the selective use of history.

Conventional practice does not ask whether the United States from roughly the mid-1800s to the early 1900s also acted like a supposed revisionist state and why its conduct did not bring about a systemic war. During those same years, imperial Japan adopted Western institutions and followed Western conventions—that is, it assiduously conformed to the then-prevailing norms and rules of the "civilized world"—but it was nevertheless denied admittance to the select club of established powers. In other words, according to this account, similar conduct produced different results (a revisionist Wilhelmine Germany compared to a revisionist United States during Theodore Roosevelt's administration with respect to resistance by the established powers and thus the occurrence of a systemic war), and different conduct produced similar results (a revisionist *Kaiserreich* and a conformist Japan with respect to their failed demand for recognition by the established powers).

One can, of course, debate about whether or to what extent the *Kaiserreich* was truly revisionist and imperial Japan truly conformist. The larger point I am trying to make is that these are empirical questions to be settled by evidence, and the revisionist and status quo orientations of a state's foreign policy should not be concluded by rhetorical assertions. The question about how Beijing's actions and policies today compare with Washington's when the United States was a rising power rarely comes up in the prevailing discourse and scholarship dominated by Americans. In narratives about contemporary

China, some historical precedents are recalled and applied to it as an instructive analogue (namely, Wilhelmine Germany), but other precedents are not (such as imperial Japan and the United States during Theodore Roosevelt's administration). Some historical precedents are presented as if they offer a natural fit with contemporary international relations, while others are seldom recalled or invoked. This phenomenon strikes me as selective recall with the intent and/or the effect of shoehorning history to fit one's favorite narrative.

In the parlance of social scientists interested in making causal attribution, the above examples are reminders about the threats posed by "idiosyncrasy" and "irrelevance" to valid analysis. These terms refer, respectively, to the phenomenon that the same putative causes have produced different effects and that both the presence and absence of these putative causes have produced the same effects. This view naturally calls into question whether a state's revisionist agenda or conduct is the key variable determining the occurrence of a systemic war and its admission as a new member of the elite club of great powers by the established states. Or are there some other variables that can offer a more persuasive explanation of these outcomes?

Conclusion

Philosopher George Santayana is usually credited with the aphorism "Those who do not remember history are condemned to repeat it." Mark Twain reminds us that "history doesn't repeat itself, but it often rhymes." Analysts of international relations routinely refer to history to provide evidence to support or refute a proposition or theory, and, as suggested earlier, they also do so because history lends an aura of legitimacy and timelessness to their arguments. Yet if policymakers remember and apply lessons of history well, these lessons should be self-nullifying in situations where analogies are employed as warnings to avoid some dire consequences. That is, if officials avoid their predecessors' mistakes, history should *not* repeat itself when we are concerned about the recurrence of some disaster. Repetition happens only when people commit the same errors again and again.

For example, if US officials had learned the supposed lesson of the Korean War well—that is, to avoid policies that can provoke Chinese military intervention—their subsequent conduct should cause the Chinese to *not* undertake intervention, the nonoccurrence of an undesirable outcome. Similarly, if Chinese leaders are able to learn from the experience of Wilhelmine Germany, they would presumably avoid adopting self-defeating policies that would antagonize other countries and cause China's isolation, as Berlin did prior to 1914. Perhaps an even stronger argument can be made with regard to strategic warning. If intelligence agencies do their jobs well and their warnings of possible enemy attacks produce actions that cause these adversaries to call off their attacks, we should then expect the predicted attacks not to happen and the warnings to be disproven (Chan 1979). People's attention, however, usually goes to the occurrence of events, especially dramatic policy failures or catastrophes, and not those occasions when disasters were avoided, or the nonoccurrence of adverse events. Leaders are typically blamed for the former but do not get enough credit for the latter.

We can imagine other situations when historical patterns are apt to be self-nullifying due to people's actions to profit from them. Say that someone notices that there is a regularity whereby stocks lose their value on Fridays only to recover on Mondays. If this pattern becomes common knowledge, people's attempts to take advantage of it by buying stocks on Fridays and selling them on Mondays will cause it to disappear. Their actions will have the practical effect of erasing any such distortion, bias, or inefficiency in the financial market. The investors' collective action would then have a self-correcting effect on the market.

The field of international relations is above all an "American social science," as the title of an article by Stanley Hoffmann (1977) suggests. It is dominated by Americans, US institutions that provide graduate training, and US journals and publishers presenting scholarship that reflects US values and perspectives (there are naturally exceptions, such as indicated by this book's publication). This dominance constitutes soft power, which Joseph Nye (1990, 2002, 2004) writes extensively about. It confers an important advantage to the United States in framing policy and scholarly agendas and in propagating and legitimating certain interpretations of history at the expense of other alternatives.

It is important to underscore that Americans do not have a monopoly in practicing selective history. The Chinese and people of other countries are also frequently guilty of the same practices. For instance, Beijing has actively promoted its understanding of the history of international relations in mobilizing nationalism and rallying support for its foreign policy. Its campaign to instruct its citizens about China's "century of national humiliation" is a case in point (Z. Wang 2012, 2018). The historical accuracy of some of its narratives, such as the alleged sign "Dogs and Chinese not admitted" posted at a public park in

Shanghai, has been questioned (Bickers and Wasserstrom 2009). Beijing has also resorted to its "historical rights" in carving out the so-called nine-dash lines in the South China Sea to advance its sovereignty claim (Chan 2016)—a claim that has been rejected by the International Arbitration Tribunal. Beijing has not only resorted to manipulating history but also sought to suppress and erase some instances of history, such as the government's brutal crackdown on peaceful protestors at Tiananmen Square in 1989. Likewise, Taiwan's current authority has sought to promote a version of history intended to enhance a Taiwanese identity that is distinct and separate from a Chinese identity. In short, although this book has focused on US discourse and practices, it should not be seen to mean others, including the Chinese, are exempt from the same criticisms. We have encountered egregious and flagrant rhetoric by those who deny the horrors of the Holocaust, with some claiming that it did not even happen.

In this connection, it is also important to note that although I have pointed frequently to instances of US and Western criticisms of China for transgressions that they themselves have also been guilty of, these examples do not deny that the same criticisms can also be raised about Chinese conduct. My references to various US and Western transgressions can engender a dismissive reaction, belittling such references as "whataboutism." Such a reaction is, in my view, unwarranted. Americans can also justifiably point to transgressions that other countries (including China) have committed even if they have engaged in similar conduct. The typical retort characterizing an interlocutor's criticism as "whataboutism" is unwarranted because it fails to address the validity of the critic's charges and because it fails to recognize that such objections do have a tangible effect on popular discourse (e.g., Chow and Levin 2024).

It would also be appropriate to remind readers that history can be used for both cognitive and instrumental reasons. The latter refers to the use of history to frame policy problems and mobilize public and elite support for a preferred course of action. As stated earlier, these uses are not mutually exclusive. It is also difficult to tell their temporal order. Do leaders use historical reasoning to arrive at a decision and then try to persuade others to support this decision? Or do they act more like political entrepreneurs rather than decision-makers, seeking to propagate a particular version of history to advance their cause without bothering to inquire about the validity of the supposed historical lesson? Oftentimes, history is exploited to inflate foreign threats and to sharpen the division between in- and out-groups (Rousseau 2006)—a typical approach in the tool kits of demagogues seeking mass approval and support.

One important point of the preceding discussion is, of course, that our narratives about and understandings of international events, including our explanations of the causes of major wars, inevitably involve and reflect power relations. Certain interpretations and conclusions appear reasonable and natural, whereas others appear to be bizarre, ludicrous, and outlandish. Significantly, the historical episodes that are introduced to support prevailing theories often do not indicate what these theories' proponents suggest. Those theories or narratives being presented by prevailing US scholarship reflect US soft power, as in Antonio Gramsci's (1971) discussion of the hegemony of certain ideas that serve to maintain and justify the dominance of the capitalist class. As I have stated at the outset of this book when quoting R. B. J. Walker, international relations theories need to be themselves explained rather than to be taken for granted as detached, objective explanations of international relations.

These theories and explanations are always self-referential. "We don't see things as they are; we see them as we are"—a wise adage that is well worth always keeping in mind (it has been variously attributed to Anaïs Nin, the Babylonian Talmud, and other sources; "We Don't See Things" 2014). Harold Isaacs reminds us, "By examining the images we hold, say, of the Chinese and Indians, we can learn a great deal about Chinese and Indians, *but mostly we learn about ourselves*" (quoted in Pan 2012, 43; italics in original). As Andrew J. Bacevich (2002, 90) also points out, "American statecraft is not, in the first instance, about 'them'; it is about 'us.'"

We would do well to remember Margaret MacMillan's (2008, 169–70) admonition: "If the study of history does nothing more than teach us humility, skepticism, and awareness of ourselves, then it has done something useful. We must continue to examine our own assumptions and those of others and ask, where's the evidence? Or, is there another explanation? We should be wary of grand claims in history's name or those who claim to have uncovered the truth once and for all. In the end, my only advice is use it, enjoy it, but always handle history with care." In a thoroughly researched and persuasive analysis of *The History of the Peloponnesian War*, Jonathan Kirshner (2019) entitled his article in a similar vein, admonishing his readers to "Handle Him with Care: The Importance of Getting Thucydides Right."

Is there a "right" way to learn from history? I think not. As I have stated repeatedly, people naturally and understandably recall different historical episodes and reach different interpretations of these episodes. Their recollections and interpretations inevitably reflect their divergent backgrounds and experiences. There are many reasons for people to misapply history, and there is not a magic wand to correct the consequent errors. These errors can be due to psychological and social psychological reasons, such as people's reliance on simple schemas to help them to process information and make decisions, their proclivity for cognitive consistency, their natural tendency to seek concurrence and conform to group consensus, and the pernicious effects of common decision heuristics that they rely on to navigate their daily lives but ones that can also incline them to cause distortions that undermine the quality of their judgments.

There have been various proposals to combat close-mindedness, cognitive rigidity, ethnocentrism, bureaucratic and political pressure to conform to orthodoxies, premature intellectual closure, the domestication of dissent, and people's self-censorship to refrain from "rocking the boat" and to save their "effectiveness" for a "rainy day" (e.g., Janis 1982a; Thomson 1973). For example, there was an exchange between Alexander L. George (1972a, 1972b) and I. M. Destler (1972) about the wisdom of instituting a bureaucratic system to advance "multiple advocacy" intended to foster contrarian views that challenge established consensus. The rationale for such a proposal is to encourage intellectual pluralism and interservice rivalry so that policymakers will have the benefit of opposing views. Other proposals call for creating an agency that serves as a depository of evidence, especially that which challenges dominant perspectives (de Rivera 1968), and designating a person to be the devil's, or Cassandra's, advocate to challenge group consensus (Janis 1982a). Such efforts, however, have serious costs and limits, such as causing delay in policymaking, entailing duplicative work that raises costs, and encouraging competition to ingratiate rather than inform leaders. Given the nature of national-security apparatus, the system is geared to exclude nonconformists and minorities (such as Communists, anarchists, homosexuals at an earlier time, and those born abroad or who have unconventional lifestyles). It is also rigged to recruit conformists who have survived bureaucratic politics by not rocking the boat. Hence, efforts to mitigate the effects of "wrong" history face significant difficulties without necessarily promoting the desired outcome (Chan 1979).

It is also necessary to emphasize that it is not so easy to distinguish between "good" history and "bad" history, even in hindsight. A person can be right for the wrong reason. Winston Churchill was as opinionated as Neville Chamberlain, although history "proved" him right.

> This does not prove, however, that Chamberlain's image of Hitler was the product of misperception, irrationality, or plain naiveté. Given the evidence available to them at the time (prior to Germany's seizure of the rest of Czechoslovakia), both British leaders could reasonably conclude as they did: Hitler's actions were generally consistent with both a limited-aims revisionist and a revolutionary state. That one of these two interpretations would ultimately prove correct does not mean that the other interpretation was the result of cognitive biases or any other type of information-processing problem. Thus, even in this seemingly clear-cut case, the process of inferring motivation from behavior is problematic and riddled with ambiguity. (Schweller 1999, 21)

Hindsight bias compounds situations such as the one just described. People tend to believe the inevitability of an event after learning its occurrence. Reported outcomes appear less surprising to the subjects in hindsight than in foresight. Paul Slovic and Baruch Fischhoff (1977, 544) summarize this bias with these two points: "(a) Reporting the outcome of a historical event increases the perceived likelihood of that outcome and (b) people underestimate the effect of outcome knowledge on their perceptions. As a result, people believe that they would have seen in foresight the relative inevitability of the reported outcome, which in fact was only apparent in hindsight. Thus, they exaggerate the predictability of reported outcomes." Janice Gross Stein (2023, 399) points to the tendency for historical analogies to engender oversimplification, remarking, "Political leaders unconsciously strip the nuance, the context, and the subtleties out of the problems they face to build simple frames." Of course, scholars are also not immune from these mistakes. Therefore, it would be useful to summarize the major conclusions from the previous discussion that can help guard against these errors.

It seems obvious but still sensible advice that before we introduce a historical episode from the past as an analogy for a current situation or problem, we should pause to ask a few simple questions. Among these questions we should ask ourselves is how the historical analogue being invoked fits the contemporary case. Is ancient Athens an appropriate analogue for modern China, and is that likewise the case regarding ancient Sparta for the present-day United States? In what specific ways are these pairs similar or different? As another example, to what extent and in what ways is contemporary China a replica of Wilhelmine Germany? As Etel Solingen (2014) points out, there are important differences between these countries' ruling coalitions and their policy outlooks, and therefore, analysts should watch out for misleading conclusions when they overlook these differences.

Similarly, were Gamal Abdel Nasser and Saddam Hussein really reincarnated Adolf Hitlers? If we had paused to ask ourselves these questions, many misapplied analogies would have quickly dissolved. Sometimes, the analogy bears only a superficial resemblance to the problem or situation at hand, such as in the mistaken application of the *Pueblo* precedent to address how the United States should respond to the *Mayaguez* affair. As another example, despite talks of "Ukraine today, Taiwan tomorrow," there are important differences between these two cases. Ukraine is an independent sovereign country recognized by the international community. In contrast, Taiwan does not enjoy this status in the eyes of an overwhelming majority of states in the world—not even the United States. Whereas Russia's invasion of Ukraine is a violation of international law, a possible armed conflict between China and Taiwan will be considered by most countries in the world a domestic issue of China's and a continuation of their unfinished civil war.

Furthermore, it behooves us to consider whether the historical episodes and characters we invoke in fact match the profiles and scope conditions of the theory in question. Do they correspond with the script presented by the pertinent theory? Does this theory get essential details right when it claims validation from history? Do the historical figures and their behavior introduced to support the theory in fact do what its proponents claim? For example, if we are interested in pursuing Thucydides's aphorism that the rise of Athens and the fear that this development had caused in Sparta was the root cause of the Peloponnesian War, we would do well to establish that Athens's power was in fact gaining on Sparta's—or at least that it was perceived by the pertinent decision-makers to be trending in this direction. It would also help if we could establish that Sparta's leaders were acutely concerned, alarmed by, and even obsessed with this development.

Likewise, given power-transition theory's explicit focus on power shifts between the two most powerful countries competing to become the world's dominant power, it would be appropriate and indeed necessary to establish that it is valid to depict both world wars as instances of Anglo-German contests motivated by Berlin's desire to replace London as the world's hegemon and to rewrite the rules of international order. Did these wars happen before, after, or in the midst of an ostensible power transition? How can we recognize that a power transition is under way? Was London still the world's dominant power on the eve of these wars, and was Berlin motivated to fight it in order to claim the mantle of global hegemon? Ja Ian Chong and Todd H. Hall (2014, 18) question the conventional script that World War I happened because a cocky Germany was eager to displace Britain as the world's dominant power rather than the opposite interpretation that Germany ended up fighting Britain because it was unable to persuade London to stay on the sidelines. Other scholars raise similar objections with respect to power-transition theory's interpretation of the two world wars.

The implications of these remarks for Sino-American relations are straightforward and enormous. Would it be accurate to suggest that Beijing is itching for a fight with the United States in order to displace it as the world's premier power, or is China's gaze focused more narrowly on its immediate neighborhood? Should war happen between it and the United States, would it be because it aspired to dominate the world as its new master, or alternatively, would it rather be because it was unable to convince Washington to stay out of its unfinished civil war? In other words, would fighting the United States be China's first preference or its last resort?

These contrasting accounts obviously offer two vastly different characterizations of Chinese goals and motivations. Power-transition theory's depiction of Berlin as a cocky upstart bent on challenging London's preeminent world position attributes to Berlin an offensive motivation in both world wars. Although Germany was the aggressor state that started these wars, the available historical evidence contradicts this attribution and tends to instead support the opposite proposition that Berlin was driven more by a sense of insecurity (especially in 1914) and a preventive motivation. Its real target in both wars was Russia / the USSR. Moreover, it would have much rather preferred Britain remain neutral in these conflicts or even act as Germany's ally. Similarly, Japan's assault on Pearl Harbor in 1941 represented more a desperate gamble to stave off economic strangulation than a bold bid for world domination. Thus, it is crucial to scrutinize potentially critical mismatches in the essential details provided by the proponents of a theory and the actual historical record claimed to support it.

Avoiding serious distortions of history is important not only for good scholarship but also for sound and prudent policy. It is important to ask whether crucial historical details claimed to support a theory actually provide this support as proponents of this theory purport. This caution includes looking into whether the historical evidence being introduced is pertinent to the theory in matching its premises and satisfying its scope conditions. If power-transition theory is about contests between the world's two most powerful countries struggling for global domination, armed conflicts such as the Franco-Prussian War and the Russo-Japanese War would not qualify as suitable cases to confirm its propositions because, evidently, neither of the belligerent states involved represented the world's top dogs. A moment's reflection would also tell us to look into the puzzle that the world's premier power, the United States, only entered these armed contests considerably after their initiation, and in World War II, its participation could have been delayed even further had Japan not attacked it in 1941. What does this timing tell us? It is a curious fact that the ruling global power only entered these armed conflicts belatedly, even though power-transition theory claims that these conflicts were fundamentally about a challenge to its preeminent position and an effort to displace it from this position.

Before hastening to declare a theory to have been vindicated, it would help to ask whether the tests we have performed are complete and credible. Have we omitted a crucial variable—namely, a latecomer's revisionist motivation—or failed to operationalize this variable in testing power-transition theory, which, after all, claims that it is the combination of power shifts *and* revisionism that causes war initiation by this upstart? For both power-transition theory and Thucydides's Trap, have we followed their criteria for admissible evidence, and have we been explicit in our measurement strategy, such as in determining how much and how quickly—and even whether—power shifts were occurring between the pertinent pairs of states? How do we identify those countries that fall within the domain of a theory and others that are outside it? Are wars supposed to happen before, during, or after the specific point when a latecomer overtakes an established leading state? How long is the period during which the danger of war is elevated, and when does this danger abate? None of these rules of interpretation and criteria for admissible evidence are currently clear.

It is also instructive to recall that in the mid and even late 1800s, China still had the world's biggest economy, largest territory (if we exclude colonies from the European countries' metropole), and the greatest number of soldiers. But obviously these numerical advantages did not prevent its diplomatic setback and military defeat in its encounters with Britain, Japan, and other foreign predators. Beware of how ostensible national power is measured (Beckley 2018; Rauch 2017)!

Chong and Hall (2014, 19) also remind their readers that "analogies invite the temptation to shoehorn new actors into old roles while providing distractions from the fact that the stage they occupy has changed." In other words, past episodes are sometimes applied to contemporary situations even when circumstances have changed significantly. Thus, before introducing an analogy from the past, it would be helpful to ask whether circumstances have changed sufficiently to alter its relevance to contemporary international relations. For example, when people invoke Thucydides's Trap, they are in effect asking us to suspend our skepticism about why this analogy from an ancient war should be relevant to the contemporary world. Have the formation of modern nation-states, the advent of nationalism, and the introduction of nuclear weapons and other awesome and sophisticated weapons systems fundamentally altered the dynamics of international conflict from that which prevailed in the ancient Greek world some 2,500 years ago?

For these reasons, Chong and Hall (2014) caution us against engaging in facile analysis transferring the experience of Wilhelmine Germany to contemporary China. In 1914, the European states faced an existential threat because they were vulnerable to being invaded and conquered by their neighbors. It is unimaginable today that any country would consider invading or conquering China or the United States. Separated by an ocean, these two countries also do not have any territorial dispute (at least not directly, even though US allies do have such disputes with China), which is the most common cause for armed conflicts (Vasquez 1993, 2009). These two countries and others in the Indo-Pacific region do not face the same existential threat today that the European countries did in 1914. Moreover, nuclear weapons have altered the basic nature of international relations, making a clash between countries armed with these awesome weapons of mass destruction much too dangerous to undertake today.

For reasons indicated earlier, it is much more difficult to imagine that the United States would want to practice nuclear brinksmanship today to protect Taiwan as it did in 1962 during the Cuban Missile Crisis to coerce the USSR to remove its missiles from that island. Even the consequences of a large war among industrial but nonnuclear states are too grim to contemplate nowadays (Levy and Thompson 2010, 2011; Mueller 1989). Certainly, territorial conquest has become an outdated idea in the age of globalization. States can acquire resources, even international influence and status, by pursuing economic statecraft, such as epitomized by Richard Rosecrance's (1987) "trading states." Moreover, nationalism and international public opinion have made the costs of foreign rule too high to warrant any thought of territorial conquest, especially at the expense of another great power (Mearsheimer 2019). In short, modern developments may have rendered supposed lessons of history from another era questionable, or they would at least counsel us to consider carefully when these lessons may have to be amended before they are made relevant and applicable to contemporary circumstances.

Robert Jervis (1976, 228; italics in original) remarks that when people reason by analogy, they "pay more attention to *what* has happened than to *why* it has happened." This remark reminds us to consider what happened could be due to other causes or reasons rather than the one(s) being given by conventional wisdom. Thus, for example, we should ask ourselves whether there are alternative plausible explanations to account for Britain's and France's conduct at the Munich Conference in 1938. Are cowardice and ineptitude the only explanations for British and French conduct lending support to the supposed lesson of Munich advising us against appeasing an aggressor state? Could Chamberlain's and Daladier's behavior have been motivated by reasons other than the one(s) offered by the supposed lesson of Munich, such as to buy time to arm their countries against Germany, which was better prepared for war in 1938? Could their consideration of prevailing domestic antiwar sentiments have inclined them to accommodate Hitler's demands for the time being?

As Jervis (1976) also reminds us, sometimes the evidence available to leaders is murky at the time of their decisions. This evidence can be compatible with multiple hypotheses about a foreign counterpart's motivation and agenda. As already indicated, Hitler's aggressive nature could not be ascertained until further evidence became available only later when he invaded countries without a sizeable German-speaking population. His demands in

1938 were congruent with competing hypotheses: that he was asking for a reasonable territorial adjustment (Why not allow self-determination of German minorities living in Sudetenland?) or he was potentially a serial aggressor with an insatiable appetite. Hindsight is always twenty-twenty.

Conventional, well-worn scripts offered by popular narratives and facile analogies may not be entirely valid until we have checked the pertinent episode for alternative explanations. It is much easier to be a "Monday-morning quarterback" in retrospect than at the time when officials are considering their response to a still-uncertain situation. Given the usual situation of severe information deficit, could it be that Winston Churchill was as opinionated as Neville Chamberlain—perhaps even more so—even though he was vindicated by subsequent events? Both were reacting to an ambiguous situation at the time of the Munich Conference in 1938, and their views were determined more by their preexisting beliefs (biases, if you will) rather than the available evidence.

My previous discussion also suggests that just because an undesirable event did not happen, it does not mean that a policy has succeeded. I have already mentioned that given their emphasis on not repeating the error of provoking Chinese intervention as in the Korean War, US officials' policy choice during the Vietnam War could be considered suboptimal when seeking to apply maximum pressure on North Vietnam. That is, they applied less coercion on Hanoi than they could have for their ostensible objective because of their fear that their policy might trigger Chinese intervention. We should also not be too quick to congratulate ourselves, say, because the Cuban Missile Crisis did not escalate into a war between the United States and the USSR. We may want to ponder whether there were good reasons for the Kremlin to introduce missiles to Cuba in the first place and seriously entertain, for example, Moscow's claim that its missiles were intended to deter another US invasion of the island and attempt to overthrow Fidel Castro. In this scenario, Moscow would be the defender of the status quo, and Washington, the revisionist seeking to overthrow it.

Can we imagine how much Beijing cares about Taiwan's status by reflecting on Washington's reaction to the presence of Soviet missiles in Cuba? Moreover, we may wish to look deeper into the reasons for the peaceful resolution of the Cuban Missile Crisis beyond the popular belief that it was an instance of successful coercive diplomacy by the United States. This attribution may be undeserved or at least less deserved in view of what we now know about the secret deal exchanging Soviet missiles in Cuba for US missiles in Turkey and Washington's pledge not to invade Cuba again.

To guard against premature intellectual closure, it would also be good for officials and scholars alike to search history for possible counterexamples to the analogy being invoked. Thus, to counterbalance the popular belief that appeasement encourages further aggression and a larger war in the future—the so-called lesson of Munich—one would want to ask whether Washington's policy of standing firm against Japan's aggression in 1941 had worked—that is, whether its deterrence effort had actually backfired to cause Tokyo to attack it directly rather than try to bypass it in Japan's plan to seize the European colonies in Southeast Asia. One may also wish to inquire whether London's accommodation of a rising United States in the Western Hemisphere had led other great powers to conclude that they could more easily coerce London to also make concessions to them. Alternatively, is it possible that Britain's appeasement of the United States did not have such an adverse effect on its reputation—that is, other countries did not conclude from its dealings with the United States that they could likewise push London around and pressure it to accommodate their interests? Similar behavior by another country would be called reasonable, legitimate, and far-sighted accommodation if these concessions were made to oneself but illegitimate, dangerous, and counterproductive appeasement if made to some other country, especially if the latter country turned out to be a future enemy.

As Daniel Treisman (2004) argues, Spain's policy of standing firm against and taking on all opponents in an effort to establish a reputation for resolve to discourage future challenges had in fact backfired. This policy depleted its resources and sapped its energy, and it had the exact opposite consequence than what Spanish officials had hoped for. Philip IV and his advisors believed a reputation for firmness was worth fighting for and, moreover, any weakness or vulnerability in one part of this monarch's vast domain would have an adverse domino effect on other parts. In the words of Count-Duke of Olivares (Gaspar de Guzmán y Pimentel), Philip IV's prime minister, "The first and most fundamental dangers threaten Milan, Flanders and Germany. Any blow against these would be fatal to this monarchy; and if any one of them were to go, the rest of the monarchy would follow, for Germany would be followed by Italy and Flanders, Flanders by the Indies, and Milan by Naples and Sicily" (quoted in Treisman 2004, 366).

These words were spoken some three hundred years before US involvement in the Korean and Vietnam Wars, but they sound very much like the public rationale given by Washington to justify its intervention in these conflicts. The logic propounded by the count-duke led Spain to fight multiple wars and sometimes simultaneously in Bohemia and Flanders as well as against England and France. The more Spain fought, the more it weakened itself and thus the more it encouraged and emboldened other challengers to its power and authority. Therefore, this commitment to fight for a reputation of firmness and resolve in the hope of deterring future challenges ironically turned out to have the opposite effect. One may recall my earlier discussion of the deterrence threat made by the United States in 1941 against Japanese aggression and the effects of its embargo to deny vital strategic resources to that country. Paradoxically, these policies produced the exact opposite results than those expected by the opponents of appeasement.

During the Habsburg rule in the 1600s, Madrid was also busy putting down rebellions in Catalonia, Portugal, Naples, and Sicily. Constant warfare exhausted Spain in money and blood, setting it on a steady course of decline, which it was never able to recover from. In short, Madrid's policy was counterproductive and self-defeating. In contrast, London's policy of selective, or smart, appeasement made all the difference in the outcomes of both world wars. It ensured that the United States would be its ally rather than its opponent in these wars. Spain's experience cautions us to be skeptical of sweeping generalizations and dogmatic assertions, such as appeasement will inevitably produce more aggression and bigger wars in the future. This comment, of course, does not deny the importance of reputation—to be seen as honest and trustworthy—in international relations (e.g., Mercer 1996; A. Sartori 2002, 2005). But as shown by Spain's experience, a blind and rigid pursuit of a reputation for firmness and resolve can have serious deleterious consequences.

Importantly, London's accommodation of the United States, or, if you will, appeasement of Washington, did not cause British leaders to be worried about being seen as weak or irresolute by other states and thus inclining them to also press London for concessions. Leaders of the other states did not draw this conclusion and perceive Britain's concessions to the United States to be a precedent that could be generalized to other circumstances. Similarly, when Beijing made concessions in settling its border disputes with its neighbors, it was apparently unconcerned that these compromises might be interpreted by other countries as a sign of Beijing's weakness and thus encourage these other countries to be more intransigent in their negotiations with China (Fravel 2009). Therefore, we cannot assume that a state's actions in one case can necessarily be transferred to infer its intentions in another case. Although US failures in Vietnam and Afghanistan hurt its reputation for reliability and steadfastness, it would be a stretch to argue that just because the United States left these countries, other states can now confidently predict that it would not fight on behalf of South Korea or Japan.

The same logic applies in reverse. Those advocates for a stronger US commitment to defend Taiwan argue that it is important to uphold Washington's credibility to support and stand by a partner. They in effect argue that reputation is generalizable so that what the United States does or fails to do with respect to protecting Taiwan will affect how other countries will perceive Washington's reliability and resolve in general. However, it is not evident that this should be the proper inference. Paul Huth (1988b, 81) explains in his study of past episodes of extended deterrence, "The potential attacker did not seem to draw conclusions about the future behavior of the defender based on the defender's behavior in disputes with other states. Rather, the past behavior of the defender was taken as an indicator of behavior in the current conflict only when the potential attacker has been directly involved in past confrontations with the defender." I have also argued earlier that there are important differences between cases that may appear to be superficially similar, such as in comparing Ukraine with Taiwan.

Another example of looking to history for possible countervailing instances to received wisdom or popular analogies is provided by imperial Japan's experience. Although it was an ambitious and aggressive state seeking to expand its empire and establish a dominant position in its home region, Tokyo was a conformist, not revisionist, power that had assiduously tried to adhere to the prevailing "rules of the game" of international relations in the late nineteenth century and early twentieth century. Yet it encountered resistance to its demand to be admitted to the select club of great powers. In contrast, the United States acted more like a revisionist state. It not only sought territorial expansion but also wanted to expel European influence from the Western

Hemisphere and to establish its regional hegemony there. It introduced and propagated a heretofore unknown principle, the Monroe Doctrine, and insisted on playing the game of international politics by its own rules. Arguably, Washington provoked the Spanish-American War, resulting in not only the eviction of Spanish influence from Cuba but also the US takeover of Puerto Rico, Guam, and the Philippines. The notion that Anglo-American relations were always cordial and friendly is an ideational construct that is contradicted by frequent turbulence and occasional outbursts of bellicosity manifested by the leaders of both countries. The discrepant experiences of these two rising states in the late 1800s and early 1900s, a conformist Japan and a revisionist United States, should give analysts pause before claiming that the revisionist tendencies of rising states are *the* cause of international tension and stability.

Moreover, my criticism of how the idea of revisionism has been deployed in current discourse on international relations not only suggests conceptual confusion, a lack of analytic transparency and rigor, and a paucity of empirical content backed up by systematic evidence but also points to a strong post hoc bias. The pertinent literature implies that because a rising latecomer was not an initial party to a systemic war, it was ipso facto not a revisionist power, as in the case of the United States. Of course, this statement would only be true when referring *just* to systemic wars of which there have been only two instances—namely, the two world wars. If one looks beyond these two conflicts, the United States was certainly involved in the Spanish-American War, and it bore the major responsibility for having instigated this conflict. The more general point of this discussion is, of course, that we need to be much more explicit in disclosing what we mean by "revisionism" and clear about those empirical indicators that purport to measure this concept. This is why I have argued previously that it is incumbent on those analysts and officials who use this concept to explain how the ways ostensible revisionist countries—such as Wilhelmine Germany, imperial Japan, Fascist Italy, and the Communist Soviet Union—conducted themselves and espoused their doctrines distinguish them from their predecessors or contemporaries, the supposed status quo states, such as Britain, France, Russia, and the United States. Similarly, what specific behavior indicates that contemporary China is a revisionist state seeking to upend the international order—behavior that distinguishes it from the United States as a status quo power ostensibly committed to the defense of this order?

I have argued that prevailing US narrative reverses the customary meaning of concepts such as revisionism and balance of power, standing these ideas on their head. Thus, China professing its support for traditional Westphalian principles of state sovereignty and noninterference in other countries' domestic affairs is nevertheless declared to be revisionist, while the United States openly pursuing an agenda promoting regime change abroad and propagating new doctrines such as "preventive war" (or the Monroe Doctrine at an earlier time) is described as a status quo state. Although, in the view of traditional realists, balancing power is supposed to be the key factor determining international peace and stability, that China has closed the power gap separating it from the United States is now construed as a source of threat to peace and stability. In discourse on Chinese aggression against Taiwan, Americans do not usually remember how they settled their own civil war—or whether Beijing has acted any more egregiously than Washington against small, "unruly" neighbors, like Grenada, Nicaragua, or Panama, which can hardly be argued to have presented a threat to US national security. Soviet action in the Cuban Missile Crisis was an unacceptable encroachment on the US sphere of influence, but the reverse situations for Ukraine (for Russia) and Taiwan (for China) do not usually enter policy or scholarly conversations in the United States. As I said, some historical precedents and parallels come more easily and readily to mind than others.

My references just now to scholarship on international relations suggest that we have to often take a large grain of salt when reading or listening to supposedly detached, impartial, and objective scholarly analyses as scholars are in fact inevitably embedded in the power relations that they study. They cannot but be a product of their backgrounds and environments. Whether they realize and acknowledge their role or not, they are deeply implicated in political entrepreneurship to construct the meaning of history, to frame policy debates, and to promote certain popular narratives at the expense of others and thus play an important and even indispensable part in legitimating certain policy courses and mobilizing public support for them relative to other alternatives. In short, scholars are complicit in the propagation of popular narratives of international relations—ones that are often based on a distorted representation of history and simplistic sound bites about its supposed lessons.

In addition to those human judgmental fallibilities mentioned above, I have pointed out on several previous occasions people's vulnerability to hindsight bias. People tend to convince themselves that past events were inevitable or more certain than they had actually expected before these events' occurrences. Luck and accident play an important role in history, which could have easily taken a different turn depending on even just a few minor alterations to the script of how events actually unfolded. For instance, Archduke Ferdinand could have followed the advice from some of his subordinates to not visit Sarajevo, he could have not altered his itinerary in Sarajevo, his driver could have avoided making a wrong turn requiring him to reverse the vehicle that the archduke and his wife were traveling in and thus slowing down their motorcade, and the assassin Gavrilo Princip could have missed his shots. Richard Ned Lebow (2000–2001) reminds his readers to recognize that history is highly contingent and historical events could often very well have turned out differently. After the botched attempt on Donald Trump's life, readers need no more evidence from me to affirm that history is highly contingent and could take a very different turn by a difference of a couple of inches—quite literally.

In discussing deliberations among the Athenians and Spartans, I have also argued that their leaders and citizens were divided in their opinion about the wisdom of starting a war, and their decisions were subject to reversal. History is replete with examples of close calls and near misses. Thus, Napoleon's defeat at Waterloo was hardly a preordained outcome. According to Thomas Jones Barker (2015, 34), this battle was "a damn close run thing." Britain's Lord Wellington also said that it was "the nearest-run thing you ever saw in your life" ("What Is the Meaning," n.d.).

To reiterate, scholars often tend to imply that those events or episodes being studied by them are somehow inevitable or at least quite probable when in fact they are highly contingent and their occurrence is due to multiple factors interacting in a complex and often unexpected way (Chan, forthcoming-a, forthcoming-c; Chong and Hall 2014, 9, 18). This is an important point—one that is also emphasized by other analysts, such as Richard Ned Lebow (2000–2001) and William R. Thompson (2003). My complaint is that analysts sometimes convey greater certitude in their conclusions than is warranted by the available evidence. They also sometimes make sweeping generalizations, such as "History teaches us that rising powers are likely to provoke war" (Shirk 2007, 4), when it is unclear what kind of historical evidence can be mustered to support such a claim, especially when relevant details about the definitions of "rising powers" and "war," controversies in assigning responsibility for instigating and starting a war, and the relevant epoch or region subject to this generalization are left imprecise or vague. For instance, would post-1945 Germany and Japan qualify as "rising states" even if their improved stature in international relations reflected their economic rather than military prowess? How about the US ascendance to its undisputed unipolar status after the USSR's demise?

The assassination of Archduke Ferdinand and his wife in Sarajevo was an accident (and it was therefore unexpected by definition), but it was a necessary catalyst to ignite the European tinderbox in the summer of 1914. The European environment then—characterized by repeated crises, armament races, bifurcated alliances, and a shifting power balance—was made of a dangerous brew. Not a single factor but rather a constellation of them made this environment highly combustible. At the same time, in the absence of a catalyst, this environment might not have blown up. World War I happened in the wake of what Lebow (2000–2001) describes as concurrent gestalt changes in the leading circles in Berlin, Vienna, and St. Petersburg, or, in other words, in the general outlook of these countries' respective high officials. He argues that had Sarajevo happened in 1916 or 1917—that is, just two or three years later—there would have been enough transformation in the European leaders' calculations and outlooks to avoid the conflagration that we now call World War I.

Robert Jervis (1976) points out that we tend to see our foreign counterpart's actions to be more coherent, centralized, and deliberate than is often warranted. We do not readily accept, for example, the proposition that Soviet missiles might have been introduced to Cuba by some low-ranking officials without the Kremlin's knowledge or approval or that the seizure of the *Mayaguez* was an unauthorized action undertaken by a local commander of the Khmer Rouge. But we want to persuade the Chinese that the bombing of their embassy in Belgrade by the US Air Force was an innocent mistake caused by a misunderstanding about where this embassy was located. Here is then an example of what attribution theory tells us about the way in which our minds tend to work. When someone does something bad to us, we are more ready to impugn this person's motive, typically explaining this behavior as a result of inherent bad faith or hostile intention. But when we do something bad to others, we tend to blame it on circumstances beyond our control, an innocent mistake, or an unintended accident.

Finally, there is the natural human tendency to recall some past events more readily than others. Those that have happened to oneself or others close to one are more easily retrieved from memory. Particularly dramatic, traumatic, or graphic episodes are also more available for officials and scholars alike in their work. In addition to saliency, there is a recency bias such that people understandably tend to remember more recent events in comparison to ancient ones, especially if these events happened a long time ago in an age that they cannot personally relate to. Motorists tend to slow down and drive more cautiously shortly after they have witnessed a horrific traffic accident. A popular adage argues that generals are often making plans to fight the last war. The converse also holds. In international relations, people are often not familiar with or even aware of those historical experiences that are important to other people living in foreign countries or coming from different cultures. Therefore, it is understandable that officials and scholars in different countries and from different cultures often operate on the basis of different historical knowledge, awareness, and referents.

As I have argued on several previous occasions, introspection and empathy are not common. People do not usually put themselves in the shoes of their counterparts, who, as already said, often remember and act on quite different historical referents. For example, why should the Chinese care less about Taiwan's status than Americans cared about Cuba's status? Can we appreciate the intensity of Chinese feelings if we consider how strongly the Kennedy administration felt about getting rid of Soviet missiles in Cuba—even to the point of risking a nuclear confrontation with another superpower? If domestic political considerations weighed heavily on Kennedy and his advisors, do we have any reason to expect that these considerations are less important or stressful for Chinese leaders when it comes to their policymaking regarding Taiwan?

If the United States had worked itself up to such an extent to invade Grenada because that tiny island's leaders had Marxist sympathies and to contravene congressional prohibition to provide covert support to the contras fighting against Nicaragua's Sandinistas, would it be unnatural for Moscow to feel equally intensely about a pro-Western government being installed in Ukraine or for Beijing to feel the same way about the prospect of a similar government established under Washington's aegis right on its border with Korea? It should not have to take a foreign policy expert or a specialist on Russia or China to answer such questions. Moscow's reaction to US encroachments on its traditional sphere of influence in Ukraine and China's response to US actions in Korea and Taiwan could have been easily foreseen and grasped by imagining how any US president would have reacted should Mexico become a Russian or Chinese ally or should there be a Russian or Chinese army marching toward Rio Grande. Had Truman and his advisors considered the latter scenario, they would have been less surprised by China's counterintervention in the Korean War when US forces advanced to the Yalu, the river separating Korea from China.

Argentinian leaders and even some US officials had dismissed the idea that Britain would send a fleet to retake some faraway islands with a small resident population and without much strategic or economic value to it to speak of. Although the Argentinian leaders knew how important domestic political considerations were for themselves in formulating and choosing their policy toward the Falklands/Malvinas, they were apparently unable to imagine that similar considerations would be important for Margaret Thatcher and the British Cabinet. Conversely, whereas the importance of Falklands/Malvinas never reached to the top of Britain's policy agenda, British officials did not appreciate the urgency and importance attached by their Argentinean counterparts to these islands' status. There is, of course, a parallel with respect to Taiwan's status here. This matter is of utmost importance to Beijing's leaders, who have repeatedly and publicly declared that this issue impinges on China's core interests. It is clearly not at or near the top of Washington's policy agenda.

Intense preference implies resolve, tenacity, and perseverance. Those states with a more intense preference will fight longer and harder. If the US experiences in Korea, Vietnam, Iraq, Somalia, and Afghanistan teach us anything, it is that raw capabilities are not everything, often not even the most important thing, in deciding the outcome of armed conflicts. In addition, government cohesion, elite solidarity, and popular support make a difference. Furthermore, intensity of preference is indicative of the allocation of policy attention to different issues by different countries. There can be an asymmetry in attention just as there can be an asymmetry of resolve and capabilities. Robert O. Keohane and Joseph S. Nye (1977) argue that Australia and Canada have made more gains in their negotiations with the United States in the past than the power disparities between these countries would have implied. The United States often suffers a disadvantage due to its fragmented bureaucracy, disjointed policy processes, and attention deficit resulting from a crowded policy agenda. "Governmental cohesion is important in determining [dispute] outcomes, and in general, the United States was less cohesive than Canada and Australia. In part this lack of cohesion is a function of sheer size and of presidential as contrasted with parliamentary government, but it is also a function of asymmetry of attention. The United States government does not focus on Canada and Australia the way that Canada, or even Australia, focuses on the United States. Greater cohesion and concentration helps [*sic*] to redress the disadvantage in size" (207–8).

One of the purposes of this book is to critically examine the historical evidence that analysts of international relations use to develop their theories of war and peace and to rally support for their diagnosis and prognosis of relations between China and the United States. Many of the prevailing explanations, predictions, and prescriptions offered by prominent US scholars appear to me highly problematic and even dubious. There is a tendency to shoehorn history and to provide a simplistic and distorted caricature from the past to analyze and interpret the present. Such works are also often self-centered and self-serving. My understanding of episodes such as the Peloponnesian War and the two world wars does not support leading theories of war and peace, such as Thucydides's Trap and power-transition theory. There is usually not enough skepticism to interrogate whether power shifts (or perceived power shifts) were in fact responsible for the war between Athens and Sparta and, if concerns with power shifts did play a role in causing the two world wars, how this factor actually affected the motivations and perceptions of the relevant leaders. The depiction of the two world wars as a failed bid by Germany to displace Britain to claim the latter's status as the global hegemon is historically inaccurate in my view.

Moreover, it is dangerously misleading when used as an analogy to interpret contemporary Sino-American relations. It implies a cocky, overconfident, and ambitious China eager to challenge the United States and take over its leadership position in the world and install a new international order based on Chinese interests and values. In fact, China does not have such an intention or agenda. With respect to Beijing's supposed historical counterpart or predecessor, Germany had wanted to stay out of a fight with Britain in both world wars, but it was unsuccessful in its effort to persuade London to stay on the sidelines. The last thing China would want is to have itself involved in a direct armed conflict with the United States. Beijing's diplomacy has in fact been designed to persuade Washington to stay out of its unfinished civil war. Although Beijing surely wants to return Taiwan to Chinese sovereignty and jurisdiction, its foreign policy hardly seeks to seize the mantle of world leadership from Washington and to rewrite the rules of international order. Attempts to apply ancient Athens and Wilhelmine and Nazi Germany as analogues for contemporary China are much too facile, presenting a formulaic depiction that overlooks important differences among these cases.

Parenthetically, no single country, however powerful, can dictate the rules of international order. Although power is important to sustain this order, legitimacy is also required. A dominant power needs followership from less powerful countries to support an international order. Moreover, it is a fundamental misconception of the nature of international order to imply that it is a static thing that can be settled once and for all, when in fact it is always in the process of evolving, being negotiated and renegotiated and with some parts of it being retained by majority concurrence, while other parts are being updated to reflect changing circumstances. All countries would like to see some rules and norms of international order changed while preserving others. Of course, they do not necessarily agree on which ones to keep and which ones to abandon. It is way too facile and simplistic to claim that rising states want to overthrow the existing rules and norms of international order, while established, dominant states are committed to retain and defend them (Chan et al. 2021).

Similarly, what is often asserted or presented as eternal truths, such as the so-called lesson of Munich, is far too simplistic, dogmatic, and sweeping. When such historical analogies are recalled, the resulting mental shortcuts and top-down processing of information can seriously mislead policymakers. The invocation of ostensible historical lessons can be dangerous to the extent that they engender self-fulling prophecy. Thus, if leaders believe in the warning of Thucydides's Trap, their views and actions can bring about a war between China and the United States, which as Lebow and Valentino (2009) indicate, history has failed to oblige. Historical aphorisms, such as the lesson of Munich, are often troubling because leaders can accept them at face value without asking whether there are alternative explanations for the historical episode in question and whether there are other historical cases that contradict it and caution against a blind acceptance of received wisdom.

My discussion of Japan's decision to attack Pearl Harbor offers a dramatic example that a resolute refusal to appease an aggressor state can have serious consequences that the anti-appeasers invoking the lesson of Munich typically overlook. Similarly, the contrasting experiences between Spain in the mid-1600s and Britain in the late 1800s—one determined to fight any and all perceived challengers to its authority and power and the other engaging in selective appeasement and accommodation—do not typically detain those people whose mind is made up about the evils of appeasement. Superficial reasoning, such as applying the ostensible lesson of Munich to justify US support for Taiwan to resist China, is dangerous. Sometimes when a popular narrative or aphorism is repeated often and legitimated by authority figures, it acquires a life of its own, and people come to accept and embrace it as self-evidently true without bothering to scrutinize it critically. Loose talk, such as regarding the so-called Thucydides's Trap and its application to characterize contemporary Sino-American relations, is concerning for this reason.

There is also the danger of willful neglect of history. As I have already stated, some historical episodes are more easily recalled than others. People also often overlook some episodes because they are unfamiliar or uncomfortable with them. For example, Americans do not typically think in terms of the historical frame provided by the Cuban Missile Crisis when they discuss or analyze China's views on and concerns about Taiwan. They are thus unable to imagine that Chinese leaders feel about Taiwan in the same way that US leaders felt with respect to Cuba. Indeed, Americans do not typically ask themselves how they settled their own civil war. Abraham Lincoln is undoubtedly one of the most popular US presidents—in retrospect if not when he was alive. Surely, his insistence on preserving the Union and his resistance to the Confederacy's secession are among the main reasons for his popularity and his preeminent position in US history. Empathy and introspection are usually not people's strong suit. Americans are opposed to Crimea's secession from Ukraine but do not usually see any inconsistency or contradiction with their support for Taiwan's continued separation and thus de facto independence from China. They do not usually consider parallels between their civil war and the Chinese Civil War.

I have taken a dissenting position against conventional wisdom and prevailing consensus throughout this book. The world does not need another book reminding its readers about the lesson of Munich to warn about the danger of appeasement. There is already plenty of such advice—and not enough contrarian arguments to challenge orthodoxies and conformist reasoning. As I have mentioned on several previous occasions, empathy and introspection are often in short supply. People are not accustomed to putting themselves in the shoes of their counterparts to appreciate how the other side feels and sees things, and they do not question their own reasoning and motivation critically to guard against ethnocentrism and self-righteousness.

As I said at the outset of this book, I get concerned when people crowd to one side of the boat. Irving L. Janis (1982a) writes persuasively about the phenomenon of groupthink—the tendency for people to engage in conformist reasoning and their reluctance to challenge group consensus. Hans Christian Andersen's fairy tale for children "The Emperor's New Clothes" also warns about concurrence-seeking behavior and people's strong inclination to follow and accept popular views even when they may have private doubts about these views. These tendencies apply as much to ordinary people as to officials in charge of foreign policy and scholars who write about international relations. When officials and scholars repeat the same memes, they create an echo chamber that has the effect of reinforcing and amplifying their views and drowning out dissident voices from a minority. The historical parallels and precedents that are usually invoked in prevailing US policy and academic discourse on China tend to be tilted rather consistently in one direction, thus causing my concerns about premature policy closure, intellectual complacency, and sanctimonious smugness.

To recapitulate, I take issue with prevailing and popular narratives and theorizing about the causes of war and peace, especially in the usual manner that they have been applied to Sino-American relations and the prospect of war between these countries. These narratives and theories are, in my opinion, highly problematic in their application of historical evidence to support their propositions. Although Graham T. Allison's rendition and propagation of Thucydides's Trap have been very effective in reaching even the highest government officials as well as the informed public, I contend that ancient Athens is a dubious analogue for contemporary China and ancient Sparta is a poor fit for the contemporary United States. Moreover, that a war occurred between these two Greek polities cannot be automatically mapped onto the modern world because we need to consider important developments, such as the advent of modern states and nuclear weapons, to decide whether a war some 2,500 years ago can still provide a valid basis for extrapolation to understand the modern world without qualifications.

Moreover, the way in which Thucydides's Trap has been presented is too deterministic, overlooking the element of chance in how history has unfolded in this and other historical cases. In offering a monocausal explanation of war, it also overlooks other factors that can engender interstate conflict and that such conflict is an equifinal phenomenon that can be the result of multiple causes and several pathways. Finally, it is a structural perspective that does not give enough consideration to human agency. The danger of war becomes elevated if Chinese and US leaders repeat the same mistakes shown by the ancient Greeks—that is, if they react almost robotically to power shifts between their countries as presented in a simplistic account of the Peloponnesian War's origin. Put differently, if Chinese and US leaders learn from history, they should be able to avoid the errors made by the ancient Greeks, thus avoiding war and causing the proposition of Thucydides's Trap to be self-nullifying. In the end, Chinese and US leaders remain coauthors of their future.

As for the two world wars, the typical portrayal in international relations scholarship on war, especially in the formulation of power-transition theory, distorts history in presenting these struggles as primarily bilateral struggles between Germany and Britain in a failed bid by Berlin to oust London from its perch as the global hegemon and to rewrite the international order. This theory's presentation of history overlooks the fact that Britain was already overtaken by the United States prior to the two world wars, that Germany never came close to matching US power, and that although Berlin was an aggressive state and responsible for initiating both world wars, it was motivated not only by an ambition for making more acquisitive gains but also by a preventive motivation to forestall its expected (relative) decline with respect to an emergent colossus to its east. In contrast to the prevailing discourse, I argue that Russia / the USSR was the main target of Germany's aggression in both world wars and that its war with Britain was an unfortunate "sideshow" for Berlin—one that it would have liked to avoid. This interpretation of history makes a huge difference in contemporary discourse on Sino-American relations because the acknowledgment and even highlighting of Germany's preventive motivation and its dread over its impending relative decline and apprehensions about a foreboding future would possibly direct attention to a similar incentive on the part of the United States in its policies toward China. The world would then have to be concerned not only about the threat coming from a rising China but also one from a declining United States.

Another major problem with power-transition theory and the associated discourse on revisionist states is that they are decidedly one-sided in their account. The prevailing narrative emphasizes an impatient and ambitious rising state seeking to push aside the established, leading state to claim global hegemony and rewrite the rules of international order without asking about the other side of the story—namely, Why do declining states refuse to accommodate the rising states' demands and insist on retaining their entitlements that are no longer warranted by their reduced power? The prevailing discourse usually takes it for granted that rising states are motivated to upend the existing international order, even though this order has enabled and even facilitated their rise, and with their rise, they should now have a larger stake in preserving this order and less incentive to undermine it. Conversely, this discourse often asserts as a matter of unalterable fact that the established, leading state and its associates are forever committed to the defense of the existing order, even though they have suffered diminished stature and reduced power under it. Why should these declining states remain satisfied with their situation? Won't these states want to alter the rules of the game to arrest and reverse their fortune, especially if they still command the greatest capabilities to do so? The prevailing discourse on this topic of revisionism fails to provide us with conceptual clarity and systematic evidence on its claims, and it overlooks the fact that the international order is never a settled matter and that states are always contesting over and negotiating about it. As just explained, its logic is also highly questionable.

Recent representation of Thucydides's aphorism about the origin of the Peloponnesian War stresses the fear of a declining Sparta in view of Athens's rise. It does not ask whether the rising states can also have fears—namely, their fear of being attacked by a declining but still dominant state. To accept this possibility would overturn the entire nature and thrust of the prevailing narratives about Sino-American relations. It would turn the tables, inviting scholars of international relations, news commentators and pundits, and officials in charge of foreign policy to confront an awkward and uncomfortable question, asking themselves and their respective audiences whether a declining United States may pose a threat to China as opposed to the conventional wisdom that a rising China is a threat to the United States. This unconventional view would open a Pandora's box, causing people to alter their accustomed reasoning and reversing their logic and, of course, for Americans, casting their country in a negative light as a potential aggressor.

Of course, paradigmatic shifts and theoretical reversals have happened before. I have mentioned briefly that there has been a sea change in recent US scholarship and popular discourse. It pertains to the question of how interstate distribution of power affects war and peace. For a long time, traditional realist thinking held sway in arguing that when there is an equal distribution of power among states, the prospects for maintaining peace and stability are brighter. Conversely, when there is an imbalance of power, the traditional realist tenet argues that war and instability are more likely. Of course, Thucydides's Trap and power-transition theory stand this seemingly unassailable pillar of realist thinking on its head, contending a stronger China that has now managed to close the gap separating its power from that of the United States is a cause for concern and a source of heighted danger of war and instability. Here is then possibly a case of academic theory trying to play catch-up in adjusting to evolving reality and changing official policies. It also presents an example of the fragility of scholarly consensus and how quickly and easily academic researchers can adapt to changing political fashions and conform to political correctness—it shows that a paradigmatic transformation can occur in the field of international relations without a vigorous debate among its members about this seismic shift.

My discussion of the Cuban Missile Crisis provides a segue via this connection. Just as in the more recent episode of the Russo-Ukrainian War, there can be an endless debate about "who started it," although the prevailing discourse in the West and the United States tends to present the origins of these conflicts as an "open-and-shut case." To imply that such a debate is warranted can appear to commit political sacrilege, hence the usual trope presenting the Russo-Ukrainian War as an "unprovoked" attack by Russia on an innocent Ukraine. The Cuban Missile Crisis is typically depicted as a successful case of US coercive diplomacy to turn back Soviet encroachment in the United States' "backyard" and Moscow's sneaky attempt to upset the balance of power by introducing missiles to an island only about ninety miles away from the US mainland. There is usually scant dissent—even among informed scholars and long after this episode's conclusion—questioning this rendition of history, which, in my view, presents a great deal of political "spin," overlooks alternative explanations, and fails to consider if the shoe were on the other foot. To present Moscow's installation of missiles in Cuba as a deterrence against another US invasion of that island casts a very different light on this situation.

It puts Washington in the role of a potential aggressor and Moscow in the role of a potential defender of the status quo.

Moreover, parallels to US missiles in Turkey and Washington's policy to protect Taiwan raise uncomfortable questions. If US officials cared so much about Cuba that they were willing to push the world to the brink of a nuclear confrontation, shouldn't Soviet leaders be equally concerned about US missiles next door in Turkey? Is it possible that Chinese leaders feel the same way about US military presence in Taiwan? If Kennedy and his advisors had reason to consider serious domestic political fallout if they failed to act or be perceived to act decisively in this case, couldn't their Chinese counterparts have the same concerns with respect to domestic reactions if they were to appear "spineless" in a situation involving Taiwan? If Washington has its reputation to protect both domestically and internationally, doesn't Beijing have its reputation to consider too? Empathy and introspection are important virtues, and much of the prevailing discourse on Sino-American relations fails to show these qualities.

The supposed lesson of Munich is that officials should never appease aggressors. According to this conventional wisdom, this mistake would only embolden these aggressors and make a future war more likely and, if it occurs, wider and more destructive. There is, however, little systematic attempt to think counterfactually and ask how history would have turned out differently, as the anti-appeasers would argue—that is, to consider the counterfactual argument that a more stern and vigorous opposition to appeasement would have made a future war more likely and destructive. Although there are clearly major exceptions, those who point to the so-called lesson of Munich also fail to consider alternative explanations of why politicians sometimes accommodate demands made by ostensibly bellicose opponents, such as with respect to Neville Chamberlain's consideration of domestic political opinion and his attempt to buy time for Britain to better prepare itself for a military confrontation with Germany at a later time. There is a certitude on the part of the anti-appeasers that at the time of the Munich Conference in 1938, it was already clear that Adolf Hitler was a serial aggressor bent on a destructive rampage, when in fact the available evidence then was still ambiguous about his future intentions. His demand at Munich to incorporate areas populated by German co-ethnics did not necessarily suggest an unreasonable or aggressive agenda; self-determination probably never occurred in this instance to those who are shouting the loudest today for the United States to support Taiwan. Of course, if Hitler was a megalomaniac with an insatiable appetite for aggrandizement, then World War II would have been inevitable whether Chamberlain decided to appease him or not.

The greatest problem with sweeping and dogmatic assertions, such as those often articulated by proponents of the lesson of Munich, is that they fail to consider the possible negative consequences of their injunction. My introduction and discussion of the Japanese decision to attack Pearl Harbor are intended to show that a resolute refusal to appease does not necessarily guarantee peace. Moreover, a determination to stand one's ground can push an adversary into a corner, forcing it to choose between unconditional surrender and lashing out against its detractor. The injunction to reject appeasement also exacerbates the bias fostered by the natural disposition of officials, remarked on by Robert Jervis (1976) some time ago, to over- rather than underestimate the threat and hostility posed by the other side.

The relative strengths of the two opposing sides cannot be assumed to be the overriding factor in deciding war or peace. Japanese leaders were quite aware that their country was much weaker than the United States, and they still decided to go to war in full knowledge of this fact and their consensus that Japan could not possibly win a protracted war against the United States. Washington's policy of extended deterrence worked in this case by convincing the Japanese leaders that they could not possibly bypass fighting the United States if they were to invade the European colonies in Southeast Asia. Yet they desperately needed to make up the shortfall of resources caused by the US-led embargo, and Southeast Asia was the natural source for them to replenish their strategic stockpile. When faced with the fate of inevitable economic strangulation resulting from the US-led embargo, they decided to take the bull by its horns but try their best to blunt one of the horns. That the Japanese leaders decided to go to war even when they realized that they were facing very long odds because they were seriously outmatched by the United States should give pause to those Americans who advocate a policy of strategic clarity in committing the United States to the defense of Taiwan even at the risk of a war with China in their apparent belief that the United States still has the military upper hand, even though China has managed in recent years to reduce the power imbalance in favor of Washington.

As just suggested in reference to Japan's decision to attack Pearl Harbor, the supposed lessons of history from the 1930s (including that from the Munich Conference in 1938) are dangerous if accepted uncritically and applied to all situations unthinkingly. I have mentioned earlier the so-called law of the instrument: give a small child a hammer, and she will use it for any and all purposes. The anti-appeasers fail to consider counterexamples from history that contradict their assertion. As mentioned earlier, Spain under Philip IV fought all challengers in the hope of establishing a reputation for resolve and firmness, and this policy exhausted it financially and militarily and led to its inexorable decline. In contrast, Britain chose selective appeasement, deciding to accommodate the United States and to conciliate and cooperate with other rising powers, such as Russia and Japan, in order to oppose Wilhelmine Germany more effectively. London was not concerned that these policies would be perceived as a sign of weakness and encourage other countries to push it around to extract more concessions from it. Obviously, it would be a huge mistake if foreign leaders conclude from the US exit from Vietnam and Afghanistan that Washington would not put up a fight to defend, say, Germany or Japan. In short, anti-appeasers who invoke the lesson of Munich or more generally the lessons of the 1930s fail to grasp that reputation is not so easily transferrable from one situation to another.

I introduced the peaceful power transition between Britain and United States to point to revisionist history, which is especially on display in this case. There is a strong tendency to ransack history in a retrospective search for evidence to explain this development. The invocation of shared democratic institutions and common cultural affinity to explain the peaceful transition of the global leadership position from Britain to the United States is unpersuasive because these countries had in fact fought on at least two occasions and had, moreover, come close to fighting on other occasions. Statements from their leaders also unambiguously indicate that they had not given up the thought of using violence to settle their disagreements. Their relationship was stormy for most of the 1800s until the bilateral balance of power shifted decisively in favor of the United States. Moreover, the proposition that shared democratic institutions was the cause for the peaceful leadership transition from Britain to the United States involves a large conceptual stretch because neither country had universal adult suffrage until much later. As for cultural affinity, a moment's reflection tells us that it has not prevented fighting among people with a common heritage, including the civil war fought by Americans against

Americans. This case of peaceful leadership transition is also significant because this is the only case of such a transition thus far in modern history—one that did not produce war as power-transition theory would have predicted. Parenthetically, the peaceful end to the Cold War provides another crucial test to traditional realism, albeit, in this case, involving the precipitous and sharp fall of Soviet power, causing a large power shift in its relationship with the United States and catapulting the latter country to the indisputable position as the world's unipolar power. Traditional realism would expect a state to fight rather than to submit to its demise peacefully. War did not break out in this case or when China overtook Japan, Germany, and Russia. Peace prevailed in these cases despite the presence of power shifts and the absence of shared democratic institutions or cultural affinity.

Finally, although the shifting balance of power among states is assigned an overriding importance in attempts to explain the occurrence of war in influential narratives, such as Thucydides's Trap and power-transition theory, this variable inexplicably disappears in the dominant narrative to explain the peaceful leadership transition between Britain and the United States. Variables traditionally favored by liberals—such as democratic institutions and cultural affinity—now figure prominently in explaining the Anglo-American case. The role played by the inexorably shifting balance of power in favor of the United States and to the detriment of Britain gets short shrift, even though, as just remarked, this very factor has been assigned a central and pivotal role in explaining wars and peace.

One would think that the same variable would command even greater recognition for its explanatory power if it could account for both the outbreak of war and the maintenance of peace. This situation, however, did not prevail, even though there are scholars, like Christopher Layne (1994), who call attention to shifting power balances as an explanation of the evolving Anglo-American relationship. Prevailing discourse on peaceful transition in this case points to shuttling logic to explain away inconvenient historical phenomena. As I have argued earlier, the prevailing discourse also does not give nearly enough recognition to the role of historical contingency, especially the influence of accidental timing and special geographic circumstances, which accounted in part for the peaceful Anglo-American transition and the successful US quest for regional hegemony in the Western Hemisphere—thus far, the only instance in which a country has accomplished this feat.

The Falklands/Malvinas War highlights the importance of domestic politics in precipitating war even when the stakes involved appear to be quite negligible if it were not for the political symbolism and its potent influence in both belligerents' domestic contexts. In addition to the proposition that states might go to war even when they appear, to outside observers, to be fighting over tangibly low stakes, this case argues that winning a war can be a Pyrrhic victory when one considers the long-term consequences, such as in the context of Britain holding on to its possession of a few small, wind-swept, barren islands located far from its homeland against an opponent that is closer to these islands and is likely to gain greater advantage in its economic and political leverage in the coming years. This consideration of the long haul is, of course, the rationale articulated by former Singapore prime minister Lee Kuan Yew when he commented on the prospect of US military intervention in the Taiwan Strait in a possible war against China.

Finally, I introduced the ongoing Russo-Ukrainian War to again raise the importance of empathy and introspection. It is risky business to intrude into another country's traditional sphere of influence—even one that is contemptuously seen as a country that has fallen from the exalted position of a superpower that it once occupied. But even a small dog will sometimes stand on its hind legs, bark loudly, and occasionally bite if pressed too hard. Even much weaker opponents, such as China in 1951 and Japan in 1941, might decide to go to war if they perceive their vital national interests to be at risk. Americans do not usually put themselves in the shoes of the Russians (with respect to Ukraine) and the Chinese (with respect to Korea and Taiwan) in imagining the political and military stakes involved for the latter countries and the psychological and symbolic importance of those contested areas for these latter countries' leaders and people. There is rarely a moment when they would pause to ponder how Washington would react if Moscow or Beijing were to try to promote an anti-US government in Mexico City or to recruit this US neighbor to join a coalition headed by them.

Talks of "Ukraine today, Taiwan tomorrow" are also too facile and glib. They point to superficial similarities without delving into important substantive differences. They overlook the distinguishing fact that Russia's invasion of Ukraine is an instance of interstate invasion by one country against another. Ukraine is recognized by the international community as an independent, sovereign country. In contrast, Taiwan does not enjoy the same status. Even the United States does not recognize it as an independent, sovereign country. An overwhelming majority of the international community sees Taiwan's status as a matter of China's domestic affairs and the dispute over its status as a continuation of its unfinished civil war. Taiwan has been able to remain as an anti-Communist bastion against its nemesis in the Chinese Civil War only because of a historical accident or break: the outbreak of the Korean War that led to Harry Truman's order for the Seventh Fleet to "neutralize" the Taiwan Strait, thus preventing the mainland side from invading Taiwan ever since.

One of the major mistakes made by Washington in the Korean and Vietnam Wars is to see these conflicts through the prism of a global struggle between the free world and the Communist world and to frame these conflicts as collective defense against a menacing threat from international Communism on an expansionist campaign. US leaders saw Kim Il-sung and Ho Chi Minh as Communists rather than nationalists, assuming that they were surrogates or stooges marching on orders from Beijing or Moscow. The refrain "Ukraine today, Taiwan tomorrow" misses other important differences between the two cases. China's economic and military position is sharply different from Russia's, and Taiwan's geographic situation is also very dissimilar from Ukraine's, thus again cautioning us to be wary of facile but beguiling analogies. The one similarity between these two cases—and one that is ironically likely to be overlooked by those Americans and Westerners who are drawn to the parallels between these two cases—is that they are both located in the traditional sphere of influence of Russia and China and indeed right at their respective doorsteps.

I may have come across in this book as being too tendentious in making my arguments. My seeming stridency, however, is motivated by what I perceive to be persistent distortions and simplifications of history to advance politically correct, convenient, and self-serving narratives. Even prevailing scholarship often belies thoughtful consideration of opposing views. That conventional wisdom and popular narratives are entrenched in people's thinking and are thus difficult to dislodge even when available evidence fails to support their claim necessitates a loud voice for dissent to be heard and to overcome the natural and powerful tendency for groupthink, intellectual complacency, ethnocentrism, and self-righteousness. I have also been knowingly guilty of being repetitive in an effort to emphasize my main arguments. I have learned from my teaching experience that repetition is often necessary to make a point sink in.

I close this book with a warning. As should be abundantly clear at this point, much of the prevailing discourse on China's rise and the danger of a possible Sino-American war is flawed in my view. Not only are popular scripts and frames offered by news commentators and pundits and official presentations provided by government leaders often mistaken or misleading in significant ways, but also scholars have produced theories and analyses whose conclusions and implications are often quite problematic. The historical evidence they introduce is sometimes quite flimsy, and their analogies, dubious. As Richard Ned Lebow and Benjamin Valentino (2009) warn, media discourse, official representations, and scholarly narratives can have serious consequences in inducing self-fulfilling prophecies. Their warning indicates that war between China and the United States is not impossible but not likely for the reasons suggested by popular narratives and prevailing theories that dominate current discourse.

Those Americans who are now advocating Washington replace its policy of strategic ambiguity toward Taiwan with a policy of strategic clarity (that is, to publicly commit the United States unambiguously to Taiwan's defense) are in effect arguing that as China narrows the gap between its military capabilities and those of the United States, Washington should up the ante by pledging itself—at least rhetorically—to Taiwan's defense to offset this unfavorable (from the US perspective) power shift. To the critics of this proposal, this sounds like putting in good money after a bad investment in the hopes of retrieving a previous loss because, with the passage of time, Washington's pledge to defend Taiwan will become more untenable. As with Vietnam and Afghanistan, the rhetorical escalation to commit US prestige to a losing cause would be all the more damaging if Washington were to stake its reputation on standing by an ally and honoring its commitments. By saying repeatedly and loudly that Vietnam and Afghanistan impinged on vital US national interests and that these conflicts were a test of US will, American officials created a rhetorical trap making a policy reversal more difficult to undertake politically and psychologically (Thomson 1973). When the end came, the damage done to the US reputation was all that much greater, and this damage was self-inflicted. Officials in Washington set up their own test question, and they failed to answer it satisfactorily, thus flunking their self-administered test. Of course, this resulting damage was not limited to just the United States' reputation and credibility as these conflicts also inflicted real and massive tragedies on people's lives. And to what end?

Robert Jervis (1976, 397) points out that the human psychological tendency to reduce cognitive dissonance may have played a role in arguments one often hears about persisting in a course of action that has failed to meet expectations despite the expenditure of large amounts of resources, remarking that "spending resources on a policy generates pressures to put in additional effort to make the policy work." Of course, ego involvement may be also present as people do not like to admit defeat or failure. One stylized fact from the world of investment claims that people sell their winning stocks too soon but hold on to their losing stocks too long. Prospect theory argues that people have an aversion to suffering loss, and they tend to take more risks in their effort to reverse a setback than in seeking gains (Kahneman, Slovic, and Tversky 1982; Kahneman and Tversky 1979, 2000). One can see this phenomenon on display in casinos when gamblers often raise their bets after encountering a series of losses. This phenomenon is sometimes referred to as "gambling for recovery." Research on foreign policy also shows a similar propensity on the part of top officials. They tend to be more acceptant of risks when they see themselves in the domain of loss, and they then try to recover their losses (Boettcher 2005; He and Feng 2012; Levy 1996; McDermott 1998d).

Graham T. Allison (2020, 38) quotes George F. Kennan, the architect of US containment policy against the USSR after World War II, saying, "There is more respect to be won . . . by a resolute and courageous liquidation of unsound positions than by the most stubborn pursuit of extravagant or uncompromising objectives." He goes on to remark, "If the balance of military power in a conventional war over Taiwan . . . has shifted decisively in China's . . . favor, current U.S. commitments are not sustainable. The gap between those commitments and the United States' actual military capabilities is a classic case of overstretch" (39). Someone has made the same point less elegantly and diplomatically: "When in a hole, stop digging!"

I have introduced earlier Lee Kuan Yew's answer to the question of whether the United States would intervene militarily against China in a contingency involving Taiwan. The premise of his response was, of course, that one needs to take into account the long run. Even though Washington might prevail militarily over Beijing in the first encounter, what about the next one? And the one after that and so on? Which side is more likely to become disengaged, distracted, and disillusioned?

Margaret Thatcher and her political colleagues should have asked themselves whether Britain would be able to—or even want to—bear the burden of defending the Falklands/Malvinas in the long run. As the Japanese thinking leading to the decision to attack Pearl Harbor attests, the passage of time has an effect that is far from being neutral. It can significantly alter the relative strengths of the contesting parties and affect their available options down the road. People are prone to make the fatal mistake of not considering seriously their "end game"—to bring the war they were about to start to a successful conclusion. As they say, all wars must end and will end somehow. But how will they end? Thinking about the long-term implications of a policy is therefore important. However, myopia is unfortunately often a professional affliction for politicians when the next election appears to them always to be just around the corner, and by time the chickens come home to roost, they will have departed from the political scene, leaving someone else to clean up the mess that they created.

Acknowledgments

I would like to thank the two anonymous reviewers of this book's manuscript for their prompt, constructive, and encouraging feedback. I am also grateful for the expert guidance of Dan LoPreto at Stanford University Press, which enabled the most expeditious and smoothest review process in my experience. Finally, I want to thank Laura J. Vollmer for her exceptional copyediting, which showed more care, thoroughness, and attention to detail than I have ever encountered in my career with publishing books. Parts of this book draw from discussions in my other past and pending publications.

References

Abeledo, Lucas Vilarino. 2016. "Britain versus the South Atlantic: The Causes of the Falklands/Malvinas War." *Historian Journal*, December 12. https://thehistorianjournal.wordpress.com/2016/12/12/britain-versus-the-south-atlantic-the-causes-of-the-falklandsmalvinas-war/.

Acheson, Dean G. 1950. "Excerpts from Acheson's Speech to the National Press Club." Vancouver Island University, January 12. https://web.viu.ca/davies/H102/Acheson.speech1950.htm.

Allison, Graham T. 1971. *Essence of Decision: Explaining the Cuban Missile Crisis*. Boston: Little, Brown.

Allison, Graham T. 2015. "The Thucydides Trap: Are the U.S. and China Headed for War?" *The Atlantic*, September 24. www.theatlantic.com/international/archive/2015/09/united-states-china-war-thucydides-trap/406756/.

Allison, Graham T. 2016. "Of Course China, Like All Great Powers, Will Ignore an International Legal Verdict." *The Diplomat*, July 11. http:thediplomat.com/2016/07/of-course-china-like-all-great-powers-will-ignore-an-international-legal-verdict/.

Allison, Graham T. 2017. *Destined for War: Can America and China Escape Thucydides's Trap?* New York: Houghton Mifflin Harcourt.

Allison, Graham T. 2020. "The New Spheres of Influence: Sharing the Globe with Other Great Powers." *Foreign Affairs* 99, no. 2: 30–40.

Allison, Grahm T., and Philip Zelikow. 1999. *Essence of Decision: Explaining the Cuban Missile Crisis*. 2nd ed. New York: Longman.

Allison, Roy. 2017. "Russia and the Post-2014 International Legal Order: Revisionism and *Realpolitik*." *International Affairs* 93, no. 3: 519–43.

Allsop, Jon. 2024. "NATO Bombed a Chinese Embassy: Twenty-Five Years On, the Battle for the Narrative Continues." *Columbia Journalism Review,* May 14. https://www.cjr.org/the_media_today/nato_bombing_chinese_embassy_belgrade_media_journalists.php.

Arreguin-Toft, Ivan. 2005. *How the Weak Win Wars: A Theory of Asymmetric Conflict.* Cambridge: Cambridge University Press.

Bacevich, Andrew J. 2002. *American Empire: The Realities and Consequences of U.S. Diplomacy.* Cambridge, MA: Harvard University Press.

Bagby, Laurie M. 1994. "The Use and Misuse of Thucydides in International Relations." *International Organization* 48, no. 1: 131–53.

Balot, Ryan K., Sara Forsdyke, and Edith Foster, eds. 2017. *The Oxford Handbook of Thucydides.* Oxford: Oxford University Press.

Barker, Thomas Jones. 2015. "A Damn Close Run Thing." *Bonhams Magazine* 42 (Spring): 34. https://www.bonhams.com/magazine/18632/.

Barletta, Michael, and Harold Trinkunas. 2004. "Regime Type and Regional Security in Latin America: Toward a 'Balance of Identity' Theory." In *Balance of Power: Theory and Practice in the 21st Century,* edited by T. V. Paul, James J. Wirtz, and Michel Fortmann, 334–59. Stanford, CA: Stanford University Press.

Barnhart, Michael A. 1987. *Japan Prepares for Total War: The Search for Economic Security, 1919–1945.* Ithaca, NY: Cornell University Press.

Beck, Robert J. 1989. "Munich's Lessons Reconsidered." *International Security* 14, no. 2: 161–91.

Beckley, Michael. 2018. "The Power of Nations: Measuring What Matters." *International Security* 43, no. 2: 7–44.

Beckley, Michael. 2023. "The Perils of Peaking Powers: Economic Slowdowns and Implications for China's Next Decade." *International Security* 48, no. 1: 7–46.

Bell, Sam R., and Jesse C. Johnson. 2015. "Shifting Power, Commitment Problems, and Preventive War." *International Studies Quarterly* 59, no. 1: 124–32.

Benson, Brett. 2012. *Constructing International Security: Alliances, Deterrence, and Moral Hazard.* Cambridge: Cambridge University Press.

Benson, Brett. 2022. "Why It Makes Sense for the U.S. to Not Commit to Defending Taiwan." *Washington Post,* March 25. https://www.washingtonpost.com/outlook/2022/05/25/biden-taiwan-strategic-ambiguity/.

Ben-Zvi, Abraham. 1976. "Hindsight and Foresight: A Conceptual Framework for the Analysis of Surprise Attack." *World Politics* 28, no. 3: 381–95.

Berghahn, Volker R. 1973. *Germany and the Approach of War in 1914.* London: St. Martin's.

Berman, Larry. 1982. *Planning a Tragedy: The Americanization of the War in Vietnam.* New York: Norton.

Bernstein, Richard. 2020. "The Scary War Game over Taiwan That the U.S. Loses Again and Again." RealClearInvestigations, August 17. https://www.realclearin

vestigations.com/articles/2020/08/17/the_scary_war_game_over_taiwan_that_the_us_loses_again_and_again_124836.html.

Betts, Richard K. 1980–1981. "Surprise Despite Warning: Why Sudden Attacks Succeed." *Political Science Quarterly* 95, no. 4: 551–72.

Bickers, Robert A., and Jeffrey N. Wasserstrom. 2009. "Shanghai's 'Dogs and Chinese Not Admitted' Sign: Legend, History and Contemporary Symbol." *China Quarterly* 142: 444–66.

Blanchette, Jude, Thomas J. Christensen, Robert Daly, M. Taylor Fravel, Bonnie Glaser, Paul Haenle, Arthur R. Kroeber, et al. 2022. "Avoiding War over Taiwan: Policy Brief by the Task Force on US-China Policy." Center on US-China Relations, Asia Society. https://asiasociety.org/center-us-china-relations/avoiding-war-over-taiwan.

Boettcher, William A., III. 2005. *Presidential Risk Behavior in Foreign Policy: Prudence or Peril?* New York: Palgrave.

Borger, Julian. 2016. "Russian Hostility 'Partly Caused by West,' Claims Former US Defence Head." *The Guardian*, March 9. https://www.theguardian.com/world/2016/mar/09/russian-hostility-to-west-partly-caused-by-west.

Boulding, Kenneth E. 1962. *Conflict and Defense: A General Theory*. New York: Harper.

Bourne, Kenneth. 1967. *Britain and the Balance of Power in North America, 1815–1908*. Berkeley: University of California Press.

Broz, J. Lawrence, Zhiwen Zhang, and Gaoyang Wang. 2020. "Explaining Foreign Support for China's Global Economic Leadership." *International Organization* 74, no. 3: 417–52.

Burns, William J. 2019. *The Back Channel: A Memoir of American Diplomacy and the Case for Its Renewal*. New York: Random House.

Burr, William, and Jeffrey Richelson. 2000–2001. "Whether to 'Strangle the Baby in the Cradle': The United States and the Chinese Nuclear Program, 1960–64." *International Security* 25, no. 3: 54–99.

Bush, Richard C. 2005. *Untying the Knot: Making Peace in the Taiwan Strait*. Washington, DC: Brookings Institution Press.

Bush, Richard C. 2013. *Uncharted Strait: The Future China-Taiwan Relations*. Washington, DC: Brookings Institution Press.

Butow, Robert J. C. 1961. *Tojo and the Coming of the War*. Princeton, NJ: Princeton University Press.

Buzan, Barry. 2004. *The United States and the Great Powers: World Politics in the Twenty-First Century*. Cambridge: Polity Press.

Buzan, Barry, and Michael Cox. 2013. "China and the US: Comparable Cases of 'Peaceful Rise'?" *Chinese Journal of International Politics* 6, no. 2: 109–32.

Buzan, Barry, and Evelyn Goh. 2020. *Rethinking Sino-Japanese Alienation: History Problems and Historical Opportunity*. Oxford: Oxford University Press.

Buzas, Zoltan I. 2013. "The Color of Threat: Race, Threat Perception, and the Demise of the Anglo-Japanese Alliance, 1902–1923." *Security Studies* 22, no. 4: 573–606.

Cabestan, Jean-Pierre. 2024. *Facing China: The Prospect for War and Peace*. Lanham, MD: Rowman and Littlefield.

Carillet, Joel. 2008. "Hidden Treasures: Shanghai Just Like Kansas City?" *Wandering Educators*, September 25. https://www.wanderingeducators.com/best/traveling/hidden-treasures-shanghai-just-kansas-city.html.

Carr, Edward H. 2001 [1939]. *The Twenty Years' Crisis, 1919–1939: An Introduction to the Study of International Relations*. Rev. ed. New York: Harper and Row.

Cha, Victor D. 1999. *Alignment despite Antagonism: The United States-Korea-Japan Security Triangle*. Stanford, CA: Stanford University Press.

Cha, Victor D. 2016. *Powerplay: The Origins of the American Alliance System in Asia*. Princeton, NJ: Princeton University Press.

"Chairman McCaul: 'Ukraine Today—It's Going to Be Taiwan Tomorrow.'" 2023. Foreign Affairs Committee, February 26. https://foreignaffairs.house.gov/press-release/chairman-mccaul-ukraine-today-its-going-to-be-taiwan-tomorrow/.

Chan, Steve. 1979. "The Intelligence of Stupidity: Understanding Failures in Strategic Warning." *American Political Science Review* 73, no. 1: 171–80.

Chan, Steve. 2004a. "Can't Get No Satisfaction? The Recognition of Revisionist States." *International Relations of the Asia Pacific* 4, no. 2: 207–38.

Chan, Steve. 2004b. "Exploring Some Puzzles in Power-Transition Theory: Some Implications for Sino-American Relations." *Security Studies* 13, no. 3: 103–41.

Chan, Steve. 2008. *China, the U.S., and the Power-Transition Theory: A Critique*. London: Routledge.

Chan, Steve. 2015. "On States' Status-Quo and Revisionist Orientations: Discerning Power, Popularity and Satisfaction from Security Council Vetoes." *Issues and Studies* 51, no. 3: 1–28.

Chan, Steve. 2016. *China's Troubled Waters: Maritime Disputes in Theoretical Perspective*. Cambridge: Cambridge University Press.

Chan, Steve. 2017. "The Power-Transition Discourse and China's Rise." In *The Oxford Encyclopedia of Empirical International Relations Theory*, edited by William R. Thompson. New York: Oxford University Press. E-book. https://doi.org/10.1093/acrefore/9780190228637.013.561.

Chan, Steve. 2019. "More Than One Trap: Problematic Interpretations and Overlooked Lessons from Thucydides." *Journal of Chinese Political Science* 24, no. 1: 11–24.

Chan, Steve. 2020a. "China and Thucydides's Trap." In *China's Challenges and International Order Transition: Beyond the "Thucydides's Trap,"* edited by Kai He and Huiyun Feng, 52–71. Ann Arbor: University of Michigan Press.

Chan, Steve. 2020b. Response to "Roundtable 12-2 on *Thucydides's Trap? Historical Interpretation, Logic of Inquiry, and the Future of Sino-American Relations*." Robert

Jervis International Security Studies Forum, November 9. https://issforum.org/roundtables/12-2-Thucydides.

Chan, Steve. 2020c. *Thucydides's Trap? Historical Interpretation, Logic of Inquiry, and the Future of Sino-American Relations*. Ann Arbor: University of Michigan Press.

Chan, Steve. 2021a. "Challenging the Liberal Order: The US Hegemon as a Revisionist Power." *International Affairs* 97, no. 5: 1335–52.

Chan, Steve. 2021b. "Why Thucydides' Trap Misinforms Sino-American Relations." *Vestnik RUDN, International Relations* 21, no. 2: 234–42.

Chan, Steve. 2022. "Precedent, Path Dependency, and Reasoning by Analogy: The Strategic Implications of the Ukraine War for Sino-American Relations and Relations across the Taiwan Strait." *Asian Survey* 62, no. 5–6: 945–68.

Chan, Steve. 2023. "Bewildered and Befuddled: The West's Convoluted Narrative on China's Rise." *Asian Survey* 63, no. 5: 691–715.

Chan, Steve. 2024. "America's Reaction to China's Rise: Power Shift, Problem Shift, and Policy Shift." In *Routledge Handbook on Global China*, edited by Maxmilian Mayer, Emilian Kavalski, Marina Rudyak, and Xin Zhang, 67–77. New York: Routledge.

Chan, Steve. Forthcoming-a. *Fuses, Chains and Backlashes: China, the United States, and the Dynamics of Conflict Contagion and Escalation*. Oxford: Oxford University Press.

Chan, Steve. Forthcoming-b. *Punctuated Equilibria and Sino-American Relations: Lulls and Lurches across the Pacific*. Cambridge: Cambridge University Press.

Chan, Steve. Forthcoming-c. *Taiwan and the Danger of a Sino-American War*. Cambridge Elements in Indo-Pacific Security. Cambridge: Cambridge University Press.

Chan, Steve, Huiyun Feng, Kai He, and Weixing Hu. 2021. *Contesting Revisionism: China, the United States, and the Transformation of International Order*. Oxford: Oxford University Press.

Chan, Steve, and Weixing Hu. Forthcoming-a. "Rising States and the Liberal World Order: The Case of China." *International Affairs*.

Chan, Steve, and Weixing Hu. Forthcoming-b. *Geography and International Relations: Ukraine, Taiwan, Indo-Pacific, and Sino-American Relations*. New York: Routledge.

Chan, Steve, Richard W. X. Hu, and Kai He. 2019. "Discerning States' Revisionist and Status-Quo Orientations: Comparing China and the U.S." *European Journal of International Relations* 27, no. 2: 613–40.

Chen, Jian. 1994. *China's Road to the Korean War: The Making of the Sino-American Confrontation*. New York: Columbia University Press.

Cheney, Kyle. 2022. "What the GOP Meant When It Called Jan. 6 'Legitimate Political Discourse.'" *Politico*, February 15. https://www.politico.com/news/2022/02/15/gop-meaning-jan-6-legitimate-political-discourse-00008777.

Choate, Pat. 1990. *Agents of Influence: How Japan's Lobbyists in the United States Are Manipulating Western Political and Economic Systems*. New York: Knopf.

Chong, Ja Ian, and Todd H. Hall. 2014. "The Lessons of 1914 for East Asia Today: Missing the Trees for the Forest." *International Security* 39, no. 1: 7–43.

Choucri, Nazli, and Robert C. North. 1975. *Nations in Conflict: National Growth and International Violence*. San Francisco: Freeman.

Chow, Wilfred M., and Dov H. Levin. 2024. "The Diplomacy of Whataboutism and U.S. Foreign Policy Attitudes." *International Organization* 78, no. 1: 103–33.

Christensen, Thomas J. 1996. *Useful Adversaries: Grand Strategy, Domestic Mobilization, and Sino-American Conflict, 1947–1958*. Princeton, NJ: Princeton University Press.

Christensen, Thomas J. 2001. "Posing Problems without Catching Up: China's Rise and Challenges to U.S. Security Policy." *International Security* 25, no. 4: 5–40.

Christensen, Thomas J. 2021. "There Will Not Be a New Cold War: The Limits of U.S.-Chinese Competition." *Foreign Affairs*, March 24. www.foreignaffairs.com/articles/united-states/2021-03-24/there-will-not-be-new-cold-war.

Christensen, Thomas J., Taylor Fravel, Bonnie Glaser, Andrew Nathan, and Jessica Chen Weiss. 2022. "How to Avoid a War over Taiwan: Threats, Assurances, and Effective Deterrence." *Foreign Affairs*, October 13. https://www.foreignaffairs.com/china/how-avoid-war-over-Taiwan.

Christensen, Thomas J., and Jack Snyder. 1990. "Chain Gangs and Passed Bucks: Predicting Alliance Patterns in Multipolarity." *International Organization* 44, no. 2: 137–68.

Claar, Martin, and Norrin M. Ripsman. 2016. "Accommodation and Containment: Great Britain and Germany Prior to the Two World Wars." In *Accommodating Rising Powers: Past, Present, and Future*, edited by T. V. Paul, 150–72. Cambridge: Cambridge University Press.

Clarke, Walter. n.d. "Ambush in Mogadishu." Interview. *Frontline*, PBS. Accessed January 14, 2025. https://www.pbs.org/wgbh/pages/frontline/shows/ambush/interviews/clarke.html.

Clinton, Bill. 2020. "Bill Clinton Tells Jim Lehrer There 'Is No Sexual Relationship' with Monica Lewinsky." Hosted by Jim Lehrer. Posted January 24, by PBS NewsHour. YouTube, 3:40. https://www.youtube.com/watch?v=XBzHnZiSv7U.

Cohen, Michael D., James G. March, and Johan P. Olsen. 1972. "A Garbage Can Theory of Organizational Choice." *Administrative Science Quarterly* 17, no. 1: 1–25.

Coicaud, Jean-Marc. 2001. "Legitimacy, Socialization, and International Change." In *Power in Transition: The Peaceful Change of International Order*, edited by Charles A. Kupchan, Emanuel Adler, Jean-Marc Coicaud, and Yuen Foong Khong, 68–100. Tokyo: United Nations University Press.

Cooley, Alexander, Daniel Nexon, and Steven Ward. 2019. "Revising Order or Challenging the Balance of Power? An Alternative Typology of Revisionist and Status-Quo States." *Review of International Studies* 45, no. 4: 689–708.

Copeland, Dale C. 2000. *The Origins of Major War.* Ithaca, NY: Cornell University Press.

Crawford, Timothy W. 2003. *Pivotal Deterrence: Third-Party Statecraft and the Pursuit of Peace.* Ithaca, NY: Cornell University Press.

Daalder, Ivo H., and James M. Lindsay. 2005. *America Unbound: The Bush Revolution in Foreign Policy.* New York: Wiley.

Danilovic, Vesna. 2001. "Conceptual and Selection Bias Issues in Deterrence." *Journal of Conflict Resolution* 45, no. 1: 97–125.

Daugherty, William J. 2003. "Jimmy Carter and the 1979 Decision to Admit the Shah into the United States." *American Diplomacy* (April). https://americandiplomacy.web.unc.edu/2003/04/jimmy-carter-and-the-1979-decision-to-admit-the-shah-into-the-united-states/.

Davidson, Jason W. 2006. *The Origins of Revisionist and Status-Quo States.* London: Palgrave Macmillan.

denisli34 [username]. 2021. "Rising Powers React to Contentious U.S.-China Relations: A Roundup." Rising Power Initiative, George Washington University, March 25. https://www.risingpowersinitiative.org/publication/rising-powers-react-to-contentious-u-s-china-relations-a-roundup/.

de Rivera, Joseph H. 1968. *The Psychological Dimension of Foreign Policy.* Columbus, OH: Merrill.

Destler, I. M. 1972. "Comment: Multiple Advocacy; Some 'Limits and Costs.'" *American Political Science Review* 66, no. 3: 786–90.

de Soysa, Indra, John R. Oneal, and Yong-Hee Park. 1997. "Testing Power-Transition Theory: Using Alternative Measures of National Capabilities." *Journal of Conflict Resolution* 41, no. 4: 509–28.

Deutsch, Karl W., Sidney A. Burrell, Robert A. Kann, Maurice Lee Jr., Martin Lichtenman, Raymond E. Lindgren, Francis L. Loewenheim, and Richard W. Van Wagenen. 1957. *Political Community and the North Atlantic Area: International Organization in the Light of Historical Experience.* New York: Greenwood.

de Vries, Karl. 2023. "Milley Says Trump Disrespected US Military with Execution Comment." CNN, September 28. https://www.cnn.com/2023/09/28/politics/milley-donald-trump-execution-comment/index.html.

DeWeerd, Harmen A. 1962. "Strategic Surprise in the Korean War." *ORBIS* 6: 435–52.

DiCicco, Jonathan M., and Jack S. Levy. 1999. "Power Shifts and Problem Shifts: The Evolution of the Power Transition Research Program." *Journal of Conflict Resolution* 43, no. 6: 675–704.

Diez Acosta, Tomás. 2002. *October 1962: The "Missile" Crisis as Seen from Cuba.* New York: Pathfinder Press.

Doran, Charles F. 1991. *Systems in Crisis: New Imperatives of High Politics at Century's End.* Cambridge: Cambridge University Press.

Doran, Charles F., and Wes Parsons. 1980. "War and the Cycle of Relative Power." *American Political Science Review* 74, no. 4: 947–65.

Ellsberg, Daniel. 1972. "The Quagmire Myth and the Stalemate Machine." In *Papers on the War*, 42–131. New York: Simon and Schuster.

Elman, Colin. 2003. "Introduction: Appraising Balance of Power Theory." In *Realism and the Balancing of Power: A New Debate*, edited by John A. Vasquez and Colin Elman, 1–22. Upper Saddle River, NJ: Prentice Hall.

Elman, Colin. 2004. "Extending Offensive Realism: The Louisiana Purchase and America's Rise to Regional Hegemony." *American Political Science Review* 98, no. 4: 563–76.

Emerson, Ralph Waldo. n.d. "Ralph Waldo Emerson." Goodreads. Accessed January 14, 2025. https://www.goodreads.com/quotes/353571-a-foolish-consistency-is-the-hobgoblin-of-little-minds-adored.

Fearon, James D. 1994. "Signal versus the Balance of Power and Interests: An Empirical Test of a Crisis Bargaining Model." *Journal of Conflict Resolution* 38, no. 2: 236–69.

Fearon, James D. 1995. "Rationalist Explanations for War." *International Organization* 49, no. 3: 379–414.

Fearon, James D. 1997. "Signaling Foreign Policy Interests: Tying Hands versus Sinking Costs." *Journal of Conflict Resolution* 41, no. 1: 68–90.

Fearon, James D. 2002. "Selection Effects and Deterrence." *International Interactions* 28, no. 1: 5–29.

Feis, Herbert. 1962. *The Road to Pearl Harbor: The Coming of the War between the United States and Japan*. Princeton, NJ: Princeton University Press.

Feng, Huiyun. 2009. "Is China a Revisionist Power?" *Chinese Journal of International Politics* 2, no. 3: 313–34.

Feng, Yongping. 2006. "The Peaceful Transition of Power from the UK to the US." *Chinese Journal of International Politics* 1, no. 1: 83–108.

Ferdinand, Peter. 2014. "Foreign Policy Convergence in Pacific Asia: The Evidence from Voting in the UN General Assembly." *British Journal of Politics and International Relations* 16, no. 4: 662–79.

Fingleton, Eamonn. 1995. *Blindside: Why Japan Is Still on Track to Overtake the U.S. by the Year 2000*. Boston: Houghton Mifflin.

Fischer, Fritz. 1967. *Germany's Aims in the First World War*. New York: Norton.

Fischer, Fritz. 1975. *The War of Illusions*. New York: Norton.

Fischhoff, Baruch. 1977. "Perceived Informativeness of Facts." *Journal of Experimental Psychology: Human Perception and Performance* 3, no. 2: 349–58.

Fischhoff, Baruch, and Ruth Beyth. 1975. "I Knew It Would Happen: Remembered Probabilities of Once-Future Things." *Organizational Behavior and Human Performance* 13, no. 1: 1–16.

Foot, Rosemary, and Andrew Walter. 2011. *China, the United States, and Global Order*. Cambridge: Cambridge University Press.

Fravel, M. Taylor. 2009. *Strong Borders, Secure Nation: Cooperation and Conflict in China's Territorial Disputes*. Princeton, NJ: Princeton University Press.

Friedberg, Aaron L. 1988. *The Weary Titan: The Experience of Relative Decline, 1985–1905*. Princeton, NJ: Princeton University Press.

Friedberg, Aaron L. 2011. *A Contest for Supremacy: China, America, and the Struggle for Mastery in Asia*. New York: Norton.

Friedman, George, and Meredith LeBard. 1991. *The Coming War with Japan*. New York: St. Martin's.

Fry, Michael G. 1989. *The Suze Crisis: 1956*. Pew Case Studies in International Affairs, case no. 126. Washington, DC: Institute for the Study of Diplomacy, Pew Case Studies Center, Georgetown University.

Gelb, Leslie H. 1971. "Vietnam: The System Worked." *Foreign Policy* 3 (Summer): 140–67.

"'Genocide' Is the Wrong Word for the Horrors of Xinjiang: To Confront Evil, the First Step Is to Describe It Accurately." 2021. *The Economist*, February 13. https://www.economist.com/leaders/2021/02/13/genocide-is-the-wrong-word-for-the-horrors-of-xinjiang.

George, Alexander L. 1972a. "The Case for Multiple Advocacy in Making Foreign Policy." *American Political Science Review* 66, no. 3: 751–85.

George, Alexander L. 1972b. "A Rejoinder to 'Comment' by I. M. Destler." *American Political Science Review* 66, no. 3: 791–95.

George, Alexander L., David K. Hall, and William E. Simons. 1971. *The Limits of Coercive Diplomacy: Laos, Cuba, Vietnam*. Boston: Little, Brown.

Gilpin, Robert. 1981. *War and Change in World Politics*. Cambridge: Cambridge University Press.

Glaser, Bonnie S., Michael J. Mazarr, Michael J. Glennon, Richard Haas, and David Sacks. 2020. "Dire Straits: Should American Support for Taiwan Be Ambiguous?" *Foreign Affairs*, September 24. https://www.foreignaffairs.com/articles/united-states/2020-09-24/dire-straits.

Goddard, Stacie E. 2018a. "Embedded Revisionism: Networks, Institutions, and Challenges to World Order." *International Organization* 72, no. 4: 763–97.

Goddard, Stacie E. 2018b. *When Right Makes Might: Rising Powers and World Order*. Ithaca, NY: Cornell University Press.

Gramsci, Antonio. 1971. *Selections from the Prison Notebooks of Antonio Gramsci*. New York: International Publishers.

Green, Brendan R., and Caitlin Talmadge. 2022. "Then What? Assessing the Military Implications of Chinese Control of Taiwan." *International Security* 47, no. 1: 7–45.

Greve, Andrew Q., and Jack S. Levy. 2018. "Power Transition, Status Dissatisfaction, and War: The Sino-Japanese War of 1894–1895." *Security Studies* 27, no. 1: 148–78.

Grigoryan, Arman. 2020. "Selective Wilsonianism: Material Interests and the West's Support for Democracy." *International Security* 44, no. 4: 158–200.

"*The Guardian* View on the Lessons the First World War Has for Today." 2014. *The Guardian*, August 3. https://www.theguardian.com/commentisfree/2014/aug/03/guardian-view-lessons-first-world-war-today.

Gurr, Ted R. 1970. *Why Men Rebel?* Princeton, NJ: Princeton University Press.

Haass, Richard, and David Sacks. 2020. "American Support for Taiwan Must Be Unambiguous." *Foreign Affairs*, September 20. https://www.foreignaffairs.com/articles/united-states/american-support-taiwan-must-be-unambiguous.

Hagstrom, Linus, and Bjorn Jerden. 2014. "East Asia's Power Shift: The Flaws and Hazards of the Debate and How to Avoid Them." *Asian Perspective* 38, no. 3: 337–62.

Hallin, Daniel C. 1986. *The "Uncensored" War*. Oxford: Oxford University Press.

Handel, Michael I. 1977. "The Yom Kippur War and the Inevitability of Surprise." *International Studies Quarterly* 21, no. 3: 461–502.

He, Kai, and Huiyun Feng. 2012. *Prospect Theory and Foreign Policy Analysis in the Asia Pacific: Rational Leaders and Risky Behavior*. New York: Routledge.

He, Kai, Huiyung Feng, Steve Chan, and Weixing Hu. 2021. "Rethinking Revisionism in World Politics." *Chinese Journal of International Politics* 14, no. 2: 159–86.

Hemmer, Christopher, and Peter J. Katzenstein. 2002. "Why Is There No NATO in Asia? Collective Identity, Regionalism, and the Origins of Multilateralism." *International Organization* 56, no. 3: 575–607.

Herrmann, David G. 1995. *The Arming of Europe and the Making of the First World War*. Princeton, NJ: Princeton University Press.

Herwig, Holger H. 1986. *Germany's Vision of Empire in Venezuela 1871–1914*. Princeton, NJ: Princeton University Press.

Higgins, Trumbull. 1966. *Hitler and Russia: The Third Reich in a Two-Front War, 1937–1943*. New York: Macmillan.

Hilgruber, Andrea. 1981. *Germany and the Two World Wars*. Cambridge, MA: Harvard University Press.

Hoffmann, Stanley. 1977. "An American Social Science: International Relations." *Daedalus* 106, no. 3: 41–60.

Holsti, Ole R. 1962. "Belief System and National Images: A Case Study." *Journal of Conflict Resolution* 6, no. 3: 244–52.

Houweling, Henk, and Jan G. Siccama. 1988. "Power Transitions as a Cause of War." *Journal of Conflict Resolution* 32, no. 1: 87–102.

Human Rights Watch. 2020a. "US Sanctions International Criminal Court Prosecutor: Trump Administration's Action Tries to Block World's Worst Crimes." September 2. https://www.hrw.org/news/2020/09/02/us-sanctions-internation al-criminal-court-prosecutor.

Human Rights Watch. 2020b. "US Sanctions on the International Criminal Court: Questions and Answers." December 14. https://www.hrw.org/news/2020/12/14/us-sanctions-international-criminal-court.

Hurd, Ian. 2007. "Breaking and Making Norms: American Revisionism and Crises of Legitimacy." *International Politics* 44, no. 2–3: 194–213.

Huth, Paul K. 1988a. "Extended Deterrence and the Outbreak of War." *American Political Science Review* 82, no. 2: 423–44.

Huth, Paul K. 1988b. *Extended Deterrence and the Prevention of War.* New Haven, CT: Yale University Press.

Huth, Paul, and Bruce M. Russett. 1988. "Deterrence Failure and Crisis Escalation." *International Studies Quarterly* 32, no. 1: 29–46.

Ike, Nobutake. 1967. *Japan's Decision for War: Records of the 1941 Policy Conferences.* Stanford, CA: Stanford University Press.

Ikenberry, G. John. 2001. *After Victory: Institutions, Strategic Restraint, and the Rebuilding of Order after Major Wars.* Princeton, NJ: Princeton University Press.

Ikenberry, G. John. 2008. "The Rise of China and the Future of the West: Can the Liberal System Survive?" *Foreign Affairs* 87, no. 1: 23–37.

Ikenberry, G. John. 2011. "The Future of the Liberal World Order: Internationalism after America." *Foreign Affairs* 90, no. 3: 56–68.

Ikenberry, G. John. 2012. *Liberal Leviathan: The Origins, Crisis, and Transformation of the American World Order.* Princeton, NJ: Princeton University Press.

Initiative for US-China Dialogue on Global Issues. 2020. "America's Taiwan Policy: Debating Strategic Ambiguity and the Future of Asian Security." Georgetown University, October 2. https://uschinadialogue.georgetown.edu/events/america-s-taiwan-policy-debating-strategic-ambiguity-and-the-future-of-asian-security.

Iriye, Akira. 1981. *Power and Culture: The Japanese-American War, 1941–1945.* Cambridge, MA: Harvard University Press.

Ives, Mike, and Elsie Chen, 2019. "In 1967, Hong Kong's Protestors Were Communist Sympathizers." *New York Times,* September 16. https://www.nytimes.com/2019/09/16/world/asia/hong-kong-1967-riots.html.

Jaffe, S. N. 2017. *Thucydides on the Outbreak of War: Character and Contest.* Oxford: Oxford University Press.

Janis, Irving L. 1982a. *Groupthink: Psychological Studies of Policy Decisions and Fiascoes.* 2nd ed. Boston: Houghton Mifflin.

Janis, Irving L. 1982b. "In and Out of North Korea: 'The Wrong War with the Wrong Enemy.'" In *Groupthink: Psychological Studies of Policy Decisions and Fiascoes,* 48–71. 2nd ed. Boston: Houghton Mifflin.

Janis, Irving L. 1982c. "A Perfect Failure: The Bay of Pigs." In *Groupthink: Psychological Studies of Policy Decisions and Fiascoes,* 14–47. 2nd ed. Boston: Houghton Mifflin.

Jentleson, Bruce W. 1992. "The Pretty Prudent Public: Post-Vietnam American Opinion on the Use of Military Force." *International Studies Quarterly* 36, no. 1: 47–74.

Jentleson, Bruce W., and Rebecca Britton. 1998. "Still Pretty Prudent: Post–Cold War American Public Opinion on the Use of Military Force." *Journal of Conflict Resolution* 42, no. 4: 395–417.

Jervis, Robert. 1968. "Hypotheses on Misperception." *World Politics* 20, no. 3: 454–79.

Jervis, Robert. 1976. *Perception and Misperception in International Politics.* Princeton, NJ: Princeton University Press.

Johnston, Alastair I. 2003. "Is China a Status Quo Power?" *International Security* 7, no. 4: 5–56.

Johnston, Alastair I. 2013. "How New and Assertive Is China's New Assertiveness?" *International Security* 37, no. 4: 7–48.

Johnston, Alastair I. 2019. "China in a World of Orders: Rethinking Compliance and Challenge in Beijing's International Relations." *International Security* 44, no. 2: 9–60.

Jones, F. C. 1954. *Japan's New Order in East Asia: Its Rise and Fall 1937–45*. Oxford: Oxford University Press.

Kagan, Donald. 1969. *The Outbreak of the Peloponnesian War*. Ithaca, NY: Cornell University Press.

Kahneman, Daniel, Paul Slovic, and Amos Tversky, eds. 1982. *Judgment under Uncertainty: Heuristics and Biases*. Cambridge: Cambridge University Press.

Kahneman, Daniel, and Amos Tversky. 1979. "Prospect Theory: An Analysis of Decision under Risk." *Econometrica* 47, no. 2: 263–92.

Kahneman, Daniel, and Amos Tversky, eds. 2000. *Choices, Values, and Frames*. Cambridge: Cambridge University Press.

Kamisar, Ben. 2023. "Almost a Third of Americans Still Believe the 2020 Election Result Was Fraudulent." NBC News, June 20. https://www.nbcnews.com/meet-the-press/meetthepressblog/almost-third-americans-still-believe-2020-election-result-was-fraudule-rcna90145.

Kang, David C. 2003. "Getting Asia Wrong: The Need for New Analytical Frameworks." *International Security* 27, no. 4: 57–85.

Kang, David C. 2007. *China Rising: Peace, Power, and Order in East Asia*. New York: Columbia University Press.

Kang, David C. 2010. "Hierarchy and Legitimacy in International Systems: The Tribute System in Early Modern East Asia." *Security Studies* 19, no. 4: 591–622.

Kang, David C. 2012. *East Asia before the West: Five Centuries of Trade and Tribute*. New York: Columbia University Press.

Kang, David C. 2020. "Thought Games about China." *Journal of East Asian Studies* 20, no. 2: 135–50.

Kang, David C. 2025. "There Is No East Asian Balancing against China." In *Reconsidering the East Asian Peace: Confluences, Regional Characteristics and Societal Transformation*, edited by William R. Thompson and Thomas J. Volgy, 181–209. New York: Routledge.

Kanno-Youngs, Zolan, and Peter Baker. 2022. "Biden Pledges to Defend Taiwan If It Faces a Chinese Attack." *New York Times*, May 23. https://www.nytimes.com/2022/05/23/world/asia/biden-taiwan-china.html.

Kastner, Scott L. 2022. *War and Peace in the Taiwan Strait*. New York: Columbia University Press.

Kastner, Scott L., and Phillip C. Saunders. 2012. "Is China a Status Quo or Revisionist State? Leadership Travel as an Empirical Indicator of Foreign Policy Priorities." *International Studies Quarterly* 56, no. 1: 163–77.

Kaufman, Chaim. 2004. "Threat Inflation and the Failure of the Marketplace of Ideas: The Selling of the Iraqi War." *International Security* 29, no. 1: 5–48.

Kegley, Charles W., Jr., and Gregory A. Raymond. 1994. *A Multipolar Peace? Great-Power Politics in the Twenty-First Century*. New York: St. Martin's.

Kennan, George F. 1997. "A Fateful Error." *New York Times*, February 5. https://www.nytimes.com/1997/02/05/opinion/a-fateful-error.html.

Kennedy, David M. 1988. *The Reagan Administration and Lebanon*. Pew Case Studies in International Affairs, case no. 340. Washington, DC: Institute for the Study of Diplomacy, Pew Case Studies Center, Georgetown University.

Kennedy, Paul. 1980. *The Rise of Anglo-German Antagonism: 1860–1914*. London: Allen and Unwin.

Kennedy, Paul. 1987. *The Rise and Fall of Great Powers*. New York: Vintage Books.

Keohane, Robert O., and Joseph S. Nye. 1977. *Power and Interdependence: World Politics in Transition*. Boston: Little, Brown.

Khong, Yuen Foong. 1992. *Analogies at War: Korea, Munich, Dien Bien Phu, and the Vietnam Decisions of 1965*. Princeton, NJ: Princeton University Press.

Khong, Yuen Foong. 2001. "Negotiating 'Order' during Power Transitions." In *Power in Transition: The Peaceful Change of International Order*, edited by Charles A. Kupchan, Emanuel Adler, Jean-Marc Coicaud, and Yuen Foong Khong, 34–67. Tokyo: United Nations University Press.

Kim, Woosang S. 1991. "Alliance Transitions and Great Power War." *American Journal of Political Science* 35, no. 4: 833–50.

Kim, Woosang S. 1992. "Power Transitions and Great Power War from Westphalia to Waterloo." *World Politics* 45, no. 1: 153–72.

Kindleberger, Charles P. 1974. *The World in Depression, 1929–1939*. Berkeley: University of California Press.

Kindleberger, Charles P. 1981. "Dominance and Leadership in the International Economy: Exploitation, Public Goods and Free Rides." *International Studies Quarterly* 25, no. 2: 242–54.

Kindleberger, Charles P. 1986. "International Public Goods without International Government." *American Economic Review* 76, no. 1: 1–13.

Kirshner, Jonathan. 2019. "Handle Him with Care: The Importance of Getting Thucydides Right." *Security Studies* 28, no. 1: 1–24.

Kofman, Michael. 2018. "The August War, Ten Years On: A Retrospective on the Russo Georgian War." *War on the Rocks*, August 17. https://warontherocks.com/2018/08/the-august-war-ten-years-on-a-retrospective-on-the-russo-georgian-war/.

Kugler, Jacek, and Marina Arbetman. 1997. "Relative Policy Capacity: Political Extraction and Political Reach." In *Political Capacity and Economic Behavior*, edited by Marina Arbetman and Jacek Kugler, 11–45. Boulder, CO: Westview.

Kugler, Jacek, and William Domke. 1986. "Comparing the Strengths of Nations." *Comparative Political Studies* 19, no. 1: 39–69.

Kugler, Jacek, and Douglas Lemke, eds. 1996. *Parity and War: Evaluations and Extensions of the War Ledger.* Ann Arbor: University of Michigan Press.

Kupchan, Charles A. 2001. "Introduction: Explaining Peaceful Power Transition." In *Power in Transition: The Peaceful Change of International Order,* edited by Kupchan, Emanuel Adler, Jean-Marc Coicaud, and Yuen Foong Khong, 1–17. Tokyo: United Nations University Press.

Kupchan, Charles A. 2010. *How Enemies Become Friends: The Sources of Stable Peace.* Princeton, NJ: Princeton University Press.

Kupchan, Charles A. 2020. *Isolationism: A History of America's Efforts to Shield Itself from the World.* Oxford: Oxford University Press.

Larson, Deborah W. 1985. *Origins of Containment: A Psychological Explanation.* Princeton, NJ: Princeton University Press.

Larson, Deborah W., and Alexei Shevchenko. 2010. "Status Seekers: Chinese and Russian Responses to U.S. Primacy." *International Security* 34, no. 4: 63–95.

Larson, Deborah W., and Alexei Shevchenko. 2019. *Quest for Status: Chinese and Russian Foreign Policy.* New Haven, CT: Yale University Press.

Layne, Christopher. 1994. "Kant or Cant: The Myth of the Democratic Peace." *International Security* 19, no. 2: 5–49.

Layne, Christopher. 2004. "The War on Terrorism and the Balance of Power: The Paradoxes of American Hegemony." In *Balance of Power: Theory and Practice in the 21st Century,* edited by T. V. Paul, James J. Wirtz, and Michel Fortmann, 103–26. Stanford, CA: Stanford University Press.

Layne, Christopher. 2006a. *The Peace of Illusions: American Grand Strategy from 1940 to the Present.* Ithaca, NY: Cornell University Press.

Layne, Christopher. 2006b. "The Unipolar Illusion Revisited: The Coming End of the United States' Unipolar Moment." *International Security* 31, no. 2: 7–41.

Leach, Barry A. 1973. *The German Strategy against Russia: 1939–1941.* Oxford: Clarendon.

Lebow, Richard Ned. 1981. *Between Peace and War: The Nature of International Crisis.* Baltimore, MD: Johns Hopkins University Press.

Lebow, Richard Ned. 1984. "Windows of Opportunity: Do States Jump through Them?" *International Security* 9, no. 1: 147–86.

Lebow, Richard Ned. 1985. "Miscalculation in the South Atlantic: The Origins of the Falklands War." In *Psychology and Deterrence,* edited by Robert Jervis, Lebow, and Janice Gross Stein, 85–124. Baltimore, MD: Johns Hopkins University Press.

Lebow, Richard Ned. 2000–2001. "Contingency, Catalyst, and International System." *Political Science Quarterly* 115, no. 4: 591–616.

Lebow, Richard Ned. 2007. "Thucydides and Deterrence." *Security Studies* 16, no. 2: 163–88.

Lebow, Richard Ned. 2010. *Why Nations Fight: Past and Future Motivations for War.* Cambridge: Cambridge University Press.

Lebow, Richard Ned, and Daniel P. Tompkins. 2016. "The Thucydides Claptrap: Prevailing Theory Argues That U.S. Conflicts with Rising Powers Are Inevitable; It's Also Flat-Out Wrong." *Washington Monthly*, June 28. https://washingtonmonthly.com/thucydides-claptrap.

Lebow, Richard Ned, and Benjamin Valentino. 2009. "Lost in Transition: A Critical Analysis of Power Transition Theory." *International Relations* 23, no. 3: 389–410.

Lee, James. 2019. "Did Thucydides Believe in Thucydides' Trap? The History of the Peloponnesian War and Its Relevance to US-China Relations." *Journal of Chinese Political Science* 24, no. 1: 67–86.

Lee Kuan Yew. 2013. "No American Intervention If Taiwan Is Invaded." Posted July 25, by SPH Razor. YouTube, 13:59. https://www.youtube.com/watch?v=q_gr3dtBaic.

Lemke, Douglas, and William Reed. 1996. "Regime Type and Status Quo Evaluations: Power Transition Theory and Democratic Peace." *International Interactions* 22, no. 2: 143–64.

Lerner, Mitchell B. 2002. *The* Pueblo *Incident: A Spy Ship and the Failure of American Foreign Policy*. Lawrence: University Press of Kansas.

Levy, Jack S. 1987. "Declining Power and the Preventive Motivation for War." *World Politics* 40, no. 1: 82–107.

Levy, Jack S. 1996. "Loss Aversion, Framing and Bargaining: The Implications of Prospect Theory for International Conflict." *International Political Science Review* 17, no. 2: 177–93.

Levy, Jack S. 2008a. "Deterrence and Coercive Diplomacy: The Contributions of Alexander George." *Political Psychology* 29, no. 4: 537–52.

Levy, Jack S. 2008b. "Power Transition Theory and the Rise of China." In *China's Ascent: Power, Security, and the Future of International Politics*, edited by Robert S. Ross and Zhu Feng, 11–33. Ithaca, NY: Cornell University Press.

Levy, Jack S. 2008c. "Preventive War and Democratic Politics." *International Studies Quarterly* 52, no. 1: 1–24.

Levy, Jack S., and William R. Thompson. 2010. *The Causes of War*. West Sussex: Wiley-Blackwell.

Levy, Jack S., and William R. Thompson. 2011. *The Arc of War: Origins, Escalation, and Transformation*. Chicago: University of Chicago Press.

Liao, George. 2022. "Taiwanese Pessimistic about Prospect of US Sending Troops to Help Defend Nation: Pollster." *Taiwan Times*, May 20. https://www.taiwannews.com.tw/news/4481985.

Lieber, Keir A. 2007. "The New History of World War I and What It Means for International Relations Theory." *International Security* 32, no. 2: 155–91.

Lind, Jennifer. 2017. "Asia's Other Revisionist Power: Why U.S. Grand Strategy Unnerves China." *Foreign Affairs* 96, no. 2: 74–82.

Lippincott, Don, and Gregory F. Treverton. 1988. *Negotiations Concerning the Falklands/Malvinas Dispute*. Pew Case Studies in International Affairs, case no. 406, pts. A and B. Washington, DC: Institute for the Study of Diplomacy, Pew Case Studies Center, Georgetown University.

Lobell, Steven E. 2016. "Realism, Balance of Power, and Power Transitions." In *Accommodating Rising Powers: Past, Present, and Future*, edited by T. V. Paul, 33–52. Cambridge: Cambridge University Press.

Ma, Xinru, and David C. Kang. 2024. *Beyond Power Transitions: The Lessons of East Asian History and the Future of U.S.-China Relations*. New York: Columbia University Press.

MacArthur, Douglas. 2005. "The Unsinkable Aircraft Carrier." *Taiwan Review*, May 1. https://taiwantoday.tw/news.php?unit=4,29,31,45&post=4186.

Mack, Andrew. 1975. "Why Big Nations Lose Small Wars: The Politics of Asymmetric Conflict." *World Politics* 27, no. 2: 175–200.

Mackinder, Halford J. 1904. "The Geographical Pivot of History." *Geographical Journal* 23, no. 4: 421–37.

Mackinder, Halford J. 1919. *Democratic Ideals and Reality: A Study in the Politics of Reconstruction*. London: Constable.

Mackinder, Halford J. 1943. "The Round World and the Winning of the Peace." *Foreign Affairs* 21, no. 4: 595–605.

MacMillan, Margaret. 2008. *Dangerous Games: The Uses and Abuses of History*. New York: Modern Library.

MacMillan, Margaret. 2013. *The War That Ended Peace*. New York: Random House.

Mahbubani, Kishore. 2020. *Has China Won? The Chinese Challenge to American Primacy*. New York: PublicAffairs.

Mandelbaum, Michael. 1997. "The New NATO: Bigger Isn't Better." *Wall Street Journal*, July 9. https://www.wsj.com/articles/SB868390552819966500.

Markovits, Andrei S., and Simon Reich. 1997. *The German Predicament: Memory and Power in the New Europe*. Ithaca, NY: Cornell University Press.

Massie, Suzanne. 2014. "Opinion: US Intervention in Ukraine Arrogant, Heavy-Handed." Sputnik, May 16. http://sputniknews.com/world/20140516/189865599.html.

May, Ernest R. 1975. *"Lessons" of the Past: The Use and Misuse of History in American Foreign Policy*. Oxford: Oxford University Press.

May, Ernest R., and Philip D. Zelikow, eds. 1977. *The Kennedy Tapes: Inside the White House during the Cuban Missile Crisis*. Cambridge, MA: Harvard University.

McDermott, Rose. 1998a. "The Decisions about Admitting the Shah." In *Risk-Taking in International Relations: Prospect Theory in American Foreign Policy*, 77–105. Ann Arbor: University of Michigan Press.

McDermott, Rose. 1998b. "The Iran Hostage Rescue Mission." In *Risk-Taking in International Relations: Prospect Theory in American Foreign Policy*, 45–75. Ann Arbor: University of Michigan Press.

McDermott, Rose. 1998c. "The 1956 Suez Crisis." In *Risk-Taking in International Rela-*

tions: Prospect Theory in American Foreign Policy, 135–64. Ann Arbor: University of Michigan Press.

McDermott, Rose. 1998d. *Risk-Taking in International Relations: Prospect Theory in American Foreign Policy*. Ann Arbor: University of Michigan Press.

McDermott, Rose. 1998e. "The U-2 Crisis." In *Risk-Taking in International Relations: Prospect Theory in American Foreign Policy*, 107–34. Ann Arbor: University of Michigan Press.

McFaul, Michael, Stephen Sestanovich, and John J. Mearsheimer. 2014. "Faulty Powers: Who Started the Ukraine Crisis?" *Foreign Affairs* 93, no. 6: 167–78.

Mearsheimer, John J. 2001. *The Tragedy of Great Power Politics*. New York: Norton.

Mearsheimer, John J. 2006. "China's Unpeaceful Rise." *Current History* 105, no. 690: 160–62.

Mearsheimer, John J. 2011. *Why Leaders Lie: The Truth about Lying in International Politics*. Oxford: Oxford University Press.

Mearsheimer, John J. 2014. "Why the Ukraine Crisis Is the West's Fault." *Foreign Affairs* 93, no. 5: 77–89.

Mearsheimer, John J. 2019. "Bound to Fail: The Rise and Fall of the Liberal International Order." *International Security* 43, no. 4: 7–50.

Mearsheimer, John J. 2022a. "The Causes and Consequences of the Ukraine Crisis." *National Interest*, June 23. https://nationalinterest.org/feature/causes-and-consequences-ukraine-crisis-203182.

Mearsheimer, John J. 2022b. "Playing with Fire in Ukraine: The Underappreciated Risks of Catastrophic Escalation." *Foreign Affairs*, August 17. https://www.foreignaffairs.com/ukraine/playing-fire-ukraine.

Mersheimer, John J. 2023. "The Darkness Ahead: Where the Ukraine War Is Headed." John's Substack, June 23. https://open.substack.com/pub/mearsheimer/p/the-darkness-ahead-where-the-ukraine.

Mearsheimer, John J., and Sebastian Rosato. 2023. *How States Think: The Rationality of Foreign Policy*. New Haven, CT: Yale University Press.

Mearsheimer, John J., and Stephen M. Walt. 2003. "An Unnecessary War." *Foreign Policy* 134 (January–February): 50–59.

Menkhaus, Ken, and Louis Ortmayer. 1995. *Key Decisions in the Somalia Intervention*. Pew Case Studies in International Affairs, case no. 464. Washington, DC: Institute for the Study of Diplomacy, Pew Case Studies Center, Georgetown University.

Mercer, Jonathan. 1996. *Reputation and International Politics*. Ithaca, NY: Cornell University Press.

Merom, Gil. 2003. *How Democracies Lose Small Wars: State, Society, and the Failure of France in Algeria, Israel in Lebanon, and the United States in Vietnam*. Cambridge: Cambridge University Press.

Miller, Manjari C. 2021. *Why Nations Rise: Narratives and the Path to Great Power*. Oxford: Oxford University Press.

Miller Center. n.d. "The 'Mission Accomplished' Moment." University of Virginia. Accessed January 14, 2025. https://millercenter.org/americas-war-in-iraq/mission-accomplished-moment.

Moise, Edwin E. 1996. *Tonkin Gulf and the Escalation of the Vietnam War.* Chapel Hill: University of North Carolina Press.

Morris, Kyle. 2021. "Milley Secretly Called Chinese Officials Out of Fear Trump Would 'Attack' in Final Days: Book Claims." Fox News, September 14. https://www.foxnews.com/politics/milley-secretly-called-chinese-officials-out-of-fear-trump-would-attack-in-final-days-book-claims.

Mueller, John H. 1989. *Retreat from Doomsday: The Obsolescence of Major War.* New York: Basic Books.

Mueller, Karl P., Jason J. Castillo, Forrest E. Morgan, Negeen Pegahi, and Brian Rosen. 2006. *Striking First: Preemptive and Preventive Attack in U.S. National Security Policy.* Santa Monica, CA: RAND.

Murray, Michelle. 2010. "Identity, Insecurity, and Great Power Politics: The Tragedy of German Naval Ambition before First World War." *Security Studies* 19, no. 4: 656–88.

Murray, Michelle. 2019. *The Struggle for Recognition in International Relations: Status, Revisionism, and Rising Powers.* New York: Oxford University Press.

Mynott, Jeremy, ed. 2013. *Thucydides: The War of the Peloponnesians and the Athenians.* Cambridge: Cambridge University Press.

Neustadt, Richard E., and Ernest R. May. 1986a. "The Seducer and the Kid Next Door." In *Thinking in Time: The Use of History for Decision Makers*, edited by Neustadt and May, 58–74. New York: Free Press.

Neustadt, Richard E., and Ernest R. May. 1986b. *Thinking in Time: The Use of History for Decision Makers.* New York: Free Press.

Norris, Pippa, ed. 1999. *Critical Citizens: Global Support for Democratic Government.* Oxford: Oxford University Press.

Norris, Pippa. 2011. *Democratic Deficit: Critical Citizens Revisited.* Cambridge: Cambridge University Press.

Norris, Pippa, and Ronald Inglehart. 2019. *Cultural Backlash: Trump, Brexit, and Authoritarian Populism.* Cambridge: Cambridge University Press.

Nye, Joseph S., Jr. 1990. *Bound to Lead: The Changing Nature of American Power.* New York: Basic Books.

Nye, Joseph S., Jr. 2002. *The Paradox of American Power.* Oxford: Oxford University Press.

Nye, Joseph S., Jr. 2004. *Soft Power: The Means to Success in World Politics.* New York: PublicAffairs.

"Obama: US, Not China, Should Set Pacific Trade Rules." 2016. Voice of America News, May 3. https://www.voanews.com/usa/obama-us-not-china-should-set-pacific-trade-rules.

Olson, Mancur, Jr. 1965. *The Logic of Collective Action*. Cambridge, MA: Harvard University Press.

Oneal, John R., Brad Lian, and James H. Joyner Jr. 1996. "Are the American People 'Pretty Prudent?' Public Responses to U.S. Uses of Force, 1950–1988." *International Studies Quarterly* 40, no. 2: 261–79.

Oren, Ido. 2003. *Our Enemies and US: America's Rivalries and the Making of Political Science*. Ithaca, NY: Cornell University Press.

Organski, A. F. K. 1958. *World Politics*. New York: Knopf.

Organski, A. F. K., and Jacek Kugler. 1980. *The War Ledger*. Chicago: University of Chicago Press.

Ortmayer, Louis, and Joanna Flinn. 1997. *Hamstrung over Haiti: Returning the Refugees*. Pew Case Studies in International Affairs, case no. 355. Washington, DC: Institute for the Study of Diplomacy, Pew Case Studies Center, Georgetown University.

Overholt, William H. 1993. *The Rise of China: How Economic Reform Is Creating a Superpower*. New York: Norton.

Owen, John M., IV. 1994. "How Liberalism Produces Democratic Peace." *International Security* 19, no. 2: 87–125.

Owen, John M., IV. 1997. *Liberal Peace, Liberal War: American Politics and International Security*. Ithaca, NY: Cornell University Press.

Pan, Chengxin. 2012. *Knowledge, Desire and Power in Global Politics: Western Representations of China's Rise*. Cheltenham: Elger.

Parello-Plesner, Jonas. 2023. "Taiwan Learns from Ukraine." Germany Marshall Fund, March 14. https://www.gmfus.org/news/taiwan-learns-ukraine.

Paul, T. V. 1994. *Asymmetric Conflicts: War Initiation by Weaker Powers*. Cambridge: Cambridge University Press.

Pickens, T. Boone, Pat Choate, and Christopher Burke. 1992. *The Second Pearl Harbor: Say No to Japan*. Washington, DC: National Press Books.

Platias, Athanassios, and Vasilis Trigkas. 2021. "Unravelling the Thucydides' Trap: Inadvertent or War of Choice?" *Chinese Journal of International Politics* 14, no. 2: 187–217.

Powell, Robert. 1999. *In the Shadow of Power: States and Strategies in International Politics*. Princeton, NJ: Princeton University Press.

Power, Samantha. 2001. "Bystanders to Genocide." *Atlantic Monthly* 288, no. 2: 84–108.

Power, Samantha. 2002. *"A Problem from Hell": America and the Age of Genocide*. New York: Basic Books.

Prange, Gordon W. 1982. *At Dawn We Slept: The Untold Story of Pearl Harbor*. New York: McGraw-Hill.

Prestowitz, Clyde V., Jr. 1990. *Trading Places: How We Are Giving Our Future to Japan and How to Reclaim It*. New York: Basic Books.

Primiano, Christopher, and Jun Xiang. 2016. "Voting in the UN: A Second Image of China's Human Rights." *Journal of Chinese Political Science* 21, no. 3: 301–19.

Pu, Xiaoyu. 2019. *Rebranding China: Contested Status Signaling in the Changing Global Order.* Stanford, CA: Stanford University Press.

"Public Less Confident in U.S. Coming to Taiwan's Defense: Survey." 2022. Central News Agency, April 30. https://focustaiwan.tw/politics/202204300009.

Putnam, Robert D. 1988. "Diplomacy and Domestic Politics: The Logic of Two-Level Games." *International Organization* 42, no. 3: 427–60.

Rapkin, David P., and William R. Thompson. 2003. "Power Transition, Challenge and the (Re)emergence of China." *International Interactions* 29, no. 4: 315–42.

Rapkin, David P., and William R. Thompson. 2013. *Transition Scenarios: China and the United States in the Twenty-First Century.* Chicago: University of Chicago Press.

Ratner, Ely. 2021. *Statement by Dr. Ely Ratner, Assistant Secretary of Defense for Indo-Pacific Security Affairs Office of the Secretary of Defense before the Committee on Foreign Relations, United States Senate.* 117th Congress (December 8).

Rauch, Carsten. 2017. "Challenging the Power Consensus: GDP, CINC, and Power Transition." *Security Studies* 26, no. 4: 642–64.

Ray, Michael. n.d. "Pearl Harbor in Context." Britannica. Accessed January 14, 2025. https://www.britannica.com/story/pearl-harbor-in-context.

Record, Jeffrey. 2007. *Beating Goliath: Why Insurgencies Win.* Washington, DC: Potomac Books.

Reiter, Dan. 1995. "Exploding the Powder Keg Myth: Preemptive Wars Almost Never Happen." *International Security* 20, no. 2: 5–34.

Renshon, Jonathan. 2016. "Status Deficits and War." *International Organization* 70, no. 3: 513–50.

Renshon, Jonathan. 2017. *Fighting for Status: Hierarchy and Conflict in World Politics.* Princeton, NJ: Princeton University Press.

Rich, Timothy S., Vasabjit Banerjee, and Benjamin Tkach. 2023. "How Has the War in Ukraine Shaped Taiwanese Concerns about Their Own Defense." *Asian Survey* 63, no. 6: 952–79.

Ricks, Thomas E. 2006. *Fiasco: The American Military Adventure in Iraq.* New York: Penguin Press.

Ripsman, Norrin M., and Jack Levy. 2008. "Wishful Thinking or Buying Time: The Logic of British Appeasement during the 1930s." *International Security* 33, no. 2: 148–81.

Roberts, Geoffrey. 2022. "'Now or Never': The Immediate Origins of Putin's Preventative War on Ukraine." *Journal of Military and Strategic Studies* 22, no. 2: 3–27.

Robertson, Esmonde D. 1963. *Hitler's Pre-war Policy and Military Plans, 1933–1939.* London: Longmans.

Rock, Stephen R. 1989. *Why Peace Breaks Out: Great Power Rapprochement in Historical Perspective.* Chapel Hill: University of North Carolina Press.

Rock, Stephen R. 2000. *Appeasement in International Politics*. Lexington: University of Kentucky Press.

Röhl, John C. G. 1994. *The Kaiser and His Court*. Cambridge: Cambridge University Press.

Rosecrance, Richard. 1987. *The Rise of the Trading State: Commerce and Conquest in the Modern World*. New York: Basic Books.

Rousseau, David L. 2006. *Identifying Threats and Threatening Identities: The Social Construction of Realism and Liberalism*. Stanford, CA: Stanford University Press.

Russett, Bruce M. 1969. "Refining Deterrence Theory: The Japanese Attack on Pearl Harbor." In *Theory and Research on the Causes of War*, edited by Dean G. Pruitt and Richard C. Snyder, 127–35. Englewood Cliffs, NJ: Prentice-Hall.

Russett, Bruce M., and John R. Oneal. 2001. *Triangulating Peace: Democracy, Interdependence and International Organizations*. New York: Norton.

Sample, Susan G. 2018. "Power, Wealth, and Satisfaction: When Do Power-Transitions Lead to Conflict?" *Journal of Conflict Resolution* 62, no. 9: 1905–31.

Sartori, Anne E. 2002. "The Might of the Pen: A Reputation Theory of Communication in International Disputes." *International Organization* 56, no. 1: 121–49.

Sartori, Anne E. 2005. *Deterrence by Diplomacy*. Princeton, NJ: Princeton University Press.

Sartori, Giovanni. 1970. "Concept Misformation in Comparative Politics." *American Political Science Review* 64, no. 4: 1033–53.

Schake, Kori. 2017. *Safe Passage: The Transition from British to American Hegemony*. Cambridge, MA: Harvard University Press.

Schelling, Thomas C. 1966. *Arms and Influence*. New Haven, CT: Yale University Press.

Schroeder, Paul W. 1976. "Munich and the British Tradition." *Historical Journal* 19, no. 1: 223–43.

Schroeder, Paul W. 2004. "Embedded Counterfactuals and World War I as an Unavoidable War." In *Systems, Stability, and Statecraft: Essays on the International History of Modern Europe*, edited by David Wetzel, Robert Jervis, and Jack S. Levy, 157–91. New York: Palgrave.

Schuster, John M. 2010. "The Deception Dividend: FDR's Undeclared War." *International Security* 34, no. 3: 133–65.

Schwarz, Benjamin. 2005. "Comment: Managing China's Rise; Contending with China's Ambitions Requires a Better Understanding of Our Own." *Atlantic Monthly*, June. http://www.theatlantic.com/magazine/archive/2005/06/managing-chinas-rise/303972/.

Schweller, Randall L. 1992. "Democratic Structure and Preventive War: Are Democracies More Pacific?" *World Politics* 44, no. 2: 235–69.

Schweller, Randall L. 1998. *Deadly Imbalances: Tripolarity and Hitler's Strategy of World Conquest*. New York: Columbia University Press.

Schweller, Randall L. 1999. "Managing the Rise of Great Powers: History and Theory." In *Engaging China: The Management of an Emerging Power*, edited by Alastair I. Johnston and Robert Ross, 1–32. London: Routledge.

Schweller, Randall L. 2015. "Rising Powers and Revisionism in Emerging World Orders." Russia in Global Affairs. http://eng.globalaffairs.ru/valday/Rising-Powers-and-Revisionism-in-Emerging-International-Orders-17730.

Schweller, Randall L. 2018. "Opposite but Compatible Nationalisms: A Neoclassical Realist Approach to the Future of US-China Relations." *Chinese Journal of International Politics* 11, no. 1: 23–48.

Scott, Esther. 1991. *The US Marines in Lebanon*. Case Program, Kennedy School of Government, case no. 1045.0. Cambridge, MA: Harvard University.

Senese, Paul D., and John A. Vasquez. 2008. *The Steps to War: An Empirical Study*. Princeton, NJ: Princeton University Press.

Sheng, Lijun. 2001. "Lee's U.S. Visit and China's Response." In *China's Dilemma: The Taiwan Issue*, 24–35. London: Tauris.

Shi, Jiangtao. 2020. "Destined for Conflict? Xi Jinping, Donald Trump, and the Thucydides Trap." *South China Morning Post*, May 21. https://www.scmp.com/news/china/diplomacy/article/3085321/destined-conflict-xi-jinping-donald-trump-and-thucydides-trap.

Shirk, Susan L. 2007. *China: Fragile Superpower*. Oxford: Oxford University Press.

Shirk, Susan L. 2023. *Overreach: How China Derailed Its Peaceful Rise*. Oxford: Oxford University Press.

Shlaim, Avi. 1976. "Failures in National Intelligence Estimates: The Case of the Yom Kippur War." *World Politics* 28, no. 3: 348–80.

Silverstone, Scott A. 2007. *Preventive War and American Democracy*. London: Routledge.

Slantchev, Branislav. 2010. "Feigning Weakness." *International Organization* 64, no. 3: 357–88.

Slovic, Paul, and Baruch Fischhoff. 1977. "On the Psychology of Experimental Surprises." *Journal of Experimental Psychology: Human Perception and Performance* 3, no. 4: 544–51.

Smith, Allan, and Carol E. Lee. 2025. "Pressure on China and Pure 'Trolling': Why Trump Is Pushing an Expansionist Agenda." NBC News, January 9. https://www.nbcnews.com/politics/donald-trump/trump-take-canada-greenland-panama-canal-rcna186591.

Smith, Anthony D. 1986. *Ethnic Origins of Nations*. Oxford: Basil Blackwell.

Smith, Steve. 1985. "The Hostage Rescue Mission." In *Foreign Policy Implementation*, edited by Smith and Michael Clarke, 11–32. London: Allen and Unwin.

Snyder, Jack. 1993. *Myths of Empire: Domestic Politics and International Ambition*. Ithaca, NY: Cornell University Press.

Solingen, Etel. 2007. "Pax Asiatica versus Bella Levantina: The Foundations of War and Peace in East Asia and the Middle East." *American Political Science Review* 101, no. 4: 757–80.

Solingen, Etel. 2014. "Domestic Coalitions, Internationalization, and War: Then and Now." *International Security* 39, no. 1: 44–70.

Spykman, Nicholas J. 1942. *America's Strategy in World Politics: The United States and the Balance of Power.* New York: Harcourt, Brace.

Spykman, Nicholas J. 1944. *The Geography of the Peace.* New York: Harcourt, Brace.

Stein, Janice Gross. 2023. "Perceiving Threat: Cognition, Emotion, and Judgment." In *The Oxford Handbook of Political Psychology,* 3rd ed., edited by Leonie Huddy, David O. Sears, and Jack S. Levy, 392–425. New York: Oxford University Press.

Strassler, Robert B., ed. 1998. *The Landmark Thucydides: A Comprehensive Guide to the Peloponnesian War.* New York: Touchstone.

Swaine, Michael D., and Ashley L. Tellis. 2000. *Interpreting China's Grand Strategy: Past, Present, and Future.* Santa Monica, CA: RAND.

Sweeney, John, Jens Holsoe, and Ed Vullimany. 1999. "Nato Bombed Chinese Deliberately." *The Observer,* October 16. https://www.theguardian.com/world/1999/oct/17/balkans.

Taiwan Documents Project. n.d. "Shanghai Communiqué: 28 February 1972." http://www.taiwandocuments.org/communique01.html (site discontinued by January 15, 2025).

Taiwan Policy Centre. 2022. "Ukraine Today, Taiwan Tomorrow." https://taiwanpolicycentre.com/wp-content/uploads/Ukraine-today-Taiwan-tomorrow.pdf.

Taliaferro, Jeffrey W. 2016. "Did the United States and the Allies Fail to Accommodate Japan in the 1920s and the 1930s?" In *Accommodating Rising Powers: Past, Present, and Future,* edited by T. V. Paul, 173–97. Cambridge: Cambridge University Press.

Tammen, Ronald L., Jacek Kugler, Douglas Lemke, Allan Stam III, Mark Abdollahian, Carole Alsharabati, Brian Efird, and A. F. K. Organski. 2000. *Power Transitions: Strategies for the 21st Century.* New York: Chatham House.

Taylor, A. J. P. 1954. *The Struggle for Mastery of Europe, 1848–1918.* Oxford: Clarendon.

Taylor, A. J. P. 1961. *The Origins of the Second World War.* New York: Atheneum.

Thies, Cameron, and Mark D. Nieman. 2017. *Rising Powers and Foreign Policy Revisionism.* University of Michigan Press.

Thompson, William R. 1996. "Balances of Power, Transitions, and Long Cycles." In *Parity and War: Evaluations and Extensions of the War Ledger,* edited by Jacek Kugler and Douglas Lemke, 163–85. Ann Arbor: University of Michigan Press.

Thompson, William R. 1999. "The Evolution of a Great Power Rivalry: The Anglo-American Case." In *Great Power Rivalries,* edited by Thompson, 201–21. Columbia: University of South Carolina Press.

Thompson, William R. 2003. "A Streetcar Named Sarajevo: Catalysts, Multiple

Causation Chains, and Rivalry Structures." *International Studies Quarterly* 47, no. 3: 453–74.

Thomson, James C. 1973. "How Could Vietnam Happen? An Autopsy." In *Readings in American Foreign Policy: A Bureaucratic Perspective*, edited by Morton H. Halperin and Arnold Kanter, 98–110. Boston: Little, Brown.

Tierney, Dominic. 2011. "Does Chain-Ganging Cause the Outbreak of War?" *International Studies Quarterly* 55, no. 2: 285–304.

Tilchin, William. 1997. *Theodore Roosevelt and the British Empire: A Study in Presidential Statecraft*. London: Macmillan.

Timsit, Annabelle. 2021. "Xi Jinping Sends Warning to the US at Davos." World Economic Forum, January 25. https://qz.com/1962084/read-xi-jinpings-speech-at-the-2021-davos-forum/.

Toal, Gerard. 2017. *Near Abroad: Putin, the West, and the Contest over Ukraine and the Caucasus*. Oxford: Oxford University Press.

Trachtenberg, Marc. 2007. "Preventive War and U.S. Foreign Policy." *Security Studies* 16, no. 1: 1–31.

Treisman, Daniel. 2004. "Rational Appeasement." *International Organization* 58, no. 2: 344–73.

"Truth behind America's Raid in Belgrade." 1999. *The Observer*, November 27. https://www.theguardian.com/theobserver/1999/nov/28/focus.news1.

Tuchman, Barbara W. 1962. *The Guns of August*. New York: Dell.

Tversky, Amos, and Daniel Kahneman. 1974. "Judgment under Uncertainty: Heuristics and Biases." *Science* 185, no. 4157: 1124–31.

Tyler, Patrick. 1999. *A Great Wall, Six Presidents and China: An Investigative History*. New York: Perseus.

US Department of State. 2022. "Secretary Antony J. Blinken at a Press Availability." January 26. https://www.state.gov/secretary-antony-j-blinken-at-a-press-availability-13/.

"US Lifts Trump Sanctions on International Criminal Court Officials." 2021. Deutsche Welle, April 3. https://www.dw.com/en/us-lifts-trump-sanctions-on-international-criminal-court-officials/a-57089520.

Van Evera, Stephen. 1984. "The Cult of Offensive and the Origins of the First World War." *International Security* 9, no. 1: 58–107.

Van Evera, Stephen. 1999. *Causes of War: Power and the Roots of Conflict*. Ithaca, NY: Cornell University Press.

Vasquez, John A. 1993. *The War Puzzle*. Cambridge: Cambridge University Press.

Vasquez, John A. 1996. "When Are Power Transitions Dangerous? An Appraisal and Reformulation of Power Transition Theory." In *Parity and War: Evaluations and Extensions of the War Ledger*, edited by Jacek Kugler and Douglas Lemke, 35–56. Ann Arbor: University of Michigan Press.

Vasquez, John A. 2009. *The War Puzzle Revisited*. Cambridge: Cambridge University Press.

Vertzberger, Yaacov. 1986. "Foreign Policy Decisionmakers as Practical-Intuitive Historians: Applied History and Its Shortcomings." *International Studies Quarterly* 30, no. 2: 223–47.

Vogel, Ezra F. 1979. *Japan as Number One: Lessons for America.* Cambridge, MA: Harvard University Press.

Wachman, Alan M. 2007. *Why Taiwan: Geostrategic Rationales for China's Territorial Integrity.* Stanford, CA: Stanford University Press.

Warlimont, Walter. 1962. *Inside Hitler's Headquarters: 1939–1945.* Novato, CA: Presidio.

Walker, R. B. J. 1995. *Inside/Outside: International Relations as Political Theory.* Cambridge: Cambridge University Press.

Walt, Stephen M. 1987. *The Origins of Alliances.* Ithaca, NY: Cornell University Press.

Walt, Stephen M. 2005. *Taming American Power: The Global Response to U.S. Primacy.* New York: Norton.

Waltz, Kenneth N. 1979. *Theory of International Politics.* Reading, MA: Addison-Wesley.

Waltz, Kenneth N. 2000a. "NATO Expansion: A Realist's View." *Contemporary Security Policy* 21, no. 2: 23–38.

Waltz, Kenneth N. 2000b. "Structural Realism after the Cold War." *International Security* 25, no. 1: 5–41.

Wang, T. Y., and Su-Feng Cheng. 2024. "Strategic Clarity and Taiwanese Citizens' Confidence in the US Security Commitment." *Asian Survey* 64, no. 1: 54–78.

Wang, Wenbin. 2021. "Foreign Ministry Spokesperson Wang Wenbin's Regular Press Conference on June 29, 2021." Ministry of Foreign Affairs, the People's Republic of China, June 29. https://www.fmprc.gov.cn/eng/xwfw_665399/s2510_665401/2511_665403/202106/t20210629_9170775.html.

Wang, Zheng. 2012. *Never Forget National Humiliation: Historical Memory in Chinese Politics and Foreign Relations.* New York: Columbia University Press.

Wang, Zheng. 2018. *Memory Politics, Identity and Conflict: Historical Memory as a Variable.* New York: Palgrave.

Ward, Steven. 2013. "Race, Status, and Japanese Revisionism in the Early 1930s." *Security Studies* 22, no. 4: 607–39.

Ward, Steven. 2017. *Status and the Challenge of Rising Powers.* Cambridge: Cambridge University Press.

Watt, Donald C. 1965. "Appeasement: The Rise of the Revisionist School?" *Political Quarterly* 36, no. 2: 191–213.

"We Don't See Things." 2014. Quote Investigator, March 9. Last updated January 20, 2021. https://quoteinvestigator.com/2014/03/09/as-we-are/.

Welch, David. 2015. "Can the United States and China Avoid a Thucydides Trap?" E-International Relations, April 6. https://www.e-ir.info/2015/04/06/can-the-united-states-and-china-avoid-a-thucydides-trap/.

Welch, David. 2020. "China, the United States, and the 'Thucydides Trap.'" In *Chi-*

na's Challenges and International Order Transition: Beyond "Thucydides's Trap," edited by Huiyun Feng and Kai He, 47–70. Ann Arbor: University of Michigan Press.

Wells, Tom. 1994. *The War Within: America's Battle over Vietnam.* Berkeley: University of California Press.

Whaley, Barton. 1973. *Codeword Barbarossa.* Cambridge, MA: MIT Press.

"What Is the Meaning of Wellington's Quote, in Modern Vernacular, of 'the Nearest-Run Thing You Ever Saw in Your Life,' When Referring to Napoleon and the Battle of Waterloo." n.d. Quora. Accessed January 8, 2025. https://www.quora.com/What-is-the-meaning-of-Wellingtons-quote-in-modern-vernacular-of-the-nearest-run-thing-you-ever-saw-in-your-life-when-referring-to-Napoleon-and-the-Battle-of-Waterloo.

The White House. 2024. "Remarks by President Biden and Prime Minister Kishida Fumio of Japan in Joint Press Conference." April 10. https://www.whitehouse.gov/briefing-room/speeches-remarks/2024/04/10/remarks-by-president-biden-and-prime-minister-kishida-fumio-of-japan-in-joint-press-conference/.

Whiting, Allen S. 1962. *China Crosses the Yalu: The Decision to Enter the Korean War.* Stanford, CA: Stanford University Press.

Wikipedia. 2024a. "Century of Humiliation." Wikimedia Foundation, last modified December 12, 04:25 (UTC). https://en.wikipedia.org/wiki/Century_of_humiliation.

Wikipedia. 2024b. "Law of the Instrument." Wikimedia Foundation, last modified September 19, 15:56 (UTC). https://en.wikipedia.org/wiki/Law_of_the_instrument.

Wikipedia. 2024c. "Weltpolitik." Wikimedia Foundation, last modified October 11, 13:16 (UTC). https://en.wikipedia.org/wiki/Weltpolitik.

Wingrove, Josh. 2022a. "Biden Says US Would Defend Taiwan in 'Unprecedented Attack.'" Bloomberg, September 18. https://www.bloomberg.com/news/articles/2022-09-18/biden-says-us-would-defend-taiwan-from-unprecedented-attack.

Wingrove, Josh. 2022b. "Biden: US Would Defend Taiwan from 'Unprecedented Attack.'" *Time,* September 18. https://time.com/6214511/biden-defend-taiwan-china-us/.

Wohlstetter, Roberta. 1962. *Pearl Harbor: Warning and Decision.* Stanford, CA: Stanford University Press.

Wohlstetter, Roberta. 1965. "Cuba and Pearl Harbor: Hindsight and Foresight." *Foreign Affairs* 43, no. 4: 691–707.

Wolf, Reinhard. 2014. "Rising Powers, Status Ambitions, and the Need to Reassure: What China Could Learn from Imperial Germany's Failures." *Chinese Journal of International Politics* 7, no. 2: 185–219.

Wood, Frederick S. 1927. *Roosevelt as We Knew Him.* Philadelphia: Winston.

Woodward, Bob. 2006. *State of Denial: Bush at War.* New York: Simon and Schuster.

Woodward, Bob, and Robert Costa. 2021. *Peril.* New York: Simon and Schuster.

Wyden, Peter. 1979. *Bay of Pigs: The Untold Story.* New York: Simon and Schuster.

Xi, Jinping. 2017. "Full Text of Xi Jinping Keynote at the World Economic Forum." China Global Television Network, January 17. https://america.cgtn.com/2017/01/17/full-text-of-xi-jinping-keynote-at-the-world-economic-forum.

Xi, Jinping. 2021. "China Welcomes Helpful Suggestions but Won't Accept Sanctimonious Preaching." *Xinhua,* July 1. http://www.xinhuanet.com/english/special/2021-07/01/c_1310037332.htm.

Yicai Global. 2017. "China 'Lacks the Gene' to Fall into Thucydides Trap, Says Xi Jinping." September 20. https://yicaichina.medium.com/china-lacks-the-gene-to-fall-into-the-thucydides-trap-says-xi-jinping-ccade48ac392.

Zakaria, Fareed. 1998. *From Wealth to Power: The Unusual Origins of America's World Role.* Princeton, NJ: Princeton University Press.

Zakaria, Fareed. 2020. "The New China Scare: Why America Shouldn't Panic about Its Latest Challenger." *Foreign Affairs* 99, no. 1: 52–69.

Zakaria, Fareed. 2024. "Fareed: Putin Doesn't Need Sanctions, He Needs Military Setbacks." CNN, March 17. https://www.cnn.com/videos/opinions/2024/03/17/russian-election-putin-the-west-fareeds-take-gps-intl-ldn-vpx.cnn.

Zarakol, Ayse. 2020. "Use of Historical Analogies in IR Theory." In "H-Diplo/ISSF Roundtable 12-2 on *Thucydides's Trap?* Historical Interpretation, Logic of Inquiry, and the Future of Sino-American Relations." H-Net, November 9. https://networks.h-net.org/node/28443/discussions/6721850/h-diploissf-roundtable-12-2-thucydides%E2%80%99s-trap-historical.

Zelleke, Andy. 2020. "'Strategic Clarity' Won't Solve the United States' Taiwan Dilemma: An Open Commitment to Defend Taiwan Won't Mean Much Unless the U.S. Has the Certain Capacity to Do So." *The Diplomat,* October 2. https://thediplomat.com/2020/10/strategic-clarity-wont-solve-the-united-states-taiwan-dilemma/.

Zeren, Ali, and John A. Hall. 2016. "Seizing the Day or Passing the Baton? Power, Illusion, and the British Empire." In *Accommodating Rising Powers: Past, Present and Future,* edited by T. V. Paul, 111–30. Cambridge: Cambridge University Press.

Zhao, Lijian. 2022. "Foreign Ministry Spokesperson Zhao Lijian's Regular Press Conference on May 30, 2022." Ministry of Foreign Affairs, People's Republic of China, May 30. https://www.fmprc.gov.cn/eng/xwfw_665399/s2510_665401/2511_665403/202205/t20220530_10694714.html (site discontinued).

Index

Routledge Frontiers of Political Economy

Human Economics
Paradigms, Systems, and Dynamics
Sara Casagrande

The Knowledge Problems of European Financial Market Integration
Paradoxes of the Market
Troels Krarup

Beyond Ecological Economics and Development
Critical reflections on the thought of Manfred Max-Neef
Edited by Luis Valenzuela and María del Valle Barrera

New Economic Statecraft
China, the United States and the European Union
Zhang Xiaotong

The Scottish Economy and Nationalism
Constructing Scotland's Imagined Economy
James Foley

The Meaning of Shared Value
New Perspective on Creating Shared Value
Paolo Ricci, Patrick O'Sullivan and Floriana Fusco

For more information about this series, please visit: www.routledge.com/Routledge-Frontiers-of-Political-Economy/book-series/SE0345